The Politics
of a Poverty
Habitat

The Politics of a Poverty Habitat

Donald V. Kurtz
University of Wisconsin –Milwaukee

Ballinger Publishing Company ● Cambridge, Mass.
A Subsidiary of J.B. Lippincott Company

Library of Congress Catalog Card Number 73–9595

International Standard Book Number 0–88410–000–6

Printed in the United States of America

Library of Congress Cataloging in Publication Data

Kurtz, Donald V
    The politics of a poverty habitat. 74– 7783
    Includes bibliographical references.
    1. Economic assistance, Domestic—San Ysidro, Calif. 2. Poor—San Ysidro, Calif. 3. Mexican Americans—San Ysidro, Calif. I. Title.
HC108.S718K87   362.5'09794'98   73–9595
ISBN 0–88410–000–6

To Jacky

Contents

List of Figures

List of Tables

List of Appendix Tables

Acknowledgments

The bulk of the research upon which this book is based was con-ducted without benefit of funding from any agency. I should, I suppose, thank the Internal Revenue Service for permitting me to write off my income tax some of the expenses I incurred. This information may be of some value to other young scholars who in the current period of tight research money may find themselves forced to utilize their own resources in order to accomplish their goals.

I financed the research out of my salary as an instructor in the Department of Anthropology at San Diego State College. I wish to thank the 1968–1969 anthropology faculty at San Diego State for extending my temporary appointment for one year. This enabled me to complete the research which I had begun in April of 1968 and which I concluded about a year later. I also wish to thank the Language and Area Center for Latin America at the University of Wisconsin-Milwaukee for the support they provided me in 1972. This assistance permitted me to return to San Ysidro for five weeks during June and July in order to investigate some of what had transpired since my departure.

Ruben Dominguez and Robert Peer introduced me to San Ysidro and its problems. They were helpful to me on many occasions during my research. Señora Angelbertha Cobb rented me the couch in her house upon which I slept for ten weeks in the summer of 1968 when I lived in San Ysidro. She and her five children were generous to a fault and Señora Cobb extended my social contacts in San Ysidro quickly and far beyond what I would have been able to accomplish on my own.

I am deeply indebted to Jane Girten and Fred Martinez. They were especially helpful to me and gave freely of their time and knowledge regarding the war on poverty in San Diego County and the problems in San Ysidro. Lily Vargas, Carmen Guzman, Eddie Cuen, Duane Scott, Wallace Van Buren and Delia Cacho all withstood my tedious and persistent inquiries with patience and their candor proved to be of inestimable value. Members of the San Ysidro Poor Families and Tenants Association, The San Ysidro Planning Group, The Economic Opportunity Commission of San Diego County, and administrators of the San Ysidro School District were patient with me and very helpful. The beleaguered troops of many of the community action organizations in San Diego County provided me with a breadth and depth of understanding into the war on poverty that I would otherwise have not been able to acquire. Frank Cervantes worked as my research assistant for a few months and acquired information that would have been inaccessible to me. My thanks to them all for making the research exciting and worthwhile.

Professor Edwin Cook and David Olmstead read the preliminary draft of this manuscript in its entirety and made valuable suggestions. Professor Cook was especially encouraging and helpful and I may not have completed the manuscript without his help. Professors Edward Wellin, James Silverberg, and Alvin Wolfe read portions of the early draft and their comments resolved many problems for me. Professor Philip Staniford read a later draft and his comments were helpful in preparing this final version.

Mrs. Dorothy Gallas typed one draft of the manuscript; Miss Jan Kendall prepared the final copy. Their perseverence and interest in this project were most gratifying.

Obviously the final interpretations in the work are my own, and I alone am responsible for any errors. The critiques and comments I received in the course of my efforts from all these individuals have resulted in a better work than I could have accomplished alone.

Finally, and most importantly, my research and this book would not have been possible without the help and understanding of my wife Jacquelyn. She was not only a source of constant support, she typed the first draft of the manuscript from my longhand copy, a herculean effort that required that she learn a new and not very valuable symbol system. She and my daughter Elizabeth made sacrifices throughout my research and the writing of this work for which no gratitude I could convey would be sufficient.

Introduction

Anthropologists increasingly are applying their analytic tools and methodological techniques to the study of sociocultural phenomena within the urban sectors of the nations of the world. One focus of these studies has been upon the causes and problems of poverty in the United States. Studies concerned with this problem have been conducted in a variety of methodological contexts: ethnographic descriptions, sociological analyses, critiques of accomplished studies, analyses of family relationships, and others.[1] However, the only anthropological model that has been available for the study of poverty has been that derived from the concept of the culture of poverty. This conceptualization has not proven especially fruitful.

As a scientific instrument the culture of poverty concept failed in two ways. First, it provided no insight into the causes of poverty. Second, it generated no body of theory by which poverty might be better understood and explained. As is well known the concept is derived from the study of the life styles and culture of a few selected families, and as Oscar Lewis applied the concept it became devoted to the proliferation of culture traits which are presumably associated with poverty. Not only does the concern with the distribution of culture traits smack of an outmoded anthropological tradition, there is serious doubt regarding whether the traits Oscar Lewis isolated are actually indicative of poverty.[2]

The culture of poverty concept also has a variety of unfortunate and insidious implications built into it. Perhaps the implication most injurious to the poor in the United States is the ways in which the concept reinforces widely held prejudices and stereotypes regarding the poor, especially the notion that the poor are themselves to blame for their impoverishment. This attitude also obtains support from the national ideology as it is derived from the Protestant ethic. According to this ethic everyone should work; those that don't are relegated to an inferior status. The culture of poverty concept becomes a covert and insidious part of this ideology because it helps to explain why some make it in the society and others do not. As a result of these considerations the majority of the nation's population and a broad and powerful segment of its decision- and policy-making structures feel themselves absolved of any blame for the existence of poverty. Thus they see little reason for providing or paying for any program designed to eliminate poverty.

However, a number of perspicacious individuals very quickly perceived the shortcomings of the concept and it became the center of a bitter polemic.[3] Since then the concept of the culture of poverty has fallen into a state of intellectual and scientific bankruptcy from which it is doubtful it will ever revive.

As a result of the polemic over the value of the culture of poverty concept there has been a plea for an alternative approach and conceptualization by which the problems of poverty might be attacked. First, there has been a call for an "ecological approach" to the study of poverty;[4] that is an approach which will provide an understanding of the relationship of populations in poverty to the larger national sociocultural system and of the adaptive strategies the poor develop as a consequence of that relationship. The assumption which underlies this point of view is that the fundamental causes and problems of poverty exist in and emanate from the larger national sociocultural system. Secondly, there has been a call for a conceptualization of poverty which will supplant the culture of poverty concept and provide the basis for a more fruitful methodology.[5] If such a methodology is to be derived from the ecological approach, then an alternative conceptualization ought to be an integral part of that approach. It should provide a theoretical framework which will take into account the fact that poverty is a part of a larger sociocultural system. For these reasons I here suggest the concept of a poverty habitat as an alternative to the culture of poverty concept.

A poverty habitat may be conceptualized as the socially bounded configuration of demographic, physical, sociocultural, and ideological features which develop and exist on the margins of a nation's dominant techno-energy system and institutional nexus, especially that concerned with economic, political, legal, and educational activity, and into which the nation's impoverished population is only marginally integrated. The concept of a poverty habitat is designed to bring into sharp focus the relationship and interaction of the poor and the larger national sociocultural system of which they are a part. The working hypothesis that derives from this conceptualization is that the causes of poverty and the social problems associated with it are influenced more by forces outside the control of poor people than by any cultural, racial, or ethnic factors peculiar to the impoverished population. The fundamental relationship between the population of the poverty habitat and the dominant technological and institutional nexus as derived from this conceptualization can be summed up quite succinctly. The technology of the United States does not adequately make use of the poor. The educational institutions of the society do not satisfactorily train or educate the poor. The economic institutions of the society do not meaningfully provide for the poor. The political institutions of the society do not equally represent the poor. The legal institutions of the society are not impartial advocates for the poor. The poor are victims of a vicious cybernation which locks them into a self-contained system of perpetual poverty that begins at birth and ends at death.

It is the contention here that the special profile of poverty which exists in the United States is the result of the rapid industrialization, automation, and cybernation of American society and culture. The persistence of poverty seems to be the result of a curious feedback between the nation's technological and institutional nexus. On the one hand this complex is able to absorb an increasing number of people. On the other hand, at the same time, it is disenfranchising an increasing number of people. Not only are a vast number of Americans with skills and knowledge being displaced by our techno-economic system, this system is finding it impossible to provide individuals without skills and knowledge access to industries and occupations. This latter category in American society is being culturally selected against for participation in the system and relegated to a condition of poverty. In short, the very forces which emanate from the national sociocultural system and which serve to stimulate growth and change in one direction also serve in a diametrically opposite direction to promote the persistence of poverty.

Without access to jobs, education, political representation, and so forth the poor are deprived of the most fundamental rewards which participation in the nation's technological and institutional nexus can provide—status, prestige, a sense of belonging—as well as the material rewards which are so richly distributed among the mainstream of the society. Excluded from meaningful participation in this complex the poor comprise a class which, like other classes, tends to cluster. In this way the special configuration of the poverty habitat is created and comes to reflect the marginal and ephemeral involvement of its population in the mainstream of the society.

The nation's dominant institutions develop structural rules and cultural values which inhibit egress of the poor in any categorical sense from the poverty habitat. The poor become defined in terms of these rules and values and the society's institutions make use of the poor in accordance with that definition. The poor find themselves underemployed, segregated, exploited, victimized by police, insulted by the welfare system, demeaned, and so forth. It is to these forces and to the special ways in which the institutions of the society penetrate into the poverty habitat and use the poor that the poor must adapt. Because the adaptive strategies which the poor develop in response to these circumstances are grossly misunderstood by the larger society these strategies are given a high negative value.

For instance, it has been argued that the prevalence of the matrifocal family among black American poor is indicative of psychosocial pathologies inherent in the culture of urban black Americans.[6] This argument displays ignorance of the cultural pressures to which this household type represents an adaptive response; it also reinforces the stereotype of the black poor in American society and the ideology which supports that stereotype; that is that the poor are themselves to blame for their plight because in this great land of unlimited opportunity if only they weren't so lazy and would "get off their ass and go to work" all their problems would be solved! In a society which is currently finding it difficult to employ some of its most highly trained technicians, one is led to wonder where the poor are supposed to obtain work? It is to this question that the existence of the matrifocal household must be addressed.

The matrifocal household represents an adaptive response to pressures in the national culture which exclude the black male from employment which will permit him to provide sufficiently for his family. Pressed to the wall, unable to provide, the black male may consciously decide to leave the household in order that his wife and children may become eligible for funds and benefits through welfare; ergo, the matrifocal household.[7] If this represents a psychosocial pathology in black culture, then the same psychosocial pathology exists among other ethnic populations in American society.

In 1968 in San Ysidro, California, the poverty habitat upon which this book is based, approximately 17 percent of the Mexican-American households were matrifocal. This percentage is the same which exists nationally among blacks in ghettos. In 1972, in a rent subsidy housing project which was recently completed in San Ysidro and which was 82 percent Mexican-American, 50 percent of the 390 households in the project were matrifocal.[8]

Since the intensity of the family tie in Mexican-American culture is frequently extolled in American society, why then do we find and how do we explain the same adaptive strategy among poor Mexican-Americans as among poor blacks? Is the Mexican-American family and Mexican-American society and culture suddenly degenerating into a pathological state? Of course not. The factors which cause the matrifocal household among urban poor Mexican-Americans are the same which cause it among poor blacks. In fact, regardless of ethnic or cultural backgrounds the matrifocal household represents a viable alternative for the urban poor to the forces which function to exclude them from participation in the affluent mainstream of American society.[9] This does not however suggest that it is a desirable alternative.

It is axiomatic that most state societies, especially those based upon an industrial technology, are composed of culturally heterogenous populations which manifest varying degrees of integration into the national sociocultural system. One of the working hypotheses upon which this work is based is that one characteristic of most nations is their attempts to reduce sociocultural heterogeneity by initiating pressures and policies which will encourage the integration of the society. One of the most important means by which a nation achieves sociocultural integration is through the decisions that are made and the actions that take place in the nation's political institutions.[10]

One gauge of the degree of integration of a population into the state's national sociocultural system is the extent to which that population controls or has access to human, material, and ideological resources. Control of or access to such resources not only permits a population to participate more meaningfully in the national sociocultural system, it provides the necessary basis by which resources may be replenished and perhaps increased. Populations which have least access to or control of resources are generally the least integrated into the nation's sociocultural fabric. They also usually exist in poverty. Poverty may in fact be defined as the lack of resources. The poor very simply are resource poor.

It is the contention here that the extent to which resources are available to the poor is directly contingent upon the decision-making processes of political authorities and the values which underlie their decisions. It is within the political institutions of society that decisions are made which are influential in determining the persistence of a nation's poverty habitats as well as the size of the population encamped within them. Since a society's political institution are sensitive to nuances in all other spheres of social activity— economic, education, legal—they become one of the most significant elements of the larger national environment to which impoverished populations must adapt.

In a complex society such as the United States any alteration in the conditions of poverty will be the result of decisions regarding such critical matters as the allocation of industries throughout the nation, changes in educational programs and curricula, the development of job training programs, the enactment of laws which will more equally dispense justice, and so forth. The lack of responsiveness of the nation's political institutions, as well as others, to the problems of poverty amid such affluence was in large measure the causes of the agitation in the urban poverty habitats throughout the 1960s. These agitations were indicative of the lack of integration of the nation's impoverished populations into the affluent mainstream of the society. They also posed a serious threat to the unity of the United States. One response to this turmoil was the declaration of a national war against poverty.

The United States war on poverty may be viewed as an adaptive response to the lack of national sociocultural integration. Although the avowed goal of the war on poverty was to alleviate poverty and the conditions which create it, its more covert purpose was to restore a degree of national sociocultural unity. The failure of the war on poverty to accomplish this goal may be revealed by the fact that most of the severe uprising in the nation's poverty habitats took place only after the war against poverty had been waged for a few years. By that time these uprisings were expressions of gross contradictions between the means and ends of the antipoverty program, between legitimate expectations and reality in the society.

The contradictions built into the structure of the society—prejudice, unequal access to resources, inequality—were also built into the organization of the war on poverty. The integrative process, whether attempted through a war against poverty or some other strategy, is always mediated by the cultural values, symbols, and ideologies which support the nation's decision-making structures. From the outset the efficacy of the war on poverty was seriously impeded by substantial disagreement regarding the best way to cope with the problems and causes of poverty.

National sociocultural integration was to be achieved through the war on poverty by the human and material resources the federal government was to make available to the poor. Through the use and application of these resources the poor were expected to significantly alter their collective status vis-à-vis the more affluent categories of American society. One important goal of the war on poverty was to shift the poor away from a dependency upon services and to provide them with the means by which they might resolve their own problems. This was the basis for the community action programs of the war on poverty. Because the community action programs placed power in the hands of the poor, no other component of the war on poverty was so suspect, so criticized, and subject to such abuse.

Across the nation opponents to the war on poverty began to marshall support and resources to counter-effect the community action program. Paradoxically, these opposing forces received a great amount of help from the poor themselves. The enthusiasm of the poor and their cohorts in response to the declaration of the war against poverty was quickly muted by the reality that the resources available to them were simply not sufficient. After this realization a great deal of the activity of the poor played directly into the hands of their opponents.

The united front which some hoped the poor would develop was rent by a vicious competition for the resources that were available. The poverty habitats of the nation became political arenas, and the arenas became populated with a field of contestants who represented a variety of organizations and levels of complexity in the society. The poor were forced to compete not only with other poor for scarce resources, but with other more powerful groups who represented vested interests of the mainstream and who often sought goals that were contradictory to the war on poverty. The conflicts in the arenas supported the charges of opponents of the war against poverty that the poor were not only incapable of handling their own affairs, they were squandering the taxpayers money as well. As the conflict in the poverty habitats increased and the disillusionment of the poor with the program spread the war on poverty gradually lost what political as well as popular support it had, shuddered, and eventually succumbed.

The accomplishments the poor made against poverty in the course of the few heady years during which the battles raged has to be chalked up to their guts and determination. They frequently had little else to go on. In fact, the political activity of the poor, their tactics and strategies, has to be understood as an adaptive response to the paucity of resources made available to them. Although the methods the poor employed in their battles frequently went unnoticed, except when they invoked some moral opprobrium from the larger society, they represented fine examples of the power of the weak. The poor learned from their fights. They acquired skills and knowledge and developed organizations which, if they do not promote the integration of the poor into the mainstream of the society, will provide some viable alternatives to what existed previously and by which the poor may now better express themselves.

This work is not a community study. Nor is it a detailed study of poverty. It does attempt to fill a lacuna in our knowledge by exploring in detail the political activity in which one war on poverty institution, The Border Area Community Action Council of San Diego County, engaged. It takes into account the forces from the local to the federal levels of government which influenced the conflict and fights in the arena. Since the major concern of this work is with the interrelatedness of forms within an environment, a consideration that is crucial to ecological thought, the methodology of this work may be conceived as "political ecology." As a political analysis the work derives methodological support from the insights presented by Marc Swartz. These also suggest ecological considerations.

> ... most politics at the local level ... is variously enmeshed or encapsulated in larger and more comprehensive systems of party politics, legal codes, national ideologies, and the toils of regional and national bureaucracies. This inclusion and encapsulation in the structures and traditions of big politics and big government is, if anything, increasing. (1968:199)

This comment applies to complex industrial nations as well as to emerging nations. In the United States one example of local level politics and the results of these politics are revealed in the war on poverty.

The methodology of this work shall be concerned with illustrating the issues over which political conflict evolved in the poverty habitat of San Ysidro, the nature of that conflict, and the character of the contestants who were involved in the fights. The work will demonstrate how the control and allocation of resources—human, material, and ideological—influence and to a great extent determine the outcome of a political fight. The significance of ethnic relationships for the political activity in the arena will be a recurrent theme. Both Mexican-Americans and Anglo-Americans were deeply involved in the fights in the arena, and ethnic identity and boundaries were influential in these fights. Finally, the outcome of the conflict in this arena and its implications for the integration of the poor into the mainstream of American society is discussed at some length.

In organizing these data the following framework resulted. Chapter 1 carries on the discussion of the concept of a poverty habitat. An evolution of these environments is suggested and the poverty habitat of San Ysidro is discussed and described in this context. Chapter 2 discusses the significance of resources for political activity, and special attention is devoted to the significance of ideology as a powerful resource in a political fight. In Chapter 3 the hierarchy of contestants who comprised the field that competed in the arena is introduced along with the goals each pursued. Chapter 4 discusses the ways in which a variety of factors within the war on poverty and other sociopolitical institutions of the society precipitated conditions which led to the political conflict with which this study is concerned. In Chapter 5 three issues over which conflict developed are analyzed in order to demonstrate the nature of the conflict and the interaction between the contestants and the various issues over which they came into conflict. Chapter 6 is concerned with the means by which political goals of the contestants are achieved and suggestions are made regarding the impact of political activity in the war on poverty upon the integration of the United States. Chapter 7 is devoted to a summary of the study. By eliciting a series of theories from the data presented in the work I provide a final analysis of the integrative process and offer suggestions regarding the future social organization of the United States. Chapter 8 concludes with a brief epilogue concerned with the events in San Ysidro since January 1969 when my research terminated.

Chapter One

San Ysidro: The Poverty Habitat

THE POVERTY HABITAT

Settings which are inhabited by ethnic, racial, or national minorities, as well as certain regional areas, such as parts of the American South or Appalachia in which the way of life of the people seems somewhat distinctive, are frequently subsumed under the anthropological concept of subculture. It has recently been recognized that one attribute of the populations of many subcultures is a condition of poverty. One major problem with the concept of a subculture is that once a distinction is made between subculture and culture the tendency is to use the latter term with some very unfortunate implications for anthropological analysis. In the study of poverty in the United States the result has been a proliferation of a vast number of "cultures": poverty culture, working class culture, black culture, dregs culture, slum culture, and the like. Although the intent of the terms subculture and culture has been to imply some kind of dynamic interaction between human social systems, the unfortunate condition which has resulted from the proliferation of these various "cultures" has been the assumption that they exist in isolation from the larger socioculture unit of which the term subculture implies they are a part.[1] In order to avoid this fallacious assumption there is a need to investigate the forces and factors which influence the external as well as the internal dynamics of presumed subcultures.

In the burgeoning studies concerned with poverty in the United States one area of investigation that has been neglected is the nature of the relationship between peoples who exist in poverty and the larger national culture of which they are a part.[2] There is an increasing awareness that patterns of social behavior among groups under investigation in complex social settings, especially state societies, are regulated by many factors and forces not embedded in the group which is under investigation but which emanate from the larger sociocultural mileau, especially its political institutions and structures. In order

1

to fully explicate this awareness and to deflect the entrenched interests of social scientists from static and synchronic conceptualizations which the terms subculture and culture in certain circumstances have come to assume, a concept more amenable to the investigation of the relationship between local populations and the larger cultural setting must be developed. As noted in the introduction, the notion of a poverty habitat represents such a concept.

 A habitat, whether characterized by poverty or some other criterion, refers to an empirically determined component of a larger national environment within which a population adapts in order to ensure its survival and existence. A poverty habitat may be conceptualized as the particular constellation of demographic, physical, sociocultural, and ideological features which exist on the margins of a nation's dominant technological system and institutional nexus, especially that concerned with economic, political, legal, and educational activity, and into which a nation's impoverished population is only marginally integrated (see fig. 1). A poverty habitat represents more than just a slum or ghetto because such concepts have assumed the unfortunate connotations associated with a subculture and do not take into account the relationship of the population in poverty to the larger sociocultural environment in which they are encapsulated. The larger, or maximal, sociocultural environment in which the habitat represented by San Ysidro is a part is that delineated by the national boundaries of the United States. Within this maximal environment the state exerts an overriding influence upon the adaptation a population makes to its habitat. In order to fully appreciate this influence it seems first necessary to differentiate between a nation and a state. Such a profitable distinction has been made by Y. A. Cohen, who suggests that:

> A nation is a society made up of many communities and regions, classes (and sometimes castes), economically and otherwise specialized groups, a variety of daily and other cycles in the life style, and the like, all of which are centrally controlled by a set of interlocking agencies (or bureaucracies) that are more or less differentiated. The latter constitute the state, and they are unified into a single administrative entity devoted to the maintenance of order and conformity . . . Thus, in these terms "nation" is the territorial representation of such a society, while "state" is its political representation. (1969:658–59)

It is this complex which comprises a nation which I will refer to as the national cultural environment. It is within this setting that decisions rendered by agents and authorities who represent the political structures of the state may stimulate or inhibit changes and new adaptations within the various habitats of the nation and, by extension, the larger environment of which the habitats are but components.

 Of course poverty may also be analyzed from a more local-level

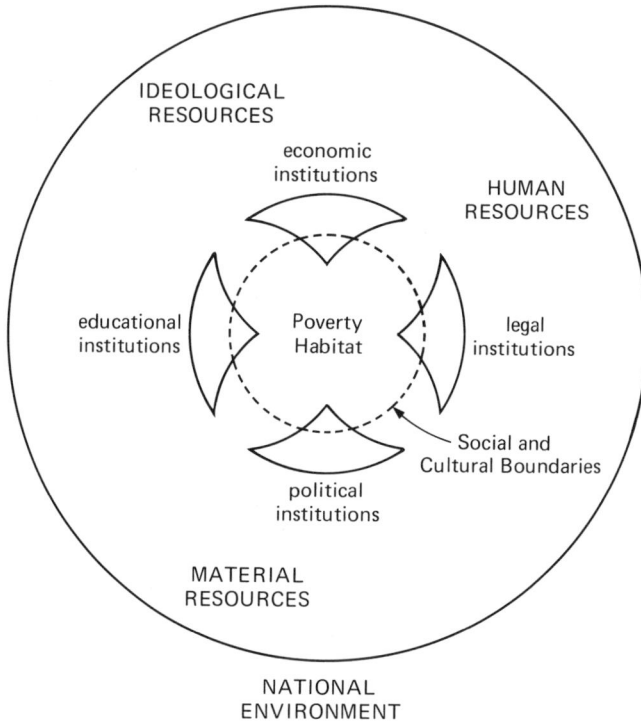

Figure 1.1. The Conceptualization of a Poverty Habitat.

perspective; a good portion of this work will be devoted to just that. However, it will also attempt to point to the relationship between politics and poverty at the local level and other, further removed political centers up to the federal government. If the state seems a far removed entity to deal with in the study of poverty it is precisely because of the overriding influence which it overtly and covertly brings to bear upon the affairs of a nation's populations and by which it may promote or alleviate poverty that it needs to be considered. This becomes increasingly significant if the fact is recognized that poverty as we know it evolved hand in hand with urban state societies. In order to demonstrate the significance of the state it seems fruitful next to introduce at a somewhat abstract level the relationship between states and local poverty.

Although the precise origin of poverty is lost in history, it may be hypothesized that poverty as we know it today and as distinct from the poverty of primitive tribal peoples represents a concomitant development of the evolution of agricultural urban states in protohistoric times in the Old World in Mesopotamia around 3000 B.C. and in the New World in the Valley of Mexico around 1500 A.D. [3] Similar developments may have occurred elsewhere, but the parallel and convergent development represented by these areas currently provides our best information on this problem. The protohistoric period in these areas was apparently characterized by a gradual population increase for which traditional horticultural techniques proved incapable of producing a sufficient supply of food. This stimulated development of a more efficient agricultural technology and utilization of energy, especially in the form of irrigation works. One result of this transition to an agricultural technology was the development of highly stratified urban state societies. Briefly, this process seems to have taken the following course.

In protohistoric Mexico and Mesopotamia shortly prior to the evolution of urban states the control of productive resources—land, material, technology—were vested in tribal horticultural populations and were available at large to all members who maintained good standing in a kinship matrix such as a lineage or clan in which lands were held commonly. Among similar horticultural populations today this still prevails. As population increased a more efficient means of producing food surpluses and allocating them to the populations became necessary. This resulted in a differentiation between choice lands, especially irrigated lands, and those less productive and the control of such lands. Irrigated lands increased in value and gradually were expropriated from tribal kin groups by state officials and incipient entrepreneurs as one means of increasing efficiency necessary to control and deploy resources and surpluses to the growing population. Centralized state and private control of these resources gradually increased and the significance of horticultural, kin-based populations near the urban states gradually decreased. As tribal social structure broke down under the intricacies of this process, many people were apparently forced into the urban centers. Once there, unable to find accommodation in urban state institutions, some apparently assumed a shifting way of life, moving between urban and rural areas as economic vicissitudes and other pressures dictated, such as attacks by marauding nomadic pastoralists operating outside state control. Others assumed a more permanent urban status in the condition we currently refer to as poverty in habitats adapted to that way of life.

As this theory suggests the role and significance of the state in this process has to be taken into account because it is as a result of state sanctions as well as its moral and material backing that private control over productive resources and technology can develop. A good case can be made that in the early phase of emerging nations, past and present, private capital and resources are so limited that it is only through the initial backing and support of state resources that private capital can begin to emerge. Although these efforts concur heavily with a socialist ideology, S. M. Lipset argues convincingly that even the economic growth and development of a capitalistic democracy such as the United States relied heavily upon state programs and direct support; that "The doctrine of 'laissez-faire' became dominant only after the growth of large corporation and private investment funds reduced the pressures for public funds"

(1963:52). Although evidence is sketchy, similar factors in a general way seem to have prevailed during the evolution of the earliest state societies, and still operate perhaps at a more significant and increased rate today. In adapting to these changing conditions, certain segments of the population would be selected against participation and integration into the urban state economic framework; it is these who would become the poor people of the time.

As suggested, it is also probable that early protohistoric urban centers served as repositories for landless peoples seeking an alternative way of life. One significant disruptive factor in the social stability of the early states may well have been the fluid and unstable populations who existed on the fringes of the urban centers and who were especially susceptible to their economic and political vicissitudes. Such populations could be construed to refer not only to nomadic belligerants on the frontiers of the early states, but also to disenfranchised, landless populations which under times of severe economic depression could emerge as a formidable city mob. Circumstances in which city mobs and rural peasants have revolted against economic conditions over which the centralized authorities had little or no control are not historical anomalies. One does not have to conjure irrationally to draw a parallel between populations who were previously peasants or tribal peoples and who exist in poverty on the fringes of urban centers today in Latin America, Africa, Asia, and elsewhere and a similarly volatile condition in protohistoric Old and New World urban centers. Some generalizations regarding possible factors which may promote the evolution and development of poverty habitats may help clarify this phenomena. In this context it may be theorized that poverty habitats in the past and currently may come about in three primary ways, none of which is exclusive of the others.

In one instance poverty habitats may evolve because social and technological resources may not exist in an area due to natural causes, because they have not been allocated to the area, or because they have not intruded into it by some other means. Also, resources that are available for exploitation may not be equally available to all members of the society because of segregation or prejudice due to ethnic background, as in the United States, South Africa, and elsewhere, or because of cultural factors, such as those which affect the socioeconomic status of Catholics in Northern Ireland. The inequality of access to desiderata and resources, an important diagnostic of poverty, may in any society be accounted for partially by historical factors. However, in industrial nations the finiteness of resources, their peculiar distribution, and the general unequality of access to them accounts in large measure for the variety of adaptations so evident in these complex state systems. The adaptation characterized by poverty may be based in part upon sociotechnological relationships reminiscent of previously dominant technological systems, such as agricultural peasants, migrant workers, and the like as well as concentrations of large numbers of urban poor and unemployed whose energies the technological system is unable to absorb. Without an infusion of meaningful human and technological resources into these areas an overadaptation may result; that is a relationship between a population, its sociocultural system, and its habitat may become characterized by a lack of dynamics and change. The persistence of this condition may help account for the hard core poverty characteristic of urban ghettoes and rural sumps, the poverty habitats where the hope of a better future is lacking or unheard of.

In another instance high level decisions in the authority structures of economic and political institutions may deploy or redeploy critical technological and human resources to certain areas which then attract or create a superfluous labor supply where none had existed previously. Although the physical sites of most urban industrial centers of the United States are the result of complex historical and geographical phenomena, their expanding urban ethnic poor and decaying inner cities may be understood at least partially as the result of this phenomenon. Of course the mere superfluousness of persons who are available for work and who congregate in a habitat characterized by poverty may also be compounded by other factors. Individuals who are relatively unskilled, who are monolingual, such as many Spanish-speakers, or who do not speak standard American English, as is the case with many blacks, who are also disadvantaged by their race, and the like, may serve as contributing factors to a populations inutility in that environment. Such populations also tend to displace other populations of higher socioeconomic status in neighborhoods and zones, and over time these become poverty habitats. Authoritarian decisions may affect and alter the relationship of the population to the environment's resource potential by selecting against certain categories of population in other ways. Increased cybernation and automation of industry, specifically the result of high level decisions, select against individuals with a variety of skills. Nor is it uncommon to discover a significant lag between the employment potential of the technology and expectations of employment by individuals in the society. Well educated and highly trained persons may find it difficult to acquire jobs in their specialized fields. Less skilled populations have a more difficult time, and under current programs in the United States large numbers of individuals are training to acquire the very skills the changes in industry are making obsolete.

Finally, and as an extension of the previous factors, a poverty habitat may result from the withdrawal of technology and resources from an area due to the depletion of certain resources or their replacement by others which the technology may utilize more efficiently. The Cumberland Plateau and other regions of Appalachia described by Caudhil (1962) represent one such case in point. Here the life-ways of a large population became dependent upon coal mining. Over time as a result of a depletion of the best coal in areas of Appalachia and competition with more efficient fuels, such as gas, oil, electricity, and nuclear power, many mining companies decided to severely cut back reproduction or leave the area. This resulted in a precipitous decline in the critical basis for employment and essential services in the region. A depressed environment with both urban and rural poverty habitats developed very quickly.

The current plight of engineers and other highly skilled personnel in the United State's aerospace and other industries graphically points out that even highly skilled and trained individuals perform at the sufferance of the technology and resources in an area. Although it is unlikely that these cutbacks will result in a poverty habitat composed of civil engineers, they are indicative of the fact that the withdrawal of resources and realignment of social and industrial priorities may affect others than the "traditional" poor. They will, however, reap the backlash of these processes. Populations in Seattle, San Diego, Los Angeles, and elsewhere have been especially hard hit because of alterations in national needs and priorities. Although highly trained and skilled professional persons are suddenly and in great number for the first time unemployed and in dire economic straits, considerably less attention is paid to the fact that as a result of the withdrawal and redeployment of technology and resources, the populations in the nation's poverty habitats who exist in even more precarious relationship to these institutional complexes suffer most severely and in greater proportion than other categories of population in the society. Unspecialized populations in American society have been increasingly selected against for participation in our industrial technology. This problem may be compounded by the currently evolving relationship between the society's social organization and its changing energy sources; in the near future this may render large numbers of highly specialized individuals as dependent upon the welfare of the state as are the poor.

Poverty habitats are at least partially the result of the general causes discussed above. They may be conceived of, in more than a metaphorical sense, as existing on the margins of the dominant institutions, technology, and resources allocated generally throughout the national cultural environment and which serve to integrate and perpetuate the national sociocultural system as a whole. Each poverty habitat is also the result of its own unique historical circumstance which places a special mark upon the racial and ethnic identity of its population, other features of its demographic composition, aspects of its institutional matrix, ideological, value, motivational system, and the like. In short, a poverty habitat can be fully understood only in the context of the historical factors out of which it emerges. San Ysidro is not an exception. In order to demonstrate this I will turn next to the historical conditions out of which San Ysidro emerged and its current status as a poverty habitat.

THE SETTING: SAN YSIDRO

San Ysidro is a small community about fifteen miles south of San Diego, California. Although it is separated from San Diego by several incorporated communities, San Ysidro was annexed to the city of San Diego in 1957. Until that time San Ysidro's solitary claim to recognition was its status as the port of entry from Tijuana, Mexico, into the United States. After annexation, for most all purposes, San Ysidro seems to have been "forgotten" by the city of San Diego until 1968. By that time poverty had been rediscovered in the United States and a "war on poverty" had been declared by then President Lyndon B. Johnson. San Ysidro had been designated a poverty pocket and the service and political institutions of the war on poverty had been founded in the area.

The area in which San Ysidro exists is within the Lower California biotic province which consists of chaparral vegetation, rolling hills, and a Mediterranean climate. Rainfall averages between 10 and 15 inches annually. There are few extremes of temperature. Summers are mild and in the winter the temperature rarely falls to the freezing point. San Ysidro is situated approximately five miles from the Pacific Ocean on the fringe of the Tia Juana River Valley. Most of the community spreads over the foothills of Otay Mesa, a large table land, agriculturally rich in celery, radishes, tomatoes and other truck vegetables, which rises up behind San Ysidro. Across the river basin the high and arid hills of Tijuana rise out of the Pacific. The river valley forms a kind of funnel between the hills of Tijuana and Otay Mesa and the lay of the land tends to regulate the air flow and climate of the area. The mild year-round climate of San Ysidro is one of the major attractions of the area as a place to live, especially for elderly and retired persons. The other major attraction is its proximity to Tijuana, one of Mexico's fastest growing cities. As a result of a massive influx of people from other areas of Mexico, over the last decade the hills of Tijuana have become corroded with a plethora of shacks that comprise the poor *colonias* of Tijuana. Except for the mile stretch of highway between the community of San Ysidro and the border which is cluttered with a variety of motels, restaurants, and shops, the shabbiness of the area is not confined to Tijuana. It spreads across the river basin and infects San Ysidro with a similar dreariness. Few people now actually see San Ysidro, for the freeway from San Diego effectively by-passes it and speeds persons on their way to Tijuana. Given the changes currently affecting San Ysidro, few people will see it again as the shabby, dreary community here described.

San Ysidro's growth and prosperity have always been based upon its relationship to the neighboring urban centers of Tijuana and San Diego. The first settlement in San Ysidro, a mission and trading post, was established in 1818.[4] By 1887 San Ysidro had evolved into a small and relatively insignificant village. It had also become a neighbor to the larger town of Tia Juana City which had grown over the years in the Tia Juana River Basin and spread without regard for the international border, which at that time was rather indifferently regarded and maintained. The ethnic mixture of Anglo-Americans and Mexican-Americans so pronounced now on the American and more affluent side of the border undoubtedly antedates this time. In 1891 one of the many periodic and severe floods for which the Tia Juana River was notorious swept out of the hills of

Mexico and washed away most of Tia Juana City. Many people did rebuild, this time on higher ground. Their enterprise laid the foundation of the present communities of Tijuana on the Mexican side of the border and San Ysidro on the American.

The slow growth of San Ysidro was augmented in 1909 by the intrusion of a group of Anglo-Americans known as the "Little Landers," who moved into the rich agricultural bottom land of the Tia Juana River and began an experiment in communal living. The experiment was in reaction to the increasing industrialization of the United States, and the ideology of the Little Landers was best expressed on a poster used to advertise the venture. It read:

Acre farms for those who prefer
"A Little Land and a Living Surely"
to
"Desperate Struggle and Wealth Possibly" [5]

The Little Landers' commune represented a cooperative marketing venture. Agricultural surpluses were trucked daily to a Little Landers' market in San Diego, and profits of the cooperative were used for such improvements of the commune as wells for irrigation and water. These wells served as the main supply of water for the community until 1958. The economic and social foundations of the commune, however, were not as substantial as they outwardly appeared. In 1916 another major flood struck the valley and the commune was destroyed. Two Little Landers were killed and 100 were left homeless and subsisted on relief funds in San Diego. The experiment ended. However, the Little Landers in San Ysidro and on the lands of Otay Mesa beyond suffered little damage. They remained and formed the nucleus of an Anglo-American aggregate within the almost exclusively Mexican community of San Ysidro. A few of the original Little Landers were still alive in 1968.

In 1916, California outlawed horse racing and betting and the first race track opened in Tijuana. Gambling and vice grew in Tijuana from that time on and gave the community a reputation that persists yet today, although with considerably less foundation. Tijuana's profligacy increased during the era of United States Prohibition and culminated with the opening of the Agua Caliente resort, race track and golf course in 1928 and the initiation of big time gambling on a large scale. San Ysidro also was officially declared a United States' port of entry into Mexico.

San Ysidro prospered during the boom years of Tijuana gambling. It became a center for horse training, breeding, and boarding, and in severely attenuated form, due to the shortage of water in Tijuana, still serves this function today. During the 1920s and early 1930s San Ysidro's population consisted of a couple of thousand people, of which approximately 60 percent were of Mexican descent and 40 percent of Anglo-American descent. The Anglos worked primarily in the gambling and racing industries of Tijuana. In 1936 a way of life was shattered. President Cardenas of Mexico outlawed gambling. This resulted in a rapid exodus of Anglos and money from the area. With its economic base gone, San Ysidro resumed its obscurity as an agricultural village and slowly slipped out of the economic mainstream of American society.

By 1940 the population of San Ysidro was estimated to be approximately 97 percent Mexican descent and 3 percent Anglo-American descent.[6] After World War II the mild year-round climate of San Ysidro began slowly to attract Anglos, especially older persons seeking a low cost area in which to retire. In the last few years the entire border area has grown considerably. Today San Ysidro has an approximate population of 7,000 persons, two-thirds of whom are of Mexican descent and one-third of Anglo-American descent. About 50 percent of the Anglo-Americans are retired (San Ysidro Community Survey 1968:16; see Appendix).[7] To a great extent San Ysidro outwardly still resembles a quiet agricultural village.

In 1953 San Ysidro was dissected by a major North-South freeway, U.S. Interstate 5, which linked San Diego to Tijuana. In a sense this also bought San Diego closer to San Ysidro. By 1955 a sizable body of influential San Ysidro citizens representing both ethnic groups wanted San Diego police and water service. As the population of Tijuana increased a severe strain was placed on the Tia Juana River. As the water table fell, the water system established by the Little Landers forty years earlier began to prove inadequate and an acute water shortage threatened. Also, there was a general feeling, never fully substantiated by fact, that thievery and burglary were rampant in the area because of San Ysidro's proximity to the border and the number of Mexicans crossing illegally into the United States. On September 26, 1957, San Ysidro and a total of some 17,750 acres of land, far exceeding the boundaries of San Ysidro itself, was annexed to San Diego. This area extends roughly from the international border north to the southern tip of San Diego Bay, eastward several miles along the Otay River Valley and then south to the international border (see fig. 1.2). Some citizens were not in favor of annexation, and still today there is widespread feeling, especially among Mexican-Americans, that San Ysidro was better off when it was part of the county. Despite this, annexation by San Diego and the introduction of city water solved the water problem, and the establishment of a police station in San Ysidro reduced the concern over theft and burglary.

Throughout this period influentials in San Ysidro were not alone in desiring annexation to San Diego. The city of San Diego had for some time been anxious to have more control over the border. There was a growing awareness of the vast tourist potential of the area, especially if San Diego and Tijuana worked together to stimulate this potential to their mutual benefit. There was also concern with the traffic of drugs across the border and lack of control of the crossing of American minors into the sin pits for which Tijuana at this time was notorious. Control of the border zone by San Diego, in conjunction with federal agencies, went a long way to promoting tourism and alleviating at least some of the latter problems.

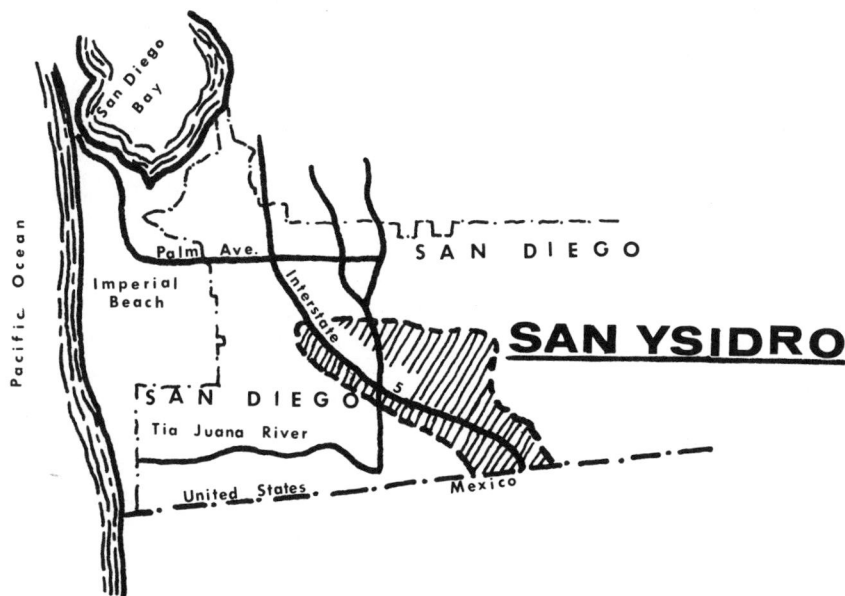

Figure 1.2. The San Diego Border Area. Source: San Ysidro Community Plan, 1970.

Despite its annexation, San Ysidro is only loosely associated with San Diego. The majority of its people have closer ties with other nearby communities. Tijuana is within walking distance of San Ysidro, and serves as a major focus for a variety of services and activities for a great portion of the Mexican-American population, as well as for a large segment of the Anglo population. Prices are considerably lower for minor services, such as haircuts, and goods that can be carried duty free across the border, such as food and clothing. There is also a deep sentimental attachment to Tijuana for a great many of the Mexican-Americans in San Ysidro. However, the proximity of Tijuana and the cheap labor it supplies as a result of the great number of Mexican citizens who possess resident alien work permits, or green cards, and maintain domiciles in Tijuana, where the cost of living is cheap, while working in the United States for far below scale wages, tends to depress the area economically. On the one hand this facilitates the survival of individuals on low or fixed incomes; on the other, because Tijuana is in a foreign country and quite poor itself, it offers nothing to the people of San Ysidro in terms of primary services, such as welfare, employment, developmental capital, and the like. The result is that there is no way in which San Ysidro can advantage itself by its proximity to Tijuana to reduce its status as a community in poverty.

Other nearby communities, especially Chula Vista, a few miles north and accessible by bus, serve many of the needs of the population of San Ysidro more effectively than does San Diego. Chula Vista is a predominately white, middle-class suburban community which, beyond the relatively close shopping facilities it offers to San Ysidro, is not overly friendly to ethnic minorities. In short, while San Ysidro is part of San Diego and has borders abutting on Tijuana, there is distance between San Ysidro and both these communities which in a real sense tends to isolate San Ysidro. The community exists between two dominant urban centers which tends to put San Ysidro in what may be described as a cultural and ethnic bind. This certainly affects and has great implications for the problems to be examined in this work.

Today the greater part of San Ysidro lies to the north of U.S. Interstate 5. Except for the few stores that exist in the funnel leading to the United States-Mexican border, all the commercial district of San Ysidro is situated in this area and extends some four blocks along the main street, San Ysidro Boulevard. Most stores along San Ysidro Boulevard are shabby or antiquated and alternate with vacant lots, dilapidated housing, trailer courts, and dusty alleys which give access to the back areas of the town. Two large feed stores and a general store which stocks bridles, saddles, and other equine paraphernalia, as well as a variety of other goods, hark back to a more bucolic past and deeper involvement of San Ysidro in the horse racing enterprises of Tijuana. Five grocery stores and a tortilleria are well stocked with Mexican foods and condiments. Several yardage shops in close proximity suggest a high degree of sartorial self-sufficiency among the people of San Ysidro. The large number of notary publics in San Ysidro, almost all of whom advertise in Spanish assistance with taxes and/or immigration matters, suggest major concerns of the Mexican-American population. The center of the town consists of a park which divides this commercial zone and which extends from San Ysidro Boulevard two blocks north. At one end on San Ysidro Boulevard is a very small library; at the other is situated the civic center, an old building in which many of the community's social and civic functions take place.

As noted, San Ysidro is a bi-ethnic community composed of Anglo-Americans and people of Mexican descent. The Anglo-American population tends to be most heavily concentrated above Cottonwood Avenue in the north section of town and in the foothills of Otay Mesa; the Mexican-American population is most heavily concentrated in the area south of Cottonwood Avenue. However, no area in San Ysidro is made up exclusively of either ethnic population. Also, the visible poverty indicators of the area, shabby housing, old cars, poor land utilization, a drab exterior, and the like are found throughout San Ysidro. The poorest section of San Ysidro, the Bolton Hall district, is situated between the freeway and the main street, San Ysidro Boulevard. This area is comprised primarily of peoples of Mexican descent, many of whom are resident Mexican nationals who possess green card visas which permit them to live and work in the United States. This is an area of high unemployment and underemployment and most of the agricultural laborers in San Ysidro live in this region. However, the quality and concentration of poverty in this area as compared to other areas of San Ysidro is simply one of degree. The only exceptions to the above overview of San Ysidro is the new housing development and the fence which encloses it, a harbinger of the changes which are about to beset San Ysidro, on the plateau half way up the bluffs of Otay Mesa. This development, Sunkist Homes, is inhabited primarily by peoples of Mexican descent. Since the price of houses in the development range from $18,000 to $21,000 the people in the Sunkist development are generally and obviously better off than most Mexican-Americans in San Ysidro. San Ysidro generally smacks of decay in its physical structure and this is especially evident south of Cottonwood Avenue in the area heavily populated by Mexican-Americans. The stores are shabby and architecurally antiquated; housing is poor. It has been pointed out that in Texas and California, Spanish-speaking families occupy worse housing for high rents than any other ethnic group (Glick 1966:107). San Ysidro does not seem to be an exception to this (see table 1.1). As indicated in table 1.1, about 25 percent of the total housing in San Ysidro is inadequate. It may be suggested that because people living in poor housing are primarily Mexican-American, and because they have the larger families, nearly half the people in San Ysidro are living in poor or substandard housing. While the correlation between rent and house quality is not made explicit in these figures, if the above assumption is correct approximately 50 percent of the Mexican-American population also pay between $70 to $100 rent for housing which in many cases was determined by the author to be of poorer quality than that inhabited by Anglos paying the same rent.

The implications for the kind of existence one leads in conditions of this sort are subtle, but not unpredictable. After reviewing all relevant studies of the affects of poor housing on residents, Alvin Schorr concludes that the following affects may spring from such housing:

> . . . a perception of one's self that leads to pessimism and passivity, stress to which the individual cannot adapt, poor health, and state of dissatisfaction; pleasure or company but not in solitude, cynicism about people and organizations, a high degree of sexual stimulation without legitimate outlet, and difficulty in household management and child rearing; and relationships that tend to spread out into the neighborhood rather than deeply into the family. (1964:20–21)

Many of these features were manifest in San Ysidro and were the basis of many of the conflicts that developed in the community during the course of this research.

A correlative feature of the poor housing in San Ysidro is the poor utilization of land in the area. South of the freeway, in the Tia Juana River Basin, horse corrals are prominent near the border and serve the Tijuana race track.

Table 1-1.   Quality of Housing in San Ysidro

	Anglo-American Houses		Mexican-American Houses						Total	
			Spanish-Speaking only		Bilingual		Mexican-American Total			
	N	%	N	%	N	%	N	%	N	%
Excellent Good	97	71	58	35	111	52	169	44	266	51
Adequate	22	16	48	29	47	22	95	25	117	23
Deteriorated-Dilapidated	18	13	59	36	57	26	116	31	134	26
	137	100	165	100	215	100	380	100	517	100

Cost of Housing in San Ysidro

	Anglo-American Houses		Mexican-American Houses						Total	
			Spanish-Speaking only		Bilingual		Mexican-American Total			
Less Than	N	%	N	%	N	%	N	%	N	%
$50	9	12	4	3	7	5	11	4	20	6
$50-59	7	11	14	10	4	3	18	6	25	7
$60-69	9	13	23	16	9	6	32	11	41	11
$70-79	12	18	23	16	22	14	45	15	57	16
$80-89	5	8	29	20	27	18	56	19	61	17
$90-99	6	9	22	16	26	17	48	16	54	15
$100-109	5	8	9	6	29	19	38	13	43	12
$110-119	4	6	11	8	11	7	22	7	26	7
$120+	10	15	7	5	19	12	26	9	36	10
	67	100	142	100	154	101	296	100	363	101

Source: San Ysidro Community Survey, 1968.

Farther north vegetable and dairy farms take advantage of the rich bottom land. Between these areas the land is scrub covered and eroded. Housing is sparse and scattered along dirt streets which irregularly dissect the river basin. In the most populated area north of the freeway approximately one-quarter of the habitable land consists of open fields, many of which are littered with junk cars, stacks of wood, dilapidated buildings, and so forth. Many of the streets are poorly laid out, also unpaved, a survival of much earlier periods of San Ysidro's growth and development, and contribute to the dusty feeling one frequently experiences in San Ysidro. This disconnected patchwork mosaic also affects the social interaction in the community and is related to the substandard housing. If apathy is the result of such housing, it is compounded by the social isolation imposed upon members of the community by the fragmented land use and street and settlement patterns. This results in a social distance between individuals and groups in the community and for many of the poorer people intensifies the frustration, alienation, lack of self-identity and apathy of individuals who are forced to exist without firm networks of relationships with their fellow. A viable role identity and sense of anchorage within a firm institutional and social complex is often lacking. In part this is because networks of social relationship and the institutions and groups which they comprise are depreciated and shallow among the poor of San Ysidro. This is not due to an internal pathology inherent in social structure of poor peoples, as Moynihan (1965) suggests for the black family. Rather it is the result of the constraints imposed by the habitats within which persons in poverty are forced to adapt as a result of pressures which emanate from the dominant institutions and culture of the larger national environment.

As discussed, one of the premises which underlies this research is that a poverty habitat, rural or urban, contains a population which is only marginally integrated into the dominant institutions and technology characteristic of the United States as a whole. This is primarily a result of barriers to ingress into these institutions and the technology imposed by the dominant national culture of the United States upon its poverty habitats. One effect of these barriers is the development of isolation from and social distance between peoples in or near poverty and those not in this condition. This isolation intrudes upon and conditions many aspects of the culture of peoples in poverty, their social organization, values, cognitive orientations, and the like. Any changes in the culture of peoples in poverty habitats must be stimulated by the forces which impose the extant condition in the first place. This is not easily achieved so long as poverty habitats exist in the kind of social isolation from the dominant cultures which to a great extent they manifest and which is perpetuated by policies and decisions emanating from the dominant national culture.

San Ysidro is no exception to this principle, but its situation is somewhat curious. While it is legally a part of the city of San Diego, it is separated from San Diego not only by fifteen miles and other communities, but also by inadequate transportation facilities. This separation effectively promotes an isolation of the community from and a lack of integration of much of its population, especially the Mexican-Americans, with San Diego and by extension, the United States. The result is that San Ysidro has maintained an agricultural character and aura reminiscent of its past, but which has been tarnished by the poverty which now affects the area. Extensive vegetable truck farms are prominent in the area. Many households maintain small backyard gardens. Cows seem ubiquitous due to the dairy farms that border San Ysidro. A few cows may be found even in the community itself. One may still be awakened in San Ysidro by the crowing of roosters at dawn. However, much of the Mexican-American population is neither rural peasant nor urban proletariat. They are simply isolated, alienated, and poor.

In 1953 the Interstate 5 freeway opened and gave direct access from San Diego to the international border. It rerouted the traffic from Alternate 101, an old two-lane highway which runs through San Ysidro and which was frequently congested due to heavy border traffic. In planning and routing this freeway the highway department argued that it would reduce congestion in San Ysidro and facilitate travel between San Ysidro and San Diego. While it accomplished both these ends and facilitated growth of the border area generally, the freeway did very little to alleviate any of San Ysidro's economic or social problems, an implicit consideration in the highway department's argument.[9] In fact, these problems have been compounded over the last decade. For example, about one-quarter of all residents in San Ysidro currently do not have a car and this correlates almost exactly to the percentage of Mexican-Americans in San Ysidro who do not have a car. One-third of the residents who speak only Spanish do not have a car (San Ysidro Community Survey, 1968:34; see Appendix). And many of the cars that are seen are old and often in poor condition.

Public transportation does not effecrively alleviate this isolation, and the existing bus service is one of the major complaints of the residents of San Ysidro. Western Greyhound Lines provides around-the-clock, round-trip service between San Diego and the international border, at half-hour intervals, but makes only one stop in San Ysidro on the north bound route, and the south bound bus stops only at the border—as much as two miles from some parts of San Ysidro. One must then walk back into San Ysidro from the border, take a taxi, or pay another bus fare to San Ysidro when the next express departs north. San Diego Economy Lines, Inc., also serves the area between San Ysidro and Chula Vista and points north to San Diego at two hour intervals from 7:00 in the morning to five in the afternoon. Residents complain that its stops also are too few and far between. The elderly, unemployed, and retired complain that fares on both lines are also somewhat high. Greyhound charges sixty cents one way to San Diego, and Economy Lines charges forty cents one way to Chula Vista.[10] Even though approximately three-quarters of the people interviewed by a poll taken for the planning department of the city of San Diego indicated that they would ride public busses if adequate service were provided (San Ysidro Community Survey 1968:34; see Appendix), the city of San Diego transit system does not feel that a sufficient need exists in San Ysidro to warrant extending service to the area.

This inadequate transportation has direct significance for San Ysidro's severely depressed economic circumstance. The agriculture of the area, dairy farms, truck farms, and several produce-packing sheds, provide employment primarily for the Mexican labor available in Tijuana. There is practically no other industry near San Ysidro that can employ people without skills or direct transportation. This is reflected in the unemployment rate among the Mexican-American population in San Ysidro (see table 1.2).

There are several salient features which may be derived from table 1.2 and which are indicative of the poverty of the area. The overall unemployment rate for San Ysidro is well over twice the national average, and over 20 percent of the residents are employed in unskilled labor. With reference to the Mexican-American population the statistics are even more striking. Among persons who speak only Spanish, 14 percent are unemployed, or four times the national average. Among the population which is bilingual, and which is almost totally of Mexican descent, 8 percent, or twice the national average, are unemployed. For the Mexican-American population, as a whole the unemployment rate is over three times the national average. Twenty-eight percent of the Mexican-American population, 33 percent of the population who speak Spanish only, and 25 percent who are bilingual are employed in unskilled labor as opposed to only 3 percent of the Anglo population. Unemployment figures of such magnitude are one characteristic common to all poverty habitats, and in San Ysidro serve as one additional factor which along with poor housing and land utilization promotes the apathetic character of poverty habitat residents.[11]

This economic depression has implications for the relationship of San Ysidro to other communities and urban centers as well as for San Ysidro itself, for another characteristic of poverty habitats is the stability of their residents.[12] A rather popular notion regarding San Ysidro is that it serves as a way station for Mexican immigrants prior to moving north to Los Angeles or other areas. This is not so, because Mexican immigrants simply do not stop in San Ysidro.

Table 1-2. San Ysidro Employment Statistics

| | Anglo-American | | Mexican-American | | | | | | Total | |
| | | | Spanish-Speaking only | | Bilingual | | Mexican-American Total | | | |
	N	%	N	%	N	%	N	%	N	%
Skilled	52	28	60	29	118	45	178	38	230	35
Unskilled	6	3	67	33	65	25	132	28	138	21
Professional	11	6	2	1	12	5	14	3	25	4
Retired	104	55	26	13	32	12	58	12	162	25
Unemployed	4	2	28	14	22	8	50	11	54	8
Housewife	1	1	19	9	2	1	21	4	22	3
Disabled	10	5	4	2	13	5	17	4	27	4
	188	100	206	101	264	101	470	100	658	100

Source: San Ysidro Community Survey, 1968.

Sixty percent of the bilingual Mexican-American population has been in San Ysidro more than four years, while about 40 percent of those who speak only Spanish have been in San Ysidro more than four years. About 90 percent expressed a preference to remain in San Ysidro (San Ysidro Community Survey, 1968:11-12; see Appendix). Almost 24 percent of the Anglo-Americans have been in San Ysidro between ten and nineteen years, and about 27 percent have been in San Ysidro for more than twenty years. About 78 percent intend to stay in San Ysidro (see table 1.3).

The Anglo population of San Ysidro is stable for reasons different than those accounting for Mexican-American residence stability. About half the Anglo population is composed of retired people. The climate of San Ysidro has been one major attraction; the relatively low tax base has been another for people living on fixed incomes. San Ysidro has also been a quiet community. However, the two latter factors are changing rapidly and may effectively aid in displacing much of this element of the population. The remainder of the Anglo population operates many of the businesses in San Ysidro, or are employed in neighboring communities.

Of overriding significance for the permanence of the Mexican-American population is the proximity to Mexico. This factor is far less important to the Anglo population. Many of the Anglos, retired people especially, expressed a real disdain for Mexico and indicated they seldom crossed the border. Still, many Anglos go into Tijuana for reasons very similar to those of the Mexican-American population. Prices for many goods and services are considerably cheaper. There is no sales tax in Tijuana. It seems that Anglos patronize Caliente Race Track more than the Mexican-American population, although movies and other entertainments not available in San Ysidro attract Mexican-Americans

Table 1-3. Years of Residence in San Ysidro

| | Anglo-American | | Mexican-American | | | | | | Total | |
| | | | Spanish-Speaking only | | Bilingual | | Mexican-American Total | | | |
	N	%	N	%	N	%	N	%	N	%
Less Than 1	19	10	26	12	27	10	53	11	72	11
1-2	11	6	30	14	18	7	48	10	59	9
3-4	26	14	61	29	55	20	116	24	142	21
5-9	36	19	45	21	64	24	109	23	145	22
10-19	45	24	31	15	62	23	93	19	138	21
20+	51	27	17	8	45	17	62	13	113	17
	188	100	210	99	271	101	481	100	669	100

Source: San Ysidro Community Survey, 1968.

to Tijuana. The Mexican-American population uses Tijuana much more as a means of stretching its restricted economic resources than does the Anglo population of San Ysidro. Also very significant is the great number of friends and relatives of Mexican-Americans in San Ysidro who live in Tijuana. Along with the ethnic, cultural, and sentimental similarities the people share, this also welds the relationship between the people of the two communities.[13] The Mexican-American people of San Ysidro didn't always express this openly, but most imply it in a number of subtle ways. They feel the people of Tijuana are friendlier than Anglos in the United States. There is no barrier imposed by language differences. The Tijuana television channel is the most popular channel among Mexican-Americans in San Ysidro. Tijuana newspapers are widely read and frequently carry news about San Ysidro not available in San Diego newspapers. And a very steady foot traffic exists between the two communities for a variety of reasons.[14]

On the other hand, the Mexican-Americans have very little attachment to the Anglo communities farther north, and for good reasons. After annexing San Ysidro, San Diego essentially lost interest in the community. It provided San Ysidro with the minimal services of police, garbage collection, water, and little else.[15] These were reflected in higher taxes for the area. Many of the people of San Ysidro resent this. A major complaint among the poorer peoples is that San Ysidro was better off, cleaner, no less efficiently policed, and not as heavily taxed, when it was part of the county of San Diego. The inefficiency of transportation to these areas is another important factor of this detachment. Even if transportation was available, the lack of skills among many of the Mexican-American population would prohibit participation in the larger economy of San Diego. The ethnic, cultural, and language differences between the Mexican-Americans of San Ysidro and many of the institutions of San Diego also prohibit an articulation with and integration of Mexican-Americans into San Diego and Anglo-American society and culture. Finally, given the economic impoverishment and lack of skills and education of so many of San Ysidro's Mexican-American population, one can legitimately ask, where else could they go? Peoples with no skills, little education, and these factors compounded by ethnic and cultural differences which alienate them from the large society, are forced to adapt to harsher realities than are persons who are part of the dominant Anglo-American society and culture. San Ysidro is one example of such an habitational reality.

The lack of skills of many of the Mexican-Americans of San Ysidro and their high unemployment is reflective of other conditions relevant to San Ysidro and San Diego. One is certainly related to the fact that approximately 41 percent of the Mexican-Americans in San Ysidro feel themselves competent only in speaking Spanish (San Ysidro Community Survey, 1968:11; see Appendix). The barrier this presents to ingress into the job market of American society is common knowledge. Although 59 percent of the Mexican-American population consider themselves bilingual (San Ysidro Community Survey, 1968:11; see Appendix), the great majority are certainly deficient in English, another factor which impedes ingress into the job market. While it may be dangerous to equate the lack of proficiency in English with a poor educational background since some of the Mexican-Americans may have been well educated in Mexico, the vast majority of Mexicans who do immigrate into the United States represent persons from lower economic and educational strata of Mexican society (Pickney 1963:359). Thus, most recent Mexican immigrants into the United States are not educationally equipped to integrate into the economic structure representative of the United States. In San Ysidro almost one-half of the Mexican-American population speaks only Spanish and over 50 percent of this population has been in the United States less than four years. This is a self-perpetuating problem, since some 700 Mexicans immigrate through Tijuana to the United States each month.[16]

It is also a profusely documented fact that educational institutions until recently have done very little to cope with the cultural and language background Mexican-Americans bring into the school systems of the United States.[17] While the quality of education is difficult to assess, there is a widespread belief among concerned Mexican-Americans as well as many Anglos, teachers, administrators, and citizens, that schools in the poverty habitats of San Diego County have much room for improvement with regard to their relationship with the Mexican-Americans of the area. There are, of course, some schools attempting to cope with this problem.

The San Ysidro elementary district is composed of three schools with a student population that is 83 percent Mexican descent, nearly half of whom speak Spanish primarily. This presents a massive confrontation for institutions not long atuned to coping with the emerging demands and expectations of Mexican-Americans. Any expectation of quick and visible changes in overcoming the English language deficiencies and cultural differences Mexican-American children bring to the schools cannot realistically be hoped for, even though it perhaps should be expected. The San Ysidro district is attempting to make changes, as will be analyzed later, though not without reluctance, not as rapidly as it could, and not without opposition from educational institutions with which it is affiliated.

For example, the San Ysidro school district runs a special program for educationally mentally retarded children—a poorly defined category—which, to a very great extent, is controlled by the county of San Diego. The program is a catchall for children with special learning problems, slow learners, children with social problems, children who cannot speak English, as well as some who are mentally retarded. The district also practices the social pass which insists that all children at age thirteen be in the seventh grade, regardless of the grade they were in previously. It is not uncommon for children in the fifth grade to skip grade six and move into a junior high school seventh grade "educationally mentally retarded program." Once students are tracked into this program they rarely leave it. The junior high school is part of a high school district which is notoriously intransigent to modernizing its programs and, as reflected in its administration and many of its faculty, is hostile to the problems of Mexican-American children. Much of the relatively good education received by Mexican-American children in the San Ysidro elementary district is dissipated with the graduation of students into the high school district, and dropout rates prior to graduation from high school are estimated to be in the eightieth percentile.[18]

Remarkably, Mexican-American parents of children in San Ysidro have very few complaints about educational conditions. In a survey taken by the local Community Action Council in the summer of 1968 only 16 respondents out of 524 felt that the schools were not satisfactory for one reason or other. This was at a time when educational problems confronting Spanish-speaking children were a matter of hot debate between concerned Mexican-Americans and school districts generally in the San Diego area. The poverty of the area, the lack of English language skills, the lack of familiarity with educational institutions, as well as a sense of inferiority common to peoples in poverty, all contribute to a lack of awareness of a very important problem area.

In short, the educational problem, while certainly not insurmountable, is not going to be quickly overcome. The result of this will be, for a long time to come, the perpetuation of individuals too poorly educated and trained to participate meaningfully in the major economic institutions of the United States. This will certainly tend to perpetuate poverty habitats.

One final result of this particular constellation of features representative of the poverty habitat is the issue of welfare recipients in San Ysidro. A prominent and stereotyped notion in San Ysidro is that poverty is primarily a result of sloth. "They're poor because they're lazy!" is a very common attitude toward the poor of Anglos and more well-to-do Mexican-Americans. While many of the individuals who express this opinion are reluctant to speculate on how many Mexican-Americans in San Ysidro are on welfare, most indicate that "lots" of them are. Figures between 40 and 80 percent are commonly given. In all cases individuals who make these extravagant claims could name at best only a few people on welfare with whom they personally are familiar.

San Ysidro does have a sizable welfare population. County welfare officials estimate that approximately 17 percent of the population in San Ysidro is accepting one form or other of welfare, and that the vast majority of these are of Mexican descent.[19] One welfare worker resident in San Ysidro pointed out that there are practically no welfare recipients north of Cottonwood Avenue, the vast majority being in the predominantly Mexican-American section of town to the south of Cottonwood Avenue. It has been pointed out that most peoples existing in poverty would prefer to work than accept welfare.[20] This is certainly the impression I gained from the people of San Ysidro. But not for any wage or at any job offered, since many of the jobs available in the area pay less than a living wage. This is directly related to the green card holders who live in Tijuana and work in the United States for low wages, a factor noted previously. Also, many of those most vehemently opposed to welfare are poor people themselves who in fact could use aid of one form or another, but whose pride will not permit them to accept it. Finally, a large number of poor Mexican-Americans also are simply not aware of the benefits available to them.

SUMMARY

The historical setting and description of the poverty habitat represented by San Ysidro could be expanded considerably. However, the salient points for the purpose of this work have been touched upon, and many of these will be examined in more detail later, for many of the considerations mentioned are directly involved in the political activities to be analyzed. San Ysidro now has to be considered in terms of other concepts: the political arena and the contestants which vie within it. It is in the poverty habitat represented by San Ysidro, as well as others throughout the United States, that political institutions representing the war against poverty were legalized for the purpose of combating poverty. In this context the poverty habitats became arenas in which the political groups and institutions proved to be, as Cohen points out (1968a:4), the most important single component which serves to alter the relationship between a population and its habitat. I will begin to investigate this matter in the next chapter.

Chapter Two

Where the Power Lies

One premise upon which this work is based is that every state system develops covertly and overtly a national political cultural policy which has as one of its primary goals the initiation of pressures and policies designed to reduce national sociocultural heterogeneity. This process of integration is effected in a variety of ways. One significant aspect of this process, and one which is an integral part of the expansion horizontally and entrenchment vertically of political institutions throughout the nation, is the increasing specialization of a nation's political institutions for the purpose of maintaining order within the society.[1] From the viewpoint of the state, it may be theorized that this is especially important with reference to those segments of the nation's population which, as a result of their lack of integration into and articulation with the nation's dominant institutions, begin to agitate actively, perhaps violently, for such integration. In the United States agitation for such integration and articulation has recently emerged among its ethnic minorities, a majority of whom exist in a state of poverty or severe economic deprivation.[2]

One of the most recent and significant post Civil War stimulus for the integration of ethnic minorities into American culture resulted from the 1954 decisions of the Supreme Court ordering integration of the nation's schools. Another major stimulus to this process came during the administration of John F. Kennedy and the "rediscovery" in the United States of widespread conditions of abject poverty. It was during this period that the foundations were laid for an attack against poverty, a project conceptualized in large part by the efforts of the president's council of economic advisors under Walter Heller. For the first time in America, economic distress and the factors which provoked it were considered in "structural" terms with reference to peoples living in "pockets of poverty" rather than in "cyclical" terms with reference to the economic cycles through which America's major economic institutions were expected to pass. The result of these efforts was the development of the antecedents to the antipoverty programs which crystalized under the subsequent administration of Lyndon B. Johnson as the war on poverty.[3]

The explicit goal of the war on poverty was to eliminate poverty in the United States by involving the poor in the policy- and decision-making processes which, it was hoped, would result in solutions to the causes of poverty and its attendant problems. Implicit in this program's goals was the integration of peoples in poverty habitats into the economic, political, educational, and other major institutions of American society. These goals were to be achieved by developing a variety of new service and political action institutions within the poverty habitats of the United States. These institutions developed under the Community Action Program of the war on poverty were to augment the efforts of more traditional agencies. However, it was primarily through the war on poverty community action institutions and the power they were to control through organizations and resources developed and supplied in large part by the federal government that a head-on attack against poverty was to be waged. One result of this process was the development of new political "arenas" in the United States. In these arenas a variety of political groups and invididuals who represented established and traditional American institutions from the local to the federal levels, as well as those institutions developed under the war on poverty, were to view for control of programs and, most significantly, the resources by which the social face and character of American society and culture was to be changed.

It has been suggested by persons actively involved in antipoverty programs that issues are abstractions of the real and immediate problems, needs, and conditions which people in poverty habitats confront. In fact, these real problems and their abstract conceptualizations are mutually reinforcing and analytically inseparable. In the arena of San Ysidro conflict developed over a variety of issues between groups and representatives of agencies and institutions which existed outside of the arena but which comprised an important segment of the field involved in its activities. The conflict in the arena of San Ysidro is significant because it was the result both of contradictions built into the super-structure of the war on poverty and of problems at the level of the poverty habitat which affected the antipoverty programs generally throughout the nation.[4] One assumption derived from this is that San Ysidro represents a more or less typical war on poverty arena and manifests many of the fundamental problems which affected and eventually nullified the nation's war on poverty. Even in San Diego County, although San Ysidro manifested the most extreme range of problems and conflict, it was not entirely unique.

At the heart of the problems in San Ysidro and perhaps nationally was the attempt to incorporate or at least bring into a functional relationship within the community action program sociopolitical organizations composed of different ethnic groups, languages, ideologies, and commitments to the war against poverty into one structure to confront the enormous problem of poverty.

The incorporation of such heterogenous elements into the superstructure of the war on poverty provided it from its inception with almost insurmountable internal contradictions, especially regarding such matters as social service and social action orientations in the program, what role the poor were to play, and formulation and interpretation of policy at different organizational levels in the structure. These contradictions were compounded by the fact that the human and especially monetary resources promised by the federal government by which local groups were to implement changes were inadequate from the start and became increasingly scarce. The increasing paucity of resources undercut the efficacy of the war on poverty programs, diluted the enthusiasm of their supporters and ultimately impugned their integrity. Rather than promoting cohesion of purpose among the organizations involved in the programs, especially those involved in the community action program, an intense competition for the scarce resources was provoked. Cynicism and disillusionment set in. As this infected an increasing number of antipoverty groups and organizations, the attack against poverty was eroded and replaced with an entrenching action. Community action organizations which were successful in acquiring some resources were forced to fight other organizations with whom they should have been cooperating and demonstrate that they could do the job better in order to justify their existence and the allocation of resources to them. Any expansion of the front was precluded and fights developed over issues and programs which a commitment by the government of sufficient resources could have avoided. The intense and well-publicized conflict in the antipoverty program reinforced establishment beliefs that the poor are incapable of helping themselves through rational action; community action programs which seemed a threat to established American institutions were gradually replaced with a "caretaker" service orientation. Administering services is not only safer, it's also easier.

Into these arenas other factors also frequently intruded to compound existing problems. Fights among groups in the arena created vacuums which permitted other groups from outside to enter the field and pursue goals which often were inimical to those of the war of poverty organizations. In San Ysidro one such vacuum-filling group was the *San Ysidro Planning and Development Association.* This association was dedicated to redeveloping the community of San Ysidro and the San Diego Border Area generally. One important factor in their program was to promote and support the construction of an interstate highway, I-805, to the United States-Mexico border at Tijuana. However, the route of the highway was directed so that it would dissect San Ysidro and displace some 270 of the poorest families in the community, almost all of whom were of Mexican descent. The Development Association argued that the highway would clear away some of the worst housing in the area and coupled with their extensive development program make San Ysidro a more desirable place in which to live. It would also, however, promote land speculation and increase land value and tax rates which few of the poor, elderly, and retired in the area could afford.

It was also obvious that several members of the Development Association would benefit handsomely from the development of San Ysidro because they had over the years built up deep economic interests in the region.

One of the major areas of conflict that emerged in the community developed around the displacement of the poor families and a housing project proposed to accommodate them. The inability of the local antipoverty action organizations to respond satisfactorily to this problem generated a schism in their ranks and fostered the rise of another organization, *The San Ysidro Poor Families and Tenants Association.* This association opposed the highway and development program and dedicated itself to helping the families who were to be displaced. As the self-proclaimed champion of the poor people in San Ysidro the Poor Families Association transformed the fight in the arena into one between the have and have-nots, or, as the leadership of the association articulated it, between "los ricos" and "los pobres." The ethnic distinctions superimposed on the socioeconomic ones already obvious in San Ysidro and between the contending groups created what has been referred to as a politico-ethnic arena. [5] The result was a complex congeries of issues, factors, and events which generated a spiraling and expanding conflict in the arena. This will be discussed in great detail later. My purpose at this point is only to indicate the significance of resources in a political contest, for in San Ysidro every fight, such as the major battle over the highway, was conditioned by the amount and kind of resources the various contestants controlled and the skill with which these resources were expended in the fight.[6]

Generally in a political contest the expenditure of political resources resides in the hands of various leaders who for a variety of reasons and in a variety of ways have developed a team of supporters. One notable feature of the struggle in San Ysidro was the frequent lack of leadership among those groups which represented the local war on poverty agencies. Much of the struggle in San Ysidro centered around these groups and was conditioned by both the general lack of leadership as well as the inability of prospective leaders to acquire necessary resources or to use skillfully the ones at hand to achieve their goals. Some individuals in these agencies attempted to become leaders and develop a following in the arena. This usually created competition and turmoil as well as an unnecessary expenditure of valuable resources; it also provided the vacuum into which other groups, such as the Development Association, who were either copiously supplied with necessary resources or who were more skillful in manipulating or creating other resources, were able to move and usurp the role of the war on poverty agencies and undermine their role and effectiveness in the arena.

The consideration of the nature of resources in the fights in the war on poverty, or in any political struggle for that matter, is of paramount importance, for political power is fundamentally the control of resources, especially human and material resources.[7] By and large, the most successful teams in political contests are those with the most power. However, the control of power does not automatically guarantee success in all political struggles. In order to avoid the tautology implicit in the argument that power is derived from control of resources and therefore resources guarantee power, it must be pointed out that there exists a variety of psychological, social, and cultural variables as well as pragmatic and more normative considerations that must be given by contestants to each issue which mediate the relationship between power and resources and makes actual application of power infinitely more complex. It is a truism that in a complex industrial society such as the United States persons and groups with power tend to be those which have control of resources, especially material resources. It is also true that not all persons who control material or other resources automatically have power; nor does an increase in resources necessarily allot to those without power an automatic increase in power. This is very simply due to the fact that any consideration of the resources upon which consideration of power is based go well beyond mere men and material. The power derived from human or material resources, while important in San Ysidro, would have proven untenable without a variety of other components, such as skill, knowledge, influence, and so forth, [8] which form an integral part of the resources which are brought into the arena.

In the war on poverty the critical resources were of three types: material, human, and ideological. Of these the most obvious and least problematical were material and human resources; they may not, however, always be the most important in winning a political contest. Material resources in the war on poverty refer primarily to money allocated in the form of grants by the federal government to underwrite community action and service programs developed by local antipoverty organizations. Monetary resources are expended primarily in hiring "experts" to study problems and, more importantly for the outcome of local level fights, to hire staff, some of whom hopefully will have the ability to become effective leaders who can implement the programs. Human resources refer most significantly to the interpersonal support networks a leader builds up from among individuals and groups in the arena and with whose aid and counsel he is able to pursue certain goals. Another kind of human resource is those individuals who are provided by the national and intermediate war on poverty organizations to the "grass roots" agencies in the form of advisors, consultants, trainers, and experts. Their task is to impart to the local organizations skills and insights which they presumably possess and by which local agencies may become better equiped to cope with the problems they confront. In San Ysidro representatives of agencies not involved in the fight in the arena, but who did comprise part of the field because of services they rendered, (presumably but not always impartially) to local contestants were known as "resource individuals."

However, in political contests even among the richest individuals, groups, or nations, human and material resources are always limited in supply. Other factors then assume subtle but real significance in determining the outcome of a political contest. For example, in any conflict contestants must estimate the cost of their machinations and actions; that is, how much of their resources they must defer to more abstract or less tangible considerations.[9] All of this involves a very high degree of skill, a resource in and of itself. Ultimately, however, the power derived from any resource in untenable without an ideological component, which also becomes an important feature of the concept of power since it provides a rationale for the actions of the contestants in the arena.

Ideology as a resource refers to the complex of ideas from which a society's values and beliefs derive and which are held or developed by an individual or social group concerning social phenomena, and by which the individual or group is provided justification for its actions. In subtle but significant ways ideology may condition the outcome of a political activity because an ideological commitment by an individual or group, whether recognized consciously or not, may not only provide them with justification for their activities, but may also instill in them a subtle, at times even arrogant, confidence. In San Ysidro this factor became significant because the attitude and actions of the development association, as one example, was conditioned by their commitment to one aspect of American national ideology, the Protestant ethic.[10]

As an ideological precept the Protestant ethic has several corollaries which become a significant part of the value and belief system among those in whom this ideology is inculcated. Work is highly regarded and an individual who does not work is conceived of as wasting time and is regarded as being if not evil, certainly of little value and worth. Work becomes a primary means by which one is expected to justify his dignity as a human being and his worth as a member and citizen of the society. Anyone who works hard enough and perseveres in an ascetic life style may well expect to achieve the pinnacles of success. Should he not so achieve, even though he works hard, then, depending upon the circumstance, failure may be explained either as a predestined and foregone fact over which the individuals simply had no control, or as the result of some personal categorical quality from which failure may be predicted, such as Mexicans being naturally lazy and blacks shiftless. The first argument provides not only a convenient "Calvinistic" rationalization for those who should make it but can't, but one that is socially acceptable. These are the "deserving" poor of the society, the elderly, the unfortunate, for whom welfare and public assistance programs were initially established. The second argument simply reinforces stereotypes and attitudes held regarding the poor and provides a simple but effective explanation for their plight: they are themselves to blame. These represent the "undeserving" poor, the welfare leaches who are poor only because they are lazy, will not work, and like to live the way they do! Individuals who make it in the system through their hard work, perserverance and initiative are able to reify these precepts by pointing to their own experience, an infallible position from which to argue; they resent those who have been forced onto welfare rolls because they have not made it and who have to be supported by the sweat of those who have. This perpetuates the invidious categorical distinction between the "deserving" poor and the "underserving" poor and the attitudes held regarding them.[11]

In the proper setting, such as San Ysidro, individuals who have acquired power can in accord with such ideological precepts develop a self-righteousness for their activities which is difficult to cope with or argue against. In a community whose population manifest two to three time the national unemployment rate and where a large segment of the population, especially those in poverty, are associated with a different cultural tradition which is already burdened with irrational "yankee" stereotypes, it is very easy for such individuals to point to the innate slothful characteristic of the poor. This conceptualization brooks no argument that postulates the existence of structural and attitudinal constraints that cause and promote poverty.

In San Ysidro the poor Mexican-Americans were the frequent brunt of comments by Anglos and individuals of Mexican descent who had passed into the national sociocultural system which impugned their worth and dignity as human beings. Two approaches, each with its own attitudinal concomitants, developed among the individuals and groups in the arena whose value system and actions were founded upon and defined by their commitment to the Protestant ethic. On the one hand, a "caretaker" attitude toward the poor was prevalent.[12] This refers broadly to the attitudes, actions, and rationalizations by which social service agencies and their representatives justify their service to the poor. This was common among the staff of services agencies in San Diego and in San Ysidro. Unfortunately, it was also prevalent among the community action groups in the arena and proved to be a significant factor in reducing their effectiveness as political action groups. On the other hand, it promoted a rather callous, self-righteous, sometimes exploitative attitude among powerful individuals and groups that may be paraphrased as "what is good for us is good for the community." This attitude was common among members of the Development Association and others and was based upon preconceptions regarding the poor: they are rather worthless, lazy, contribute little to the society. They do not deserve a say in the affairs and policies of which they are the most direct and wounded recipients.

One important consideration which affects the political activity of people living in poverty is that they are resource poor. Material resources are non-existent. Leadership is shallow, capricious, and also frequently nonexistent, as are their networks of support. Skills, credit, access to legal aid and support, and the like are in extremely short supply. Any ideology which the poor expound or develop to support their current agitation in the society will be an artifact of an adaptation forced upon them by their exclusion from the rewards of participating in America's dominant institutions. While nascent ideologies are fostered among the poor and expressed in slogans and epithets such as "*Viva La Raza*" or "Power to the People," even among the poor they provide an identity for only a few and have little credibility in the dominant culture.

The general lack of resources of people in poverty habitats has a variety of repercussions on their political activity. For one thing, this resource deficit leaves people in poverty habitats susceptible to policies which nullify the modicum of political effectiveness they demonstrate. For example, prior to the war on poverty, poor peoples in their contests with the power establishment of American society had nothing to lose by their actions. Then, through the war on poverty and its community action component, the government gave them a legal right to act and promised them resources with which to do so. However, as noted, the material resources allocated, after much prosaic rhetoric by the federal government, to antipoverty agencies were inadequate from the start and have become increasingly so. Still, in the early years of the program, when perhaps the only resource poor people had was enthusiasm, there was a real display of vitality and action in many areas of the country. The early enthusiasm generated among the poor by the war on poverty instilled a fear in local city halls that their power and control over the community would be usurped by "rabble" from the slums.[13] This obviously did not develop. Still, one may realistically argue that this concern over arming poor peoples in such a way was to some extent the result of stereotypes held regarding the poor and resulted in a subtle, covert counteraction from a variety of fronts. Much of this was a natural outgrowth of the program, but other factors may well be interpreted as part of a covert national cultural policy to nullify any meaningful or serious threat from the poverty habitat.[14]

For example, one high ranking Mexican-American official in the San Diego Economic Opportunity Commission argued that many of the antipoverty programs are covertly designed to create divisiveness between blacks and Mexican-Americans in San Diego and other areas of the nation. He pointed out, for example, that federal manpower training programs accommodate blacks because of their propensity for political agitation and that the attitude of the government is that if Mexican-Americans want any of the job slots allocated they should "get them from the blacks." The result of this policy is a high degree of friction between blacks and Mexican-Americans in the war on poverty programs in the San Diego area. The ethnic minorities are quite aware of this friction. Many of the meetings I attended broke down into shouting matches between blacks and Mexican-Americans over aims of programs and the utilization of funds allocated for them. The plea to "stop fighting among themselves and get on with the job" generally cooled things, but only until the next issue emerged. These conditions are also explainable as a principle of divide and rule, and many of the poor peoples and officials in the antipoverty programs saw these conditions in terms of the latter consideration. In short, these factors which I choose to call national cultural policies exacerbate the original hopes and goals of the program to combat poverty because they serve best those who adhere to covert national goals, aims, and ideologies.

For those who are able to extricate themselves from the morass of poverty, the national ideology does provide a solid anchorage from which they may proclaim the infallibility of the system and its ideology. When latent middle-class aspirations and goals are suddenly fulfilled individuals all too frequently, but predictably, adopt the value system of the national culture with a vengeance. Inclusion into the structural hierarchy and receipt of its economic and social rewards not only usurps energies previously dedicated to the cause of the abolition of poverty, but also creates an intense dedication to the mainstream life ways of American society. While this did not affect many individuals, in San Diego at least it became one other significant yet subtle means by which the war on poverty was undermined. This process may best be understood as a natural outgrowth of the process of bureaucratization in the war on poverty program.

For example, persons who had lived all their lives in poverty suddenly found themselves with full-time, permanent jobs which paid better than many had ever experienced. While an implicit aim of the war on poverty program was to serve as on-the-job-training for some persons who would eventually move into other job categories in the private or other public sectors of American society, many people in San Diego very quickly became entrenched in their job positions. For the first time many poor people were given a sense of power. Many frequently misapplied it. Many others obtained a heretofore unexpected respectablilty. Job categories, often with titles such as "Executive Secretary" or "Consultant" were unionized, reenforcing the individual's job consciousness and permanently stabilizing his prestige status. Not only are most people not willing to surrender such jobs and respectability, many poor people for the first time now had something to lose.

At the same time many others found themselves even more excluded from the system and frustrated in their attempts to cope with it through the War on Poverty Program. They began to question just how much more energy and effort they were expected to expend in order to experience the rewards the society had to offer. The result frequently was an even greater frustration because even the programs designed to improve their condition seemed merely techniques for reinforcing their social disenfranchisement. Though this process is certainly not meant to be a blanket accusation, it represents one among other ways, all of which will be dealt with in detail later, that the action orientation of the war on poverty was to a great extent neutralized. The achievers became unwilling to "rock the boat" and endanger the federal granting which supported the bureaucratic structure upon which they were now dependent. Frequently they impeded the efforts of those who worked for real community action. In effect, many poverty program people suddenly became petty bureaucrats.

Though in terms of gross numbers they were still pitifully few, they did impede the ingress of others and the infusion of new blood into the program and thwarted its implicit training goal. One unfortunate result is that poor people fought hard in competition with other poor people to maintain their own jobs and status. In some cases, where funds permitted, they expanded the bureaucracy so others, frequently friends, could acquire a job, though the lack of increased funding and the increasing inflation tended to reduce rather than increase positions. The fact that these tactics and problems precluded hard confrontations with the established institutions of San Diego and the larger culture of the United States also resulted in these new bureaucrats becoming living proof to the establishment of the validity of one of America's dominant ideologies—the Protestant ethic. They had succeeded through hard work and initiative in pulling themselves up by their boot straps. The administration was pleased. So were those newly entrenched in their positions. The status quo was reestablished. In this and other ways the war on poverty was neutralized and became respectable.

SUMMARY

Resources are a very important component of power. Ideology provides one resource to which members of groups with other kinds of power must subscribe if the group is to be effective in the political activity it undertakes. Without an ideology underwriting the orderly functioning and cohesion of the groups in the field, any other resource must be considered tenuous and the resource itself capricious and unreliable. Competition over goals and issues is always conditioned, if not determined, by the disparity between the available resources and the power they offer to political groups. In the next chapter, preparatory to discussing and analyzing the actual struggles and conflict that developed the contestants who comprised the field and participated in the arena, the goals the contestants sought and the issues over which they came into conflict are presented.

Chapter Three

Contestants in the Arena

In order to understand the issues over which conflict developed in San Ysidro and the goals the various contestants sought, as well as their significance for the integration of poverty habitats into American national culture, it is necessary to understand the structure, organization, and affiliations of the contestants. The contestants as conceived here may be separated into primary and secondary political groups or teams. The primary contestants included a variety of organizations, all but one of which were developed through the War on Poverty Program and which were indigenous to the area and persisted in it throughout the course of my research.

     Bailey (1969) has analyzed in great detail the relationship between political teams and their leaders, recruitment of individuals into teams, and relationships among team members. He separates these political groups into *moral teams* in which individuals are bound together in some common cause without a necessary expectation of reward for service rendered and *transactional teams* in which members do expect some return for their service. Although as models there are fundamental differences between these teams and by which they may dichotomized and typed, such as the way a leader allocates his resources, selected variations in tactics in the pursuit of goals in a political fight, methods by which team unity is maintained, and others, they are similar in that interpersonal relationships and motivations are rarely totally moral or purely transactional. Even the "hard core" members of the teams frequently are recruited and join for diverse reasons. This was certainly true among the teams in San Ysidro.

     Recruitment of members into the various teams which comprised the field of activity in San Ysidro involved a mixture of moral and transactional as well as pragmatic considerations which were often difficult to distinquish in practice. Individuals became involved in the CAC, for example, for a variety of reasons, many of which blended especially moral and pragmatic considerations; to acquire better housing, to eliminate poverty, to acquire personal power, to maintain one's image of oneself as a dedicated citizen, or merely to acquire a regularly paying job, a rare commodity for many poor people. The group perhaps most dedicated to the transactional consideration of turning over a profit as a result of their activities, *The San Ysidro Planning and Development Association,* also had in its ranks individuals who believed they were serving social progress, and the community at large. Similarly, many of the members of the *San Ysidro Poor Families and Tenants Association,* the team in the arena which most vocally and literally addressed the moral issue of what was to happen to the poor families that were going to be displaced by the freeway, candidly admitted that what they really wanted was a better house for themselves. The larger problem of the impact the routing of a major freeway through the community would have upon it was of little interest to them.[1] In one way or another, then, each of the primary contestants who comprised the political field in the arena of San Ysidro manifested a similar congeries of considerations by their membership for participating in that particular team.

The secondary political contestants are composed of those organizations and their representatives which became ephemerally and to some extent dispassionately involved in the conflict. In some instances these contestants had vested interests in the outcome of the conflict; more usually, however, these contestants had a fluid and unstable position within the field. They were drawn into the conflict at various times by an extension of certain issues; upon the resolution of the issue the contestants once again withdrew from the arena. Frequently these individuals served as political "brokers" or middlemen between their organization and primary contestants in the field, and on occasion, as was the case with other war on poverty agency personnel, between the primary contestants that represented local level war on poverty agencies, such as the CACs.

Significantly, all the contestants eventually, in one way or another, interacted with the war on poverty organizations. As a result of this interaction they became significant factors in the far-reaching ramifications of the conflict in the arena and an integral part of the networks of relationships that extended throughout and beyond the local war on poverty bureaucracy. These are the critical factors which determine their inclusion here as contestants.

The primary contestants in the arena were *The Border Area Community Action Council* (CAC), *The Mexican-American Advisory Committee Service Center in San Ysidro* (MAAC), *The San Ysidro Poor Families and Tenants Association* (PFTA), and *The San Ysidro Planning and Development Group* (SYPDG). The secondary contestants included representatives of *The Economic Opportunity Commission of San Diego County* (EOC), *The Mexican-American Adivsory Committee of San Diego County* (MAAC), the parent or umbrella agency which supervised the activities of the local MAAC center in San Ysidro, *The Planning Department of the City of San Diego, The San Ysidro Elementary*

School District, The State of California, representatives of other Community
Acion Councils in the South San Diego Bay Area, and representatives of departments of the federal government. As a means of introducing the contestants a
brief description of each and a statement of the goals each pursued will follow.

THE BORDER AREA COMMUNITY ACTION
COUNCIL (CAC)

Community Action Councils are neighborhood organizations whose purpose is to
involve the poor in the war on poverty as a means of satisfying the expectation
of maximum feasible participation of the poor in the program. The Border Area
Community Action Council, or CAC, is one of thirteen such functioning councils
in San Diego County. It was established in January 1966 by the Economic
Opportunity Commission of San Diego County and was the first council in the
county.[2]

The Border Area CAC represents one of the poorest areas in San
Diego County, and as a result of the way it was organized it incorporates three
communities. These are San Ysidro, which is part of urban San Diego, and Otay
and Woodlawn Park, which are unincorporated communities of San Diego
County. This division between city and county communities had significant
implications for the political activity which developed, for two reasons: (1) there
are differences in many of the programs available to urban-city and rural-county
war on poverty participants and each of the communities, and (2) each community, as well as having its own problems, is somewhat distinct ethnically. San
Ysidro is two-thirds Mexican-American, one-third Anglo, and both groups had
an intense identification with the area. Woodlawn Park is about 75 percent black
and 25 percent mixed Mexican-American, Anglo, and others. It is a tightly knit
community, invisible from the highway that skirts it, and, like San Ysidro, one
with which the inhabitants have a strong identification. Otay is a sprawl of
houses between San Ysidro and Woodlawn Park. It is predominantly Mexican-
American, but with little sense of community identity or awareness.

The Community Action Councils in San Diego County were
established for the functional purpose of involving residents and agencies serving
the habitat into a joint effort to first identify the specific problems of poverty
in the area and then to determine how best to attack these problems.[3] For the
purpose of carrying out these goals each CAC has an identical structure and
organization (see fig. 3.1). The description of the CACs which follows may be
considered descriptive of the Border Area CAC, except where differences are
specifically noted.

The membership of each CAC is composed of the people of the
poverty habitat which it serves. After attending a specified number of consecu-
tive meetings, two in the Border Area CAC, an individual is considered to have
demonstrated his commitment to the CAC and may become a voting member.

CAC Board of Directors
Officers

CAC Staff
Executive Secretary
Community Aide
Clerk Typist

Community Action Council
Residents
of the
Poverty Habitat

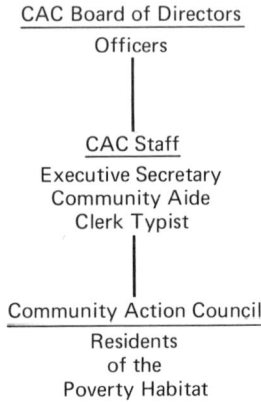

Figure 3.1. Organizational Structure of Community
Action Councils.

Each CAC also has a board of directors which is comprised of a slate of officers
which may vary in number, ethnic and racial composition, and social status,
depending on the nature of the poverty habitat. The Border Area CAC board of
directors has fourteen members composed of Mexican-Americans and Anglos
representing all three communities incorporated into the CAC, and blacks who
represent Woodlawn Park only. Most all of the members represent lower or
lower-middle-class social statuses. The members of CAC boards are volunteers
and elected from the community by the community in a democratic manner.
Each board also elects officers: a president, vice president, recording secretary,
and perhaps a parliamentarian and a sergeant at arms. The primary function of
the board is to interpret the needs of the community and serve as a clearing
house for ideas and programs to combat the poverty of the area.

CAC staffs are composed of three salaried positions: an executive
secretary, a community aide, and a clerk-typist, as well as volunteer help. The
primary tasks of the executive secretary are to run the office, maintain contact
with other antipoverty agencies serving the area, and to work closely with the
CAC board and membership in determining the poverty problems of the area and
the best way in which to solve them. The primary tasks of the community aide
are to maintain contact with the people in the habitat, to be aware of their
problems and to convey these to the executive secretary, and to attempt to
organize the community for the purpose of combating poverty. Clerk-typists
provide all clerical functions for the CAC office, though, as will be demonstrated
for the Border Area CAC, they can assume a role of great influence.[a]

a.The functions and duties of CAC boards and staff are more complex and
varied than outlined here, and were spelled out in detail in various documents that are
undoubtedly available from the Economic Opportunity Commission of San Diego County.

Organizations and Personnel*

Economic Opportunity Commission of San Diego County (EOC)	*Mexican-American Advisory Committee (MAAC)*
Mr. Flores	John Diaz (project director)
Delia Garcia	Yolanda Chaca (center director)
Executive Director	
Director of Area Development	
Bordern Area Community Action Council (CAC)	*Poor Families and Tenants Association (PFTA)*
Mr. Jim Duran (third exec. sec.)	Ramon Cervantes (president)
Mrs. Esmerelda Hurtado (community aide)	Esmerelda Hurtado
Mrs. Sally Horton (clerk typist;	Maria Soto
fourth exec. sec.)	Mercedes Paredes
Mrs. Dominguez (clerk typist)	Pablo Guzman
Mrs. Osmond (CAC board president)	Mrs. Mercado
Ramon Cervantes (CAC board)	
Mercedes Paredes (CAC board)	
Pablo Guzman (CAC board)	
Tex Stillman (CAC board; ex-pres.)	
Mr. Von Lutz (CAC board)	
Mr. Brown (ex-pres.; member)	*San Ysidro Planning and*
Mr. Amos Proud (ex-pres.)	*Development Group*
Mrs. Parker (first exec. sec.)	
	Mr. De Leon
	Mr. De La Torre
	Joe Boswell
	John Presser
San Ysidro School Superintendent	Tex Stillman
	Mr. Von Lutz
Mr. Herman	Mr. Herman

*-------- indicates cross-affiliation.

      The following is a somewhat idealized format for the operation of a CAC. Meetings of the CAC general membership, including the board which presides, the staff which is expected to attend, and interested persons from outside the habitat are held monthly. These meetings serve as open forums in which problems of the habitat may be discussed and out of which action by the CAC may emanate for the purpose of solving these problems. At the meeting the people make known to the board of directors problems which need attention in the habitat. Of course, the board and staff should have some prior idea of these problems as a result of contact with people in the habitat. However, at the meeting, the "total" community can express its wishes regarding these problems and possible ways of solving them. Where there is sufficient agreement that a particular problem is indeed serious, such as poor housing conditions, the board will act on the majority wishes of the council. In attempting to solve the problem, the board may appoint a committee of council members to look into the problem. It will also confer with the staff about the problem, either at that time, later in private, or at the monthly board of directors meeting, at which time the agenda for the next meeting is determined. The staff then attempts to effect the solution with the help and support of the council and people in the habitat and by drawing upon the resources, personnel, funds, and information made available to them through the war on poverty.

The Community Action Councils are the action components of the war on poverty in San Diego County. The CAC board of directors is a policy-making body; the paid staff implements the policy; and the persons who live in the poverty habitat and comprise the council are supposed to inform the board and staff of the problems confronting their community and assist in whatever way possible in their solution. Community Action Councils are also responsible for approving each project for their area, such as a teen post where the community's young people can meet, or a job training program, and for conducting periodic reviews and evaluations of every on-going program. CAC members and staff also serve as liaisons between the community at large and individuals and groups within and outside of the habitat, such as service agencies, police, and welfare organizations.

Beyond this rather idealized structure, Community Action Councils operate in a manner along a continuum ranging from total ineffectiveness to relative efficiency. The difference between the real and ideal in the operation of the Community Action Councils is quite varied and correlates generally with the effectiveness of the CACs in responding to the wishes of the people in the poverty habitats. Dissension or factionalism in any one of the three components that comprise the CAC, board, staff, or membership, generally is sufficient to disrupt the effectiveness of the CAC. In the Border Area CAC dissension within each of these components was rampant and affected not only the CAC but the local service center as well.

The major goal of a CAC is to organize the people of the poverty habitat for the purpose of combating and, hopefully, eliminating poverty. The effectiveness of a CAC in accomplishing this goal is based upon the way issues are translated into action by the CAC, its staff, and individuals charged with this task. In the Border Area CAC very few of the people understood the basic goal of the CAC. Everyone understood that the "war" was against poverty. The concept and practice of community organization and action, however, is not easy to comprehend;[4] the notion of social services is much more intelligible. Many of the CAC members, its board and staff were oriented toward administering services rather than promoting community organization. Most of the people seemed to have a very unclear idea of what their role in the CAC and the war on poverty should or could be. Interest in the CAC program was generally low. For example, throughout San Diego County, as of March, 1967, two-thirds (67.4 percent) of all persons who had attended CAC meetings had attended only once.[5] Apparently it is more difficult to get people to return to meetings than to get them there in the first place. And rarely do the CACs represent more than a small percentage of the total population in the habitat. One indication of the interest, involvement, and knowledge of the CAC and service center in San Ysidro is suggested in table 3.1,[6] which shows responses to two questions asked in an interview schedule conducted in San Ysidro.

Due to a general lack of familiarity with the purpose of the CAC the proposed goals of the Border Area CAC were replaced by a variety of personal interpretations. Most of the CAC board members believed the CAC should administer more services, and several frequently questioned why requests for service made to the CAC were always referred to the service center, the agency established to handle such matters. An explanation of the role and purpose of the CAC was met with looks of bewilderment. One member asked pointedly and angrily, "Well, if we're supposed to be organizing the community, then why aren't we doing it?" There were several reasons besides the board's ignorance.

The primary reason was the dissension within the CAC generally. This severely limited "out reach" by the CAC staff into the community for the purpose of educating the community and involving it in the CAC and the war on poverty. As a result community support for the program was always insufficient. As well as being saddled with an inefficient board of directors, individual staff members were also to blame for the lack of community organization and action. Given the abilities of the staff, and the commitments members had to the war on poverty as opposed to commitments they had to other organizations and their goals, it is doubtful that much would have been accomplished had there been no dissension.

Jimmy Duran, the executive secretary who was in charge of the CAC during much of the period in which I conducted research, was a young Mexican-American, the son of a well-to-do businessman in San Ysidro. The Anglo-

Table 3-1. Local Awareness of the CAC and Service Center

The following questions attempted to appraise the involvement in and knowledge of the CAC and Service Center in San Ysidro; they were asked of a random sample of San Ysidro citizens.

1. While living in San Ysidro have you ever contacted the:

	N	*Yes*	*%*	*No*	*%*
CAC	220	7	3.2	213	96.8
Service Center	225	30	13.3	195	86.7

2. Do you know anything about the activities of the:

	N	*Yes*	*%*	*No*	*%*
CAC	221	21	9.5	200	90.5
Service Center	221	56	25.3	167	74.7

American board and staff initially had high hopes that this young man would provide the CAC with badly needed leadership. He was married to an Anglo school teacher and this, the Anglos believed, would aid him in crossing ethnic boundaries. However, he was unable to comprehend the complexity of the program, the basic purpose of his job, and, as a result, to inform the CAC board and membership of the programs and resources available to them. Whatever competency he might have had was also quickly undermined by the forces that aligned against him and eventually forced him to resign. These originally emanated from the Mexican-American members of the organization who believed that because his father was a well-to-do businessman and because he had married an Anglo woman his aspirations seemed pointed to goals and interest divorced from those of the poor Mexican-American population.

The community aide, Esmerelda Hurtado, was a Mexican-American woman in her early fifties. She had been in the CAC for some time and was liked by the Mexican-American community at large, primarily because she gave them the services they desired. The idea and concept of community organization and action, one of the basic requisites for her job, was totally alien to her character and intentions, and she refused to accept any such orientation. "These poor people need help, and if I don't give it to them, who will?" was the way she frequently and disarmingly responded to suggestions about how she might better assume the responsibilities of her position.

The only staff member who had any awareness of the purpose and goals of the CAC was the clerk-typist, Sally Horton, an Anglo woman in her early thirties. She lived in Otay and her husband was in the navy. She was dedicated to the war on poverty and had familiarized herself with the programs over a long period. She too had been in the CAC for some time and had considered applying for the position of executive secretary. She decided against this because she was not Mexican-American and believed that because the community and its poor were predominantly Mexican-American a person of Mexican descent should hold that office in the Border Area of CAC. However, when Jimmy Duran resigned under stress, she applied for the job. By that time she had become convinced that someone who knew something about the programs and goals of the war on poverty generally was essential for the community. By this time, also, the schisms in the CAC were so deep that she was unable to develop any support. The Anglos were disenchanted, afraid, and deserted her; the Mexican-Americans rejected her totally, attacked her, and nullified any efforts she made to fulfill the goals of the CAC.

The goals and purposes of the CAC in San Ysidro then were subverted by a variety of factors. These will become increasingly evident in this work. Though persons hired as staff in the CAC were supposed to know the purpose of the organization, the board of directors itself, Anglos and Mexican-American alike, which did the hiring of the staff was so uninformed that the staff simply reflected its lack of knowledge and its service-oriented disposition to combating poverty.

THE MEXICAN-AMERICAN ADVISORY COMMITTEE
(MAAC): THE MULTIPURPOSE SERVICE CENTER

It has been quite well established that welfare- and service-oriented programs perpetuate dependency of the recipients upon such programs.[7] Complementing this is the reality that agencies and organizations which administer the programs are also quite dependent upon them since administering services contributes to the institutional strength of the agency and provides it with a rationale for requesting additional public funds. Gans (1962) has referred to the relationship of a welfare agency to the poor as that of a "caretaker." A more important role such agencies might play is to attempt to reduce the dependency upon welfare and service programs by people in poverty habitats and to develop organizations and institutions within poverty habitats which will take the services directly to the people and assist them in organizing for the purpose of solving their own problems. This is in great part what the war on poverty is all about and the approach which it represents is suggested in the Economic Opportunity Act of 1964, As Amended, Sec. 224:

> The director shall encourage the development of neighborhood centers, designed to promote the effectiveness of needed services in such fields as health, education, manpower, consumer protection, child and economic development, housing, legal, recreation, and social services, and so organized (through a corporate or other appropriate framework) as to promote maximum participation of neighborhood residents in center planning, policymaking, administration and operation. In addition to providing such services as may not otherwise be conveniently or readily available, such centers shall be responsive to such neighborhood needs, such as counseling, referral, follow-through, and community development activities, as may be necessary or appropriate to best assure a system under which existing programs are extended to the most disadvantaged, are linked to one another, are responsive and relevant to the range of community, family, and individual problems and are fully adapted to neighborhood needs and conditions. (1967:41)

In San Diego the Economic Opportunity Commission of San Diego County (EOC) established through federal grants four delegate agencies, whose primary goal is to provide services—employment, educational, legal, recreational—and also to make the existing services of private and public agencies more accessible to the people. Each delegate agency had one or more centers in San Diego County under its authority.[8]

One of these agencies, the Mexican-American Advisory Committee (MAAC), has four centers in San Diego County, one of which was in San Ysidro. MAAC has dedicated itself to providing services to the Mexican-Americans of San Diego County, for until MAAC was established this population had very few places to go where it could obtain help and even fewer where help was offered in Spanish. MAAC officials argue that approximately 10 percent of the population in San Diego County is Mexican-American, and that within this population unemployment varies between 20 percent and 30 percent, the school dropout rate varies between 30 percent and 50 percent, and a variety of other problems, such as English language deficiency, are prevalent. MAAC, in its attempt to cope with these problems, does serve a real need for the Mexican-American community of San Diego County.

MAAC is a corporation made up of nine Mexican-American organizations, e.g., the American G.I. Forum, IMPACT, Association of Mexican-American Educators, and others. This board serves as the policy-making body of MAAC (see fig. 3.2). From funds acquired through war on poverty grants provided by the EOC the corporation employs an executive director for the entire project and loan project directors and staff who work out of the offices located in the communities they serve. The executive director oversees the entire MAAC project and is intimate with programs available to and developed by each MAAC center. These programs are also funded by an EOC grant. Each local MAAC center has a basic staff which is salaried and consists of a project director, community aide, and clerk-typist. One of these local centers is in San Ysidro. It is up to the local staffs to implement the services concerned with manpower training, job placement, and transportation, and make them available to the population of the habitat.

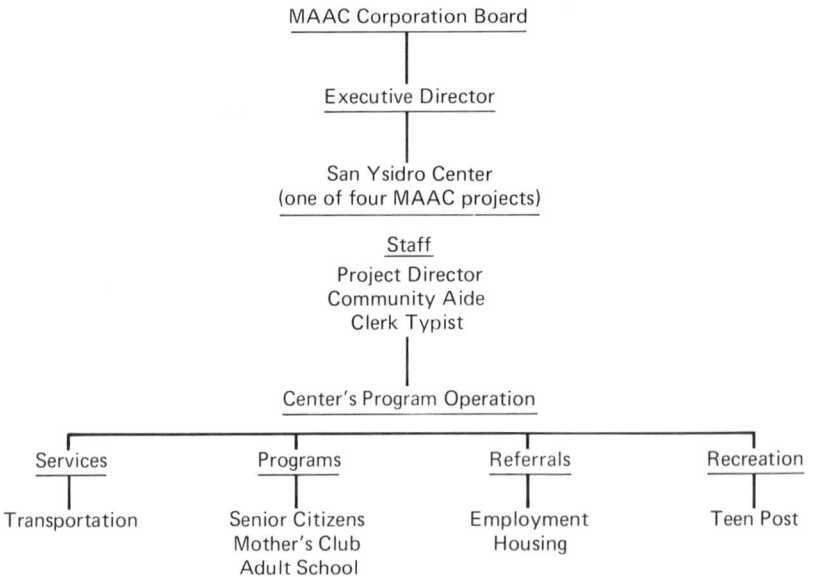

MAAC Corporation Board

Executive Director

San Ysidro Center
(one of four MAAC projects)

Staff
Project Director
Community Aide
Clerk Typist

Center's Program Operation

Services	Programs	Referrals	Recreation
Transportation	Senior Citizens Mother's Club Adult School	Employment Housing	Teen Post

Figure 3.2. The Mexican-American Advisory Committee.

MAAC service centers in San Diego County have a curious relationship with CAC, which in all cases, but especially in San Ysidro, serves as a point
of contention. Although all delegate agencies in San Diego County have a very
similar relationship with CACs, since this was part of the EOC program in the
county, only MAAC, because of its militant ideology, developed any real conflict
with CACs.

Whereas the CAC is a direct extension of the EOC, each MAAC
service center is directly responsible to the MAAC corporation. The MAAC
corporation and its local agencies, in turn, even though they are delegate agencies
of the EOC, are responsible to the CACs in the areas which it serves; this is the
expected relationship between service centers and community action councils
throughout San Diego County. Each MAAC project designed or proposed for an
area has to be evaluated and approved by the CAC, and the CAC representative
who sits on the MAAC board of directors is supposed to keep the CAC informed
regarding the operations and intentions of the MAAC corporation. Many
individuals in MAAC, but especially its executive director, John Diaz, resented
the control the CAC had over MAAC policies and considered the CACs bumbling
interlopers who only duplicated MAAC services, and badly at that, and really
served as nothing more than spies for the EOC.

Ideally, the primary task of the San Ysidro MAAC service center is
to provide a variety of services to the residents of San Ysidro, e.g., transportation
to hospitals and medical or dental clinics, job referrals, a recreation center for
the local youths, etc. The director's job is to keep abreast of all the programs and
services available to the people of the community, and to work with the CAC,
especially the executive secretary, in coordinating programs and operations to
combat poverty. The task of the community aide is to be knowledgeable about
the community's problems, to communicate these to the center director, and to
assist the people in obtaining needed services. Local volunteers frequently assist
in this function, as well as assisting the clerk-typist with clerical duties.

In addition to its service functions, MAAC vigorously adheres to a
general policy designed to reduce the dependency of the people upon service.
MAAC, through its board, project director, and staff generally developed a
militant action-oriented ideology that went far beyond administering service and
proclaimed community organization and action as a major goal of MAAC. As a
political group in the arena the MAAC team, as with all other contestants, was
held together by a congeries of moral, pragmatic, and transactional considerations.
MAAC, in short, attempted to organize through a variety of pragmatic and transactional strategies an agency through which the maximum feasible participation
of the poor, expecially Mexican-Americans, might be effected. While this was not
a totally anomalous position for a service to adhere to it did conflict with the
prupose of the CAC and resulted in a competition which, especially in San
Ysidro, impaired the function and operating procedures of both agencies.[9]

The MAAC center in San Ysidro operated for almost a year in San

Ysidro prior to the opening of the CAC office. During that period it attempted
to develop a community action program as well as allocate services, despite
the fact that resources, monetary and human, were insufficient to accomplish
this dual task. The project director, Yolanda Chaca, and her staff came to regard
San Ysidro as MAAC's private territory and, since Yolanda (a young, "middle-
class", Mexican-American female with two years of college), her community
aide, and a few volunteer aides (all females) were passionately dedicated to the
goal and purpose of community organization and action, a deep conflict
developed between the staff of the CAC and the service center in San Ysidro.
Each resented the other, felt its territory was being intruded upon, and spent
more time attempting to slander and undermine the other than in serving the
community. This prolonged and intense conflict, compounded by other issues to
be discussed, certainly contributed to the low "out reach" of each agency into
the community, and a rather low opinion of each agency that was held widely
throughout the community. This is reflected in the low-participation index
suggested by table 3.1. The elimination of any CAC control over MAAC projects
and of the CAC office in San Ysidro became one of the primary goals of MAAC.
The image of the MAAC center also suffered in the community because Yolanda,
in an attempt to build up support, promised services, such as transportation,
which she was unable to deliver. As her support waned she became increasingly
offensive to the people and attempted to blame other groups for the center's
failures. Eventually the MAAC team succumbed to attacks by other groups and
was replaced by another more service-oriented staff.

THE POOR FAMILIES AND TENANTS ASSOCIATION
OF SAN YSIDRO

The Poor Families and Tenants Association of San Ysidro (PFTA) was an outgrowth of conflict which divided the CAC, its board, and its staff. It also served
to fill a void in the arena of which many of the Mexican-Americans were aware;
that is the lack of an exclusively Mexican-American organization to represent
their interests at a time when they were being trod upon. The PFTA also
generated a tremendous amount of conflict as well as some changes in San
Ysidro; it is perhaps best viewed and analyzed as an adaptation to the reality
of the politics of the poverty habitat of San Ysidro. For example, the tactics used
by the PFTA, the contestant in the arena with the least amount of obvious
power, often seemed unfair, slanderous, and vicious to observers. Their tactics
may be better understood as adaptations to the reality of the paucity of
resources they controlled vis-à-vis more powerful groups in the arena. Without
the particular tactics it employed, which will be discussed later, the PFTA
would have been powerless in the arena.

       The core membership of the PFTA was welded together by a com-
mitment to improve services to the Mexican-American population of San

Ysidro which it felt were not being provided by the MAAC center, and to organize the families that were being displaced by the freeway so that they might acquire houses to replace those which they were to lose, a task which the CAC had been conspicuously unable to accomplish. The PFTA also fought to have Yolanda Chaca, the MAAC project director, removed from office and the CAC staff and board of the CAC reconstituted so that they were exclusively Mexican-American. Although the PFTA attempted to recruit a base of support on the promise of better services, community action, and better housing, their tactics in the fight with the CAC and MAAC center alienated the vast majority of the Mexican-American population, many of whom were despondent about the problems confronting them, but who also could not identify with the intense and evolving conflict. With its limited and yet not insignificant support the PFTA represented the purest moral team in the arena, and the commitment of its members was such that they did achieve many of their goals, although the long range and heavy issues regarding the housing dilemma went unresolved.

The PFTA leadership was composed of dissident members of the CAC board of directors and staff and much of its membership was drawn from the council itself. It acquired and maintained its base of support because it offered the hope of solutions to problems which the CAC could not and its members provided to some of the population limited services that were either lacking in the MAAC center or not well handled. The PFTA also elected a board of directors, issued membership cards and, as a tactic for acquiring additional community support, gave honorary and titular memberships, such as advisor, consultant, and translator to such local luminaries as the superintendent of the San Ysidro Elementary School District, the local priest,[10] and a teacher in the English as a second language program in the San Ysidro school district. Beyond the honorary positions the PFTA offered a few Anglos its membership was exclusively Mexican-American and to a great extent confined only to Spanish-speaking individuals.

The board of directors of the PFTA was comprised of a president, the founder and leader of the organization, Ramon Cervantes, and a tightly knit core of followers that held the offices of the vice president (Mercedes Parades), treasurer (Esmeralda Hurtado), recording secretary (Maria Soto), and first and second "vocal" (Pablo Guzman and Mrs. Mercado). This group was recruited by Ramon Cervantes and maintained its composition and integrity throughout the fight in which it became involved.

Ramon Cervantes was a middle-aged, Mexican-American welfare recipient. He spoke no English and was not a citizen. He claimed to have been an affluent rancher in Mexico and contended that his ranch had been stolen by Communists. He was a fiery speaker, and exuded more than a little charisma. He expressed the belief that in his struggle against the "rich Anglos" of San Ysidro "God was on [his] side." He also boasted of having warned John F. Kennedy of an impending assassination plot in Tijuana on a visit Kennedy was supposed to make to that city. Until impeached by the CAC and removed from his position he served as a member of the board of directors for the Border Area CAC.

The other significant member for our purposes here was the treasurer, Esmeralda Hurtado, the community aide for the CAC. As described previously, she felt a deep and sincere need to help the poor Mexican-Americans of San Ysidro. However, in her job she was stubborn, not open to suggestion, and resented undertaking any activity which could not be immediately translated into a service for the poor. Once she aligned with the PFTA her activities as the CAC community aide were carried out in service of the PFTA. She was fired from her CAC job for participating in PFTA activities on CAC time and for other reasons to be discussed later.

Of the remaining members, Pablo Guzman and Mercedes Paredes were also CAC board members and were impeached and removed from office along with Ramon Cervantes. Mrs. Mercado was a fiery and outspoken member of the CAC. Only Maria Soto had not been involved in any of the war on poverty institutions prior to achieving status in the PFTA. She had, however, one year of junior college and was the most proficient in English of the group.

Beyond this group, there was a membership that probably never exceeded forty persons, while fifteen to twenty persons made up the remainder of the hard core group. While this might seem an insignificant figure it should be remembered that participation in CAC meetings was low, rarely exceeding fifty people, although some meetings, such as the one held in April 1968 to discuss the freeway and housing problem, drew around two hundred people. It was, however, one of the more solidly knit contestants in the field, and given its composition of poor people, factory workers, housewives, unemployed, underemployed, welfare recipients, and Spanish speakers, and its relative lack of power, it in fact became a force to contend with in San Ysidro.

For example, though the active PFTA membership stabilized at about twenty members, in one heated confrontation attended by representatives of the EOC, CAC, MAAC, and the State of California over the appointment of the CAC's Anglo clerk-typist, Sally Horton, to the role of executive secretary, about forty persons from San Ysidro, all Mexican-American, turned out in support of the PFTA against the appointment. This was the largest constituency the PFTA fielded during the course of this research. Much of the power of the PFTA, however, lay in its claims of a membership in the thousands, which many of the secondary contestants, not continuously involved in the arena, tended to believe, and which, taking account of the noise and furor the PFTA created, often did not seem unreasonable.

The PFTA hammered away at a few narrow and pointed issues which directly affected the Mexican-American population. The major goal the PFTA sought was to attempt to do something about the excessive rents in San Ysidro, the relatively poor housing and the lack of housing available for the large number of families which were to be displaced by the freeway. Those were emotional issues of which the leadership of the PFTA took full advantage. Still, PFTA did confront a great amount of apathy and resignation within the community and never developed the membership and power it really wanted. In part, this was due to the fact that it involved itself in goals many interpreted as beyond its original purpose, but which the PFTA saw simply as a means to its end. For example, the great energies the PFTA devoted to either the control of or destruction of the CAC and service center was carried out at the expense of working for solutions to the housing problems, though the PFTA hoped by controlling these agencies to use their resources for that end. The PFTA did organize a following in the arena more easily than the CAC and service center, agencies expected to perform that function, because it provided a better sounding board than the CAC through which the grievances of the Mexican-Americans could be heard. As a result its following did represent the poor people of San Ysidro.

However, the battle with the CAC and service center also cost the PFTA support. For example, the superintendent of the San Ysidro schools insisted that his name be removed as a consultant from the PFTA letterhead because the PFTA was going far beyond its original purpose. Some of the poor people who were sympathetic with the PFTA were put off and frightened by some of the tactics and threats and the repercussions they might incur. The PFTA did, as a result of its tactics, do more to make the city government, the EOC, the State of California, the federal bureaucracy of the war on poverty, and perhaps other federal bureaus aware of San Ysidro than any other single group. Even with its lack of resources and power the PFTA demonstrated that there are tactics which can compensate to an extent for this lack and give to a group what may be referred to as the power of the weak.

THE SAN YSIDRO PLANNING AND DEVELOPMENT GROUP (SYPDG)

In many aspects of urban politics, local businessmen frequently have more influence over certain issues than do elected officials; while these businessmen may not actually run the town or city, they certainly influence the way it is run.[11] This may be demonstrated in San Diego by the activities of the San Ysidro Planning and Development Group. This particular group is one of several such planning groups in the City of San Diego. Each of these planning groups represents a particular area of the city and is supposed to be representative of and serve the viewpoints of the constituents in that area with reference to long-term planning, growth, and development. Each local planning group meets regularly in City Hall with the Planning and Development Department of the city of San Diego and in conjunction with their staff attempts to work out the logistics and strategy of the development of their particular area.

When it became known in the mid-1960s that a freeway was scheduled to pass through San Ysidro and that a major redevelopment of the area was proposed, the San Ysidro Planning and Development Association became active and presented itself to the city of San Diego as a concerned group representative of San Ysidro. It was recognized by the city as representing San Ysidro in 1967. Its current membership is estimated at about 100 persons.[12] However, only about a dozen are active, and they, almost all businessmen or professional people, make up the board of directors. Their activities suggest that they are serving primarily their own interest and only tangentially those of their membership, and certainly not the immediate needs of San Ysidro as they are perceived by the people.

The membership of the development association to a great extent represented a transactional team based upon the reward several of them or the companies they represented, especially local banks and railroad and real estate interests, will reap from the development of San Ysidro. Public statements by some of their members express a deep concern for the poor people of San Ysidro; private statements and actions often reveal a less indulgent disposition toward the poor as well as a less philanthropic concern for the community at large. Some of them conceive of the poor as mean and lazy and others indicate that San Ysidro in the future should be unburdened of their presence.

Much of this was couched in very pragmatic terms. The houses in the area of San Ysidro to be destroyed for the freeway were largely dilapidated and the area was blighted. The freeway, the development association argued unassailably, would remove this unsightly mess and permit new and better housing and business to be built and promoted. This sentiment was shared by other city officials. Little consideration was given to the fact that the dilapidation had been allowed to grow and spread for a decade because landlords and property owners in the area knew of the impending freeway and made no repairs or improvements. If tenants complained they were evicted, and there was no problem acquiring other tenants at high rents because the entire South San Diego Bay Area was suffering from a severe housing shortage. Maintaining housing in such condition was rarely proven illegal by city housing inspectors; in fact they rarely appeared in San Ysidro and alleged, when challenged to do so, that they were understaffed.[13] Several members of the community did seriously question the morality as well as the legality of the landlords and property owners, some of whom served on the San Ysidro Planning and Development Association. In fairness, it should be noted that Tex Stillman, one member of the association, upon instigation by the PFTA, was forced by the city to make extensive repairs at considerable expense on the "slum" trailer park he operated. He was also perhaps one of the landlords least able to afford such action.

"Moral" statements made by members of the association to justify their activities were frequently tempered by the ideological commitment and affiliation they maintained. "Morality" was work. There would be no poor in San Ysidro, at least undeserving poor, if only the Mexicans in the area would get jobs. One day as Tex and I argued over the degree of poverty in San Ysidro, he said, "Joe Boswell," who was also a member of the SYPDG, "has been trying to get someone to pump gas in his station for months now, and he can't get any of these Mexican to work."

"What's he paying?" I asked.

"A dollar and a quarter an hour."

When I suggested to Tex that was just minimum wage and would not support a family he replied that he had worked for less, and that's what was important: to work and not live off the dole.

Almost all the individuals who participated in the group stood to gain from the redevelopment of San Ysidro. Joe Boswell, for example, had managed with the group's help to have the freeway plans changed so that an off-ramp would feed cars into his gas stations and garage. Those who did not participate, such as Mr. Von Lutz, who considered himself a hippie and who will be discussed later, either tacitly or actively supported almost all that transpired. The core membership also seemed to fluctuate in response to circumstances regarding the community's development. One man appeared only once during the times I observed the group in order to thank it for its efforts in having an area adjacent to the border rezoned to accommodate his warehousing and trucking enterprises. He had been quite active prior to this time.

The San Ysidro Planning and Development Group is primarily concerned with long-term development of the San Diego Border Area. For example, the planning and development of the Border Area, of which San Ysidro is the hub, is projected to the year 2000. Still, on occasion, the group will involve themselves with immediate problems, such as having a stop sign or traffic light installed. A concern for long-term development would in and of itself tend to isolate such a group from the broad constituency of a poverty habitat, the inhabitats of which are less concerned with the development of freeways, recreation areas, marinas, and industries than with the daily problems of contending with poor housing, poor health, cockroaches, low incomes, and inadequate diets.[14]

The San Ysidro Planning and Development Group hold very infrequent meetings, which are rarely advertised. Members contact each other by phone and much of the group's business seems to be conducted this way or in private meetings. I attended one meeting. It was concerned with traffic problems near the border and a representative of the state highway department was present. When that business was concluded and the highway department representative had departed, two visiting representatives of the CAC and I were asked to leave because the board had to discuss personnel problems. However, the group has no staff that would give rise to problems that need discussing. The CAC representatives were quite disturbed about this and referred to it as just one more example of the secretiveness of the group.

Membership in the group is supposed to be open to anyone, but application may be a problem. By four different persons, members and applicants to the group, I was told that membership was open to anyone—free of charge, for a three dollar fee, a five dollar fee, and a ten dollar fee. Tex told me that the association probably was not started in the most democratic way since the orignial members of the board, many of whom still served, were self-appointed. He also pointed out that when he first called to inquire about joining the group, the chairman was suspicious and reluctant to give any information, and that only after he had "hung around" for a while was he made a member. I was also alternately told that the group had no by-laws or charter, and that I could only get a copy of the by-laws if I was a member! The strongest complaint registered against the group is that it is not representative of the community, because no poor people are members. When, on occasion, representatives of the poor of San Ysidro did attempt to obtain representation they were rebuked and given "the run-around", which discouraged their efforts. This allegation was made to the mayor of San Diego on an occasion when people from San Ysidro met with him to protest the route of the freeway. This is one aspect of the long-term development of the area in which the group is intimately involved. Although the mayor argued that the group was representative of the people of San Ysidro, the heated complaints by the people forced the mayor to tell an aide to check into the matter. Nothing tangible regarding the organization or tactics of the group developed.

In some areas of the city the groups are representative of the constituents of the area. Southeast San Diego, for example, the black "ghetto" of the city, has an especially concerned and sensitive representation. The San Ysidro group, on the other hand, is notorious among some of the other groups and among certain members of the City Planning Department of San Diego for its lack of representation of and sensitivity to the people of San Ysidro. In a sense, this can be construed as one aspect of American national political culture. As Dahl (1961:183) has pointed out, "Leaders in redevelopment are with a few exceptions officially, professionally, or financially involved in its fate." In the black area, however, due to civil organizations, the representatives are, in fact, of the people. In San Ysidro almost all of the group members with whom I spoke were representative of the Protestant ethic, frequently in its more severe, Calvinistic sense, and not at all in touch with the reality and sociocultural "nature" of a poverty habitat. As noted previously, the basic theme, either overtly or covertly expressed, is that what is good for business, especially theirs, is good for San Ysidro.

The composition of the San Ysidro Planning and Development Association and the attitudes some of its members express may make some of the previous statements more pointed. As a general introduction, two members of the group are businessmen of Mexican descent. One member is a female, the wife of a San Ysidro realtor. Another is a retired gentleman. All the others are property oweners, and/or businessmen, influential and involved in the long-term development of the area. Less than half the members are residents of San

Ysidro, and those who are the most influential and in control of the most power and resources in the area live outside San Ysidro.

Mr. DeLeon is chairman of the group and is of Mexican descent. He is president of a local bank situated near the border. Most of its employees and some of its biggest depositers, who also have deep economic interests in the development of the border area, come from Tijuana. Mr. DeLeon's attitude toward the CAC, and by extension, the war on poverty, as suggested by several comments, was quite negative, at best paternalistic. When, for one project, Tex suggested in a meeting at the city hall that the CAC be involved, he responded, "O.K., you select a couple of them (CAC members) and have them attend; we'll pat them on the ass and send them home and then do what has to be done." He lived outside San Ysidro.

Mr. De la Torre is also of Mexican descent and owns considerable property in San Ysidro. Among the people of San Ysidro he was one of the better known influentials. Most people knew him as a large property owner and many stories, most of them fanciful, if not apocryphal, circulated about him. However, he had been in the early 1960s president of the Public Works Commission of Mexico. He became involved in a scandal regarding misappropriation of a considerable sum of money and moved to the United States. He lived outside of San Ysidro

John Presser also lived outside San Ysidro. He was an insurance broker and maintained an office in the neighboring community of Chula Vista. He owned and had been buying considerable property in the area for years in anticipation of its growth. Much of this property was adjacent to routes of the freeway complex scheduled for the area and which had been projected into the area several years before.[15] He also owned property in other areas of the community which was strategically located to take advantage of its development.

Mr. Hermann was the superintendent of the San Ysidro Elementary School District. His primary concern was with the development of a proposed University of the Americas in the flats of the Tia Juana River Basin. However, he gave general support, to the interests and projection of the other members of the group. Although he too lived outside San Ysidro, he was also involved in several other organizations in the community. He was, however, quite ignorant about, and at times hostile, to the CAC. His solution to the problem of poverty was for the people to go to work, with improved services for those who really could not work, rather than community organization and action. He got along quite well with Yolanda Chaca, project director of the San Ysidro MAAC Service Center, who as we shall see, had special ideas regarding community action. Yolanda and Mr. Hermann were instrumental in nullifying the one large community action movement that got started in San Ysidro because it was aimed at possibly disrupting a San Diego City Council meeting. This will be discussed in detail in the next chapter.

Mr. Hermann's attitude toward the CAC, especially, as happened and will be discussed later, when it took issue with one of his school's programs, was that it was composed of radical left-wing outsiders bent on creating disturbance in the community. His attitude toward the people generally was quite paternalistic. He told me that he had been instructed by the school board to get involved and to become a member of all the significant organizations in order to get to know the community and its problems. He did not become a member of the CAC and did not attend their meetings.

There are other members of the group who live outside the area. The head of the Bank of America branch in San Ysidro is active in the redevelopment of the area. The San Deigo and Eastern Railroad, which runs a line through San Ysidro to the border, owns considerable property in the area and is deeply involved in the industrial development of the area. A representative of the railroad, a traffic manager, is active in the group and has taken stands on issues oriented to railroad interests in San Ysidro. Another active member is listed as an investment counselor by the group, but is better known to the people of San Ysidro as an immigration and naturalization consultant.

Besides these seven individuals and a few other less significant members, all of whom live outside San Ysidro, there are five others who maintain residences in the community, all of them Anglos. A brief description of each will demonstrate, I think, that they are far less powerful and in many ways less influential than those who live outside the area. They include Tex Stillman and Jerry Bauman—each of them owns one of the several trailer courts in San Ysidro; Joe Boswell, the owner of a large service station; Mr. Von Lutz, an elderly, retired white-collar worker; and Mrs. Williams, the wife of a local realtor. For this work Tex and Mr. Von Lutz are most significant since they were also affiliated with the CAC.

Jerry Bauman had been a member of the group for about two years and had joined because Tex, whose trailer facility was across the street, had told him about the development group. Bauman's trailer court is the neatest and best kept in San Ysidro and is surrounded by a wire mesh fence. By his own admission, he is not in favor of all that the San Ysidro Planning and Development Group has done, although he spoke very rarely on any issues at any of the meetings which I attended. He does believe the freeway is necessary for the growth of the community and also because it would get rid of some of the very worst housing in San Ysidro. He also believes that poverty is due to a lack of jobs, and that the only solution to poverty is to supply more jobs. This, he believes, should be the primary task of the war on poverty. Since it is not doing this, it is, in his opinion, a failure.

Joe Boswell is a long time resident of the community and inherited his service station from his father. When the exact placement of the off-ramps into San Ysidro was being determined, an adjustment was made so his facility would be served by an off-ramp. He occasionally hired Mexican-American attendants and paid minimum wages, a dollar and a quarter an hour. He had some difficulty keeping help and believed Mexican-Americans would rather live on welfare than work.

Mrs. Willimas, the wife of the local realtor, was quite outspoken at meetings of the group which she attended. She complained of the prejudices of the Mexican-Americans of San Ysidro against the Anglos. One of a series of public meetings whose total content and purpose will be discussed later, was concerned with job opportunities that would open up in the area because of the redevelopment of San Ysidro. Less than forty persons attended, and it was the most poorly attended meeting of the series. With some vehemence Mrs. Williams pointed out that this truly indicated the laziness of the Mexican-Americans and the fact they all chose to live on welfare rather than work. At the meeting at which she expressed these sentiments there was no open and overwhelming agreement among the members of the group. But neither was there a denial of her statements.

The other side of this incident is worth a comment. A principal of one of the elementary schools pointed out to me that attendance at the meeting dealing with jobs was low because it conflicted with the annual P.T.A. bazaar in which many of the Mexican-Americans of the community were actively involved. He attempted to have the date of either the bazaar or the public meeting changed, but without success. Perhaps more to the point, one Mexican-American resident summed up the sentiment of many others in the community about the meeting and its topic: "So what if they open up a lot of jobs in the area with their stores and gas stations and motels and businesses. They'll just hire Green Carders like they do now and we won't be any better off."

The two remaining individuals, Tex Stillman and Mr. Von Lutz, were similar to and yet different from other members of the group. They both were very civic minded and active in the CAC. Both, however, gave primary allegiance to the San Ysidro Planning and Development Group. Both also served as unofficial and unassigned liaisons between the CAC and the San Ysidro Planning and Development Group. However, they tended to carry information beneficial to the SYPDG from the CAC, but rarely from the SYPDG to the CAC.

Tex was a self-made man. He took pride in his ability to get the "facts" on all issues and arrive at independent decisions representing the "truth" of the matter. He firmly believed all men, through their initiative, thrift, hard work, and sacrifice, could achieve in American society. After all, he had done it! He argued that there were sufficient jobs for anyone who wanted to work, and pointed out the difficulty Joe Boswell had in obtaining help as an example of the innate sloth of certain types of people. To him, any person with self-respect would work for any wages just to experience the dignity of work. Poverty was not due to a lack of jobs: it was due primarily to a lack of individual worth.

A corner of his trailer court was going to be cut away by the freeway. He accepted this as a part of his civic duty. He also served in other organizations because he believed it was his duty. He was the first president of the CAC when it opened in San Ysidro. His trailer court, however, was rather run down, composed primarily of old trailers he rented for what many people claimed to be exorbitant prices. Such accusations, he argued, were based on ignorance and a lack of the facts on the cost of operating a business. He served as CAC president until the housing issue developed, and then resigned. In part he was sensitive to charges and accusations leveled against him by members of the then incipient PFTA. He also argued that he resigned because of demands of his business. Members of the PFTA had reported to the city the inadequate sanitary facilities in his court and he was order to improve them within a specified period or be fined and possibly closed. He claimed he also was tired of being a "puppet" for the EOC. He did, however, remain a member of the CAC, attending meetings, and after this research concluded, again became a member of the board of directors.[16]

Mr. Von Lutz was somewhat of a local character. He was retired, though he had worked for a local corporation and also had been involved in real estate. He was 67 years old, loud, outspoken, flamboyant in dress and considered himself a "hippie" and wore a set of "love-beads" to prove it. He spoke often of his civic-mindedness and proved this by being active in several organizations. However, I was left with a strong impression that his actions were as much a response to passing the time in an interesting way as fulfilling some civic duty. He rarely took strong stands on any issue, and was notorious for quickly backing off a stand taken in an anxious moment lest it result in some kind of conflict. This manifested itself increasingly as the conflicts intensified in San Ysidro.

He had a firm moral commitment to the San Ysidro Planning and Development Group and commented on many occasions that they had done more for San Ysidro than any other single organization. Mr. Von Lutz had also been active for several years in helping John Presser acquire land along the freeway routes. When asked why he participated in the CAC, many members of which openly spoke against the activities of the San Ysidro and Development Group, he would deplore their comments and suggest sadly that they were merely uninformed and ignorant and against progress. He also believed that the service center was more valuable to the community than the CAC, and in this way betrayed a significant aspect of his attitude toward poverty.

He was firmly committed to a patronizing "service" orientation to helping people. Regardless of how many times the community organization and action role of the CAC was explained, he never grasped the concept and always saw the CAC as a mere extension of the service concept proferred by the San Ysidro MAAC center. Had the service center a local board of directors upon which he as a member of the community could have served, he probably would have done so in preference to the CAC board. He revealed a significant part of his philosophy to me one day with reference to his commitments. "The service center," he said, "has certainly done much more for the community than the CAC. You ought to know this. After all, as an anthropologist, you know as well as I do, the reason you're a college professor, the reason I was only a high school graduate and worked all my life in an office, and the reason so many of the people here are poor is because of the seeds they inherit from their parents and ancestors and pass on to their children. You have a better seed in you than I do; and poor people have the poorest quality seeds of all. There's nothing you can do for them except try to help them. That's all."

The San Ysidro Planning and Development Group was the most influential and powerful organization in the arena of San Ysidro. It had the sanction and support of the city of San Diego. As the presumed representative of an area of San Diego the group is theoretically open to anyone. However, in one meeting members of the group discussed the degree to which they should keep their membership select and free from "kooks." No decision was reached but the implication was clear; to the best of their ability they would keep their membership select. This group is viewed by the city as critical and instrumental in making changes in San Ysidro. The attitude of the city, as expressed by a member of the city managers staff, was that there would be no change or improvement in San Ysidro without this group.

The officials at this level considered the CAC and war on poverty institutions simply as vehicles for communicating what they chose to have communicated to the community, but not, as the ideology of the CAC dictated, as agents of change in the community. This represents an expression of American political policy. Even though the war on poverty demanded "maximum feasible participation" of the poor in policies and decisions affecting their lives, this was never fully realized, and is one more example of the means by which the political efficacy of these antipoverty organizations were neutralized and made respectable by American cultural standards.

POLITICAL BROKERS: THE ORGANIZATIONAL REPRESENTATIVES

A number of individuals were active at various times who were affiliated with organizations which in one way or other had interest in the political activity in the arena. They represent the secondary political contestants. Their activity depended primarily upon the particular events which were occurring and their effect upon these organizations. In order to complete the picture of the contestants in the arena a brief description of these contestants is in order.

The Economic Opportunity Commission of San Diego County—the EOC— is the umbrella agency for the Office of Economic Opportunity's war on poverty in San Diego County. It is in charge of all the local community action programs in the county and is responsible to state, regional, and federal Offices of Economic Opportunity for the programs in San Diego County. The EOC is composed of a board of directors and a staff. The board represents a variety of organizations in San Diego County. Ideally the board is divided between fourteen representatives from the poor, or one from each CAC in the county, fourteen from community groups, and fourteen elected public officials. The EOC also employs a large staff which works out of a variety of departments (see fig. 3.3).

The EOC generally oversees the community action programs in the county and the variety of delegate agencies funded by it through grants from the federal government. At the local level the EOC has ultimate control over both the human and financial resources available to delegate agencies. It also approves programs for the area and the funding necessary to implement them, enforces policies and guidelines regarding these programs, gathers information on the problems and poverty in the area, coordinates and integrates all the antipoverty programs and evaluates them. The primary responsibility of the board of directors is to investigate the feasibility of the delegate agencies to carry out their tasks. This involves review of delegate agency effectiveness, their fiscal responsibility, compliance with OEO guidelines, resolution of personnel problems, and the like. The primary task of the EOC staff is to assist the poor in the development of community action programs and to serve as liaison between the EOC, and its delegate agencies, e.g., service centers, the CACs, and other public and private agencies which participate in the community action programs of San Diego County. It was the liaison members between the EOC and the CAC and delegate agencies who became most involved in the activities in San Ysidro.

One category of EOC staff members are the consultants to the CACs in the country.[17] Their task is to help resolve CAC problems and assist the CACs in utilizing the resources the EOC has to offer. There are three consultants and the CACs are divided among them. The consultant to the Border Area CAC, is Delia Garcia, a Mexican-American female. She also is consultant to the two other South Bay Community Action Councils in Imperial Beach and National City. However, both these CACs function quite effectively compared to the Border Area CAC. As a result Delia devotes almost all her time to the Border Area CAC, and her activities were quite significant in the events in the arena.

The structure, organization and ideology of MAAC has been discussed previously. To a great extent MAAC's militant orientation is the result of its project director, John Diaz. However, most of his board and staff, including Yolanda Chaca in San Ysidro, shared his point of view. As noted, it is a point of view which directly conflicts with the stated aims and goals of the CAC, and in each of the four areas where MAAC Centers and CAC coexisted they were in conflict. This conflict culminated in the arena of San Ysidro and the involvement of MAAC, through John Diaz, in the attempt to close down the Border Area CAC.[18]

John Diaz is a Mexican-American of somewhat unlikely background

EXECUTIVE OFFICE OF THE PRESIDENT

```
┌──────────────┐   ┌──────────────┐   ┌──────────────────┐
│ Econ.        │   │  Director    │   │ Natl Advsry      │
│ Opportunity  │   ├──────────────┤   │ Council on       │
│ Council      │   │Deputy Director│  │ Economic         │
│              │   │              │   │ Opportunity      │
└──────────────┘   └──────────────┘   └──────────────────┘
```

Executive Secretary

OEO Offices: Inspection, Civil Rights, Information, Health, Inspection, etc.

| Asst. Direct. Job Corps | Asst. Direct. VISTA | Asst. Direct. CAP | Asst. Direct. Administr. |

Regional Offices

| N. East New York | Mid-Atl. Wash. DC | S. East Atlanta | Western San Franc. | S. West Austin | Grt. Lks. Chicago | N. Cent. Kan. Cty |

State OEO, Sacramento, Calif.

Economic Opportunity Commission of San Diego County, California

EOC Board of Directors

Executive Committee

Executive Director

Administrative Asst.
Public Info. Off.
Personnel Director
Training Director

CAC Representatives to the EOC Board

| Fiscal Operations | Program Development | Area Development | Program Evaluation | Head Start Control |

CAC Reps to Dlgt. Agency Brds.

Community Action Councils of San Diego County, California (13)

CAC Boards of Directors

CAC Staff

Economic Opportunity Commission Delegate Agencies

| Head Start | Legal Aid | Service Centers | Manpower Training |

Delegate Agencies' Boards of Directors

Delegate Agencies' Staff

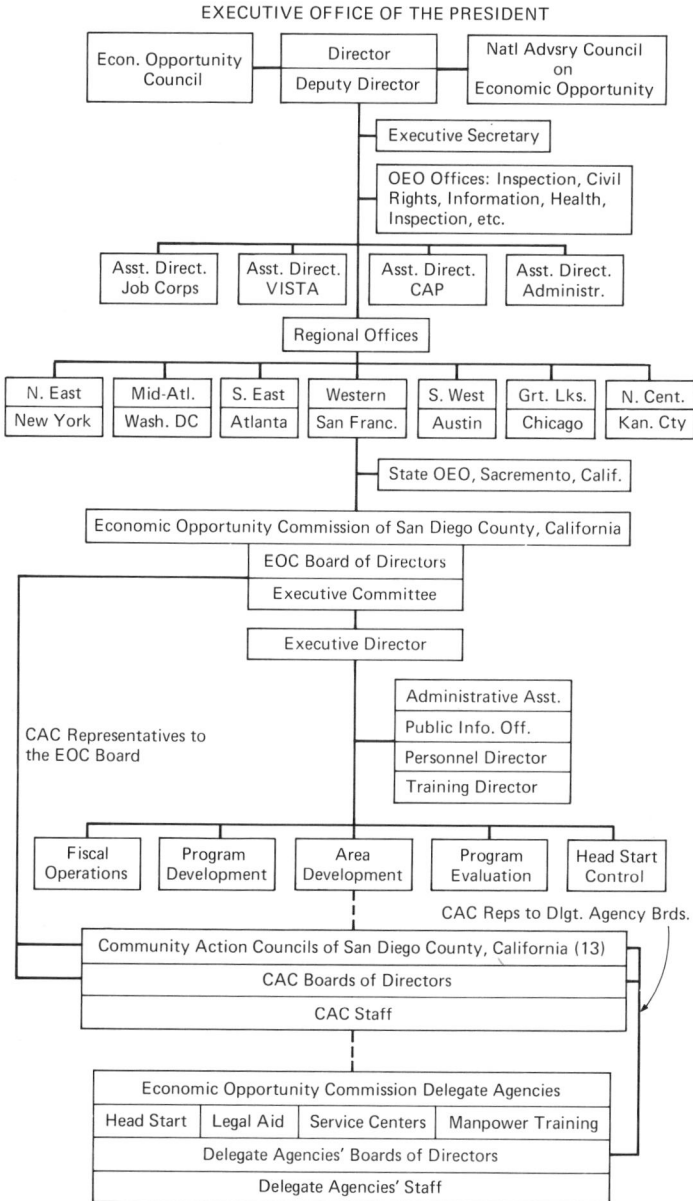

Figure 3.3. Organizational Chart: Office of Economic Opportunity, with Special Focus on the Economic Opportunity Commission of San Diego County, California, 1968.

for the executive directorship of MAAC. He had been an active Republican and in the construction business. He was reported to have failed in business and in politics and became active in the early formulation of the MAAC project and the development of the war on poverty programs in San Diego County. He is, however, representative of the MAAC Corporation membership, which is largely "middle class." When the political hostility began between the PFTA and the CAC in San Ysidro he became actively and deeply involved on the side of the PFTA. While one goal of the PFTA was either to take control of the CAC and the service center of close them down, the MAAC director, tacitly supporting the PFTA in its drive to take over the CAC, actively supported every action they took to close it and, in effect, return control of the area to the MAAC center in San Ysidro. In committing himself this way he became subject to charges of incitement to violence and conspiracy by the Anglo CAC board members. They complained to the MAAC Corporation board and the EOC and John Diaz was finally ordered by his board and the EOC to stay out of San Ysidro and its problems. He did remove himself physically from San Ysidro, but he continued to advise the PFTA privately.

As the issues ramified in the arena representatives of other agencies and groups were drawn into the conflict. Although the Mexican-Americans of Otay were very uninvolved in the problems in San Ysidro, several persons from Woodlawn Park, all black, were drawn into the conflict. Although the blacks were not concerned with control of the Border Area CAC, they did want representation on it, or some other CAC, because they believed the war on poverty was important for their community. The vice president of the CAC board and two other members were black. In almost all issues they sided with the Anglos and in the later hostilities in the arena were viciously slandered by the PFTA and for a period of time withdrew from the CAC.

A number of officials representing various departments of the City of San Diego were active at various times. Mr. John Thom, the local councilman for the area, attempted at a CAC meeting to point out to the people all that San Diego had done for San Ysidro. It was the meeting in April 1968, just after the people in the community had become cognizant of the imminent loss of homes for many of them as a result of the freeway. They shouted Mr. Thom down in anger. As a result of this and other events, and the efforts of the San Ysidro Planning and Development Group, a series of public meetings were organized in which a variety of city and county officials, representing among other agencies the local schools, welfare department, highway department, police, even the mayor personally, would attempt to explain to the people the rationale for the development of San Ysidro and the beneficial impact it would have upon their lives. By and large, these were attempts to quiet the clamor of the people over the development of San Ysidro.

Officials and teachers from the local elementary school district were drawn into the conflict. Mr. Hermann, the superintendent, remained visibly aloof from the conflict, although his role in the school issue was certainly significant. More noticeable were the assistant superintendent and two of the three school principals in San Ysidro. The special classes, or Educationally Mentally Retarded Classes (EMR), came under fire by a few mothers in the community and the CAC staff, and the school was forced to justify its role and activities in these programs. At least as a partial result of the agitation, the school district did become involved in a bilingual education program and promised changes in its special class program.

Personnel from other CACs in the area were drawn into the conflict. Executive secretaries of all the CACs met regularly with EOC staff to discuss problems, programs, and progress in their areas. As a result of this and other communications many became familiar with the problems in the Border Area CAC. Although some offered to help, there was very little they could do beyond advise and give moral support for one contestant or other.

The Border Area CAC shared an office with Mr. Flores, the local representative of the United Farmworkers Union of California. Mr. Flores is considered here a secondary contestant only because of the aloofness and neutrality he maintained throughout most of the conflict. In fact, he potentially wielded a tremendous amount of power and influence. Although he was on the scene for all of the conflict he maintained a neutral position because of a potential conflict of interests due to his other affiliations. He was a Mexican-American and president of the National City CAC board of directors. He also represented the National City CAC on the EOC board, and had been elected as vice chairman of the executive committee of the EOC board of directors. His potential for involvement, given his affiliations, could have had a profound effect on the events which transpired. Although he remained generally neutral and aloof from the infighting, he did serve as an invaluable source of information regarding policy and tactics for some of the people involved in the conflict. He was philosophically, morally, and politically committed to the goals of the war on poverty, and served as selflessly as possible to make the community action programs work.

The conflict in San Ysidro also drew into the arena the governor's advisor on Mexican-American affairs. As a Republican and a Mexican-American, he was called into the fray by John Diaz of the MAAC project. He was very closely affiliated with the PFTA and had practically nothing to do with the Anglos or the CAC.

Finally, there was the influence of the federal government upon the events in the arena. Representatives did occasionally appear, although their presence often was merely assumed. Rumors were frequent that congressional investigators were about to descend upon San Ysidro because of the conflict. The director of the EOC presumably received many communications from departments of the government inquiring into the problems of the war on poverty in the San Diego area. Officials from the Department of Housing and Urban

Development (HUD) made appearances in the area to discuss a rent subsidy housing development proposed for San Ysidro to accommodate the families being displaced by the freeway. Individuals running for state and federal offices in the 1968 national election came into the area and made political speeches. In all but one of the instances that I observed, these individuals were affiliated mainly with members of the San Ysidro Planning and Development Group or other such influentials. Only one candidate addressed a Community Action Council meeting. He lost his race. Most of these latter individuals had little or no overt influence on the activities in San Ysidro, but many of them must have carried back to their respective state and federal legislature memories and attitudes unaccommodating to the war on poverty.

There was a general paranoia among many persons at all levels of the war on poverty in San Diego during the summer and fall of 1968 to the effect that the war on poverty program would be abolished should there be a change in administration. Many resented the conflicts in the Border Area CAC and a few other CACs and programs in the county, because they reflected adversely on the program. Others complained somewhat justifiably, that the war on poverty was the least funded and most investigated program in the history of the United States, that not enough attention was given to the good things the program was accomplishing and too much attention was directed toward its shortcomings. Many other persons feared the loss of their jobs. In the few months prior to the elections there were many discussions at all levels of the local war on poverty organizations about what course the community action programs generally should assume in the event funds were cut off. Informal contingency plans were numerous. The fact that the war on poverty and its community action programs generally did survive is perhaps a credit more to its bureaucratization and resultant neutralization than a result of any tangible and overt gains it made against poverty.[19]

SUMMARY

Chapter 3 served several purposes. The political teams and contestants who conflicted in the arena were introduced. Their group and individual roles were discussed in detail and the composition and interrelationships of some of the organizations which comprise the war on poverty bureaucracy in San Diego County were described. In this way the variety of affiliations some contestants hold and the covert and overt nature of the goals they pursue are made understandable. In the next chapter the complex factors which gave rise to the issues over which the contestants conflicted are discussed in depth.

Chapter Four

It Will Be a Long War

INTRODUCTION TO THE ISSUES

Before entering into a discussion of the factors which led to the conflict in San Ysidro it may be advisable to briefly introduce the issues over which this conflict developed. From among the number of possible issues I have chosen to investigate three because they have implications, first, for the political processes by which poverty habitats may be integrated into the national culture of the United States, second, for understanding the political activity of people who live in poverty, and third, for providing insight into the forces which operate outside of the poverty habitat and which impinge upon it and influence not only the adaptation populations make to poverty but the attempts to alter this condition. All the specific issues over which contestants came into conflict may be subsumed and analyzed under these three broad issue areas: the control and survival of the Border Area CAC, the development of San Ysidro, and changes in the special education programs conducted by the San Ysidro Elementary School District.

These issues are not isolated and discrete one from the other. They intermesh in a variety of ways which give the conflict in San Ysidro its particular aura. It is, however, fair to say that the first of these is the most significant, for all other political activities in the arena were contingent upon the action and conflict which ensued in the CAC. Still, none of the issues was stimulated by events restricted to San Ysidro, or even the city and county of San Diego. Their roots lie in a complex and farther removed matrix of events which extends upward to the federal government of the United States and back through time to some indeterminate "primordial" period and condition out of which the institutions and attitudes characteristic of American national culture evolved.

Derived from this point of view is the assumption that the conflict within the CAC should not be viewed exclusively as a local problem; the conflict has more general implications for the ability of persons who live in poverty to control their destiny in the face of pressures which emanate from more powerful adherents to a national cultural pattern, tradition, ideology, and value system. Both other problems represent issue areas with some national significance and scope since the education of poor minority children and the decimation by highway construction of poor communities are current problem areas in the United States. The modest contribution offered here to understanding the way people may attempt to come to grips with these problems may be beneficial to persons in similar straits in other areas of the country and may be significant in effecting real and meaningful changes in American national culture.

The first issue, the most important because almost all other conflicts in the arena were related to it and were conditioned by it, is concerned with whether Mexican-Americans, Anglo-Americans, blacks, or some coalition of these people would control the Border Area CAC and whether the CAC would continue to serve the original three communities as designated or San Ysidro exclusively. At the heart of this issue was the ethnic composition of the CAC, its board, and staff. Interethnic hostility and conflict developed very early in the CAC and almost all issues became cast in ethnic terms.

Given the ethnic and social composition of the three communities which comprised the Border Area CAC, the emergence of such conflict might well have been predicted. However, the Border Area CAC was a product of the early, heady period of the war on poverty in San Diego County. The intention of the team who organized the CACs was to activate the war on poverty and the Community Action Council program as quickly as possible. Any problems, it was believed and hoped, would be resolved as they developed. The magnitude of the problems were probably never fully anticipated; shortage of funds, interethnic and intra-ethnic hostility, untrained personnel in authority positions, duplication of programs, hostility from a variety of sectors in the society. Almost immediately the Border Area CAC, and others, segmented along several lines over a variety of issues and problems. In the Border Area CAC, and a few others, this resulted in over two years of hostility and conflict and very few gains against poverty.

The second issue developed in the spring of 1968 and was concerned with the impending development of San Ysidro. About this time the community suddenly became aware of and reacted to the fact that an interstate highway, I-805, was going to cut through the southeast section of San Ysidro and, in conjunction with other proposed developments in the area, displace around 270 families. For a while vast numbers of persons from the community, as well as persons from Otay and Woodlawn Park, were concerned and actively involved in attempting to do something to allay this threat to San Ysidro. A massive march was proposed to descend upon San Diego City Hall in protest. Personnel from the EOC, MAAC, it local service center, and other CACs were in active support and the community was geared to act. Then counterforces were set in motion by some influential people which effectively and for some time stifled any community action.

From the outset the CAC had been involved in this issue and much of the blame for the failure to alleviate this problem fell upon it. The Mexican-Americans who were concerend about the way their community was to be drastically altered blamed this on the presumed interests of certain "rich" Anglos on the CAC board, and the conflict between PFTA and the CAC began. Since, in fact, the freeway had been planned at least since 1959, there is probably little that could have been done at this time to eliminate it or even reroute it.[1] However, the fighting between the PFTA, the CAC, and the service center over this and other issues created a void which, over the next year to eighteen months, permitted other interests, such as the San Ysidro Planning and Development Group, the City of San Diego, the City Planning Department, and others, to continue planning and acting on the development of the area without any serious opposition.

The third issue that developed was concerned with the Special Educational Programs, known as Educationally Mentally Retarded (EMR) classes, conducted by the San Ysidro Elementary School District. A letter circulated by the director of the San Ysidro service center in the early summer of 1968 listed educational reforms as one primary problem to which the war on poverty organizations in the community should address themselves. Schools of the South San Diego Bay Area are notorious among Mexican-Americans and some Anglos for their intransigence—even hostility—in dealing with problems that Spanish-speakers confront in the schools. However, in fairness to the San Ysidro School District, it needs to be pointed out that it was much more enlightened and responsive to change than many other in the area. Its EMR was its most vulnerable area and while it may well have deserved to be changed, the basic reasons that elements in the CAC attacked it when they did were based upon motives other than altruistic ones.

The educational issue developed in the fall of 1968, much later than the previous issues, and lasted for a considerably shorter duration. It represented the last attempt by the CAC as constituted to regain the support of the people in the community. It forced individuals not previously concerned with grass roots problems of a poverty habitat to become more directly and intimately involved. It revealed bigotry and ignorance on the part of some school personnel and genuine concern by others. It also brought to light serious inequities in the teaching and handling of Spanish-speaking children and, if not instrumental, certainly hastened changes in the educational system which, hopefully, will better meet the needs of children from homes where only Spanish is spoken and which adhere to a Mexican culture and value system. It did little, however, to alter the fate of the CAC.

COVERT CONJUNCTIONS AND CONTENTION

At the height of the Great Depression President Roosevelt, in an often quoted remark, referred to "one-third of a nation ill-housed, ill-clad, ill-nourished." Over thirty years later another president, Lyndon B. Johnson, would refer to the same general condition in the United States and argue that "our aim is not to relieve the symptoms of poverty, but to cure it and above all, prevent it." On this note in 1964 a war on poverty was instituted as a significant facet of American domestic policy. Upon the mandate President Johnson received from the people as a result of his landslide victory over Senator Goldwater, forces hostile to the war on poverty were muted and for several glorious months afterward enthusiasm for and excitement over this great social experiment ran at a fever pitch.

Yet, within months after the initial blush of hoped for victory over poverty, concerned individuals were to begin referring to the war on poverty as a "piddling joke" or "pitiful ."[2] It is easy to point to features of American foreign policy, such as our Southeast Asian commitment, as salient forces which undermined the efficacy of the war on poverty. However, more subtle and, perhaps, significant forces which are part of the fabric of American institutions and political arrangements and ideological systems worked to counteraffect the war on poverty and nullify it as a significant force in American society.[3] This is not to imply that the war on poverty was a total failure; though, indeed, the gains at the local level are not likely to be terribly significant unless they are backed, matched, and supported by a major national commitment, and they simply are not.

Still, much good did develop as a result of it. Most significant, I think, was the stimulus it gave to a variety of actions and activities by persons in poverty habitats to do something about their plight. Despite counterforces and influences which emanated from American national culture, such as withdrawal of the moral support of the president, insufficient funding, hostility at a variety of levels in the society, etc., there are things which the poor have shown that they can do to improve and change their condition, although the degree is certainly a moot point. Much of the activity in San Ysidro indicates this. However, the events also indicate the depth and extent of the forces persons in poverty have to confront in order to effect a meaningful change in their condition. The factors which precipitated the issues in San Ysidro ultimately have their roots in a variety of conditions far beyond San Ysidro itself, existing at best on the perimeter of the poverty habitat. Further, the vast majority of the people involved in the community action programs in San Diego were quite aware of these factors.

Scoble (1969) has suggested that the war on poverty was merely an attempt at the national level to resolve ideological and political conflict within the Democratic party. Though some truth may adhere to this it is not a very relevant explanation. The fact that during the mid-1960s the United States was experiencing deep unrest from its ethnic and racial minorities is more pertinent, and points to another condition more relevant for explaining the inception of the war on poverty and the issues at the local levels which it precipitated.

The minority disturbances were and are yet today symptomatic of an increasing social distance between ethnic, racial, and socioeconomic categories of people which comprise American society, a condition which, I theorize, is the result of the specific evolution of a society which is becoming institutionally more complex and specialized. [4] It may be postulated that a society experiencing the dual characteristics of a large and economically deprived minority population and rapid change in its social, technological, economic, and political institutions confronts a real problem of either structurally, or at least cognitively, reducing the social distance between categories and classes of persons or else suffering the loss of its national integrity and unity. The distinct possibility of this happening to American society is graphically demonstrated by the *Report of the National Advisory Commission on Civil Disorders* (1968), otherwise known as the Kerner Commission Report, and its prediction of the possibility of two unequal nations, one black and one white, developing within the national boundaries of the United States. In this context, the "war on poverty" becomes a euphemism for an attempt by the political sphere of America's complex state system to reduce poverty, not as a result of any particular altruistic motivation, but necessarily in order to effect a meaningful integration of the society in the service of national sociocultural unity and integrity.

However, as a result of decades, centuries even, of social inequality, any such attempt would be bound to confront categories of individuals who on the one hand had vested interest in the institutions of the dominant society in which they participated, and on the other who had effected more or less satisfactory adaptations to their condition in settings such as poverty habitats. As a result of commitments made to the status quo of American society, of adaptations made to a seemingly stable social order, and to ideologies which validate this condition, any sudden attempt to effect sociocultural integration, regardless of its motivation and rhetoric, is bound to confront resistance, suspicion, and hostility from a variety of sectors in the society at large. In the face of such opposition, counterforces will be set in motion to reduce the potential conflict.

Any resource committed to this reduction of conflict must by expediency and limitation of the resource be at the expense of the war on poverty. One result of such a complex interaction between federal, state, county, city, and grass roots institutions will be a condition in which those who control the most power will persist at the expense of those controlling the least; the emergence of new qualitatively different institutions by which significant change in the social system might be stimulated will be nullified, and if the initial goal of significantly reducing the socioeconomic inequality for which the program was established in the first place is achieved, the program, especially its institutions, will either become defunct or a permanent, respectable, and innocuous part of the larger sociocultural system. As the result of a variety of factors which existed in different forms and degrees from the level of the federal government down to the grass roots, the war on poverty institutions tended to manifest this latter characteristic.

Promises of action and a meaningful war on poverty very quickly came to be replaced with increasingly hollow rhetoric as other national commitments and priorities withdrew resources from the war on poverty. In San Diego and elsewhere, this led to a variety of interrelated events. As the teeth were pulled from the war on poverty and its political muscle allowed to atrophy, city and state governments which had been hostile to the war on poverty came to accept it. Funds for the war on poverty stabilized and as a result of inflation were actually depleted, and programs suffered accordingly. Amendments were made to the Economic Opportunity Act of 1964, viz., the Green Amendment of 1968. This amendment requires that the board of directors of each community agency which "is a state or political subdivision of a state," e.g., the EOC of San Diego County, shall be so constituted that one-third of the members are elected public officials, one-third represent the poor in the area served, and one-third are officials or members of business, industry, labor, and community groups generally.[5] While this amendment indisputably gives to community action agencies a more truly democratic character and does not alter the prescribed representation of poor on the boards as required by national directives in 1966, many of the war on poverty personnel in San Diego saw it as a threat to the community action programs because ostensibly conservative elements now had the door open for them to affect community action programs and policies.

By this time the 1968 national elections were becoming a topic of concern for the war on poverty in San Diego. It was feared that a change in administration would result in the demise of the war on poverty and this resulted in an intense feeling of insecurity among war on poverty participants in San Diego. There was also concern that new programs would not be funded, that some, such as the Manpower Training Program and Headstart would be "spunoff" to the Department of Labor and Department of Education respectively. Rumors of congressional investigations of various programs and agencies intent upon demonstrating inefficiency and inaffectiveness of the war on poverty were widespread.

A number of personnel were quite concerned that the problems in the Border Area CAC and others at this time would reflect unfavorably on the entire San Diego community action program and give ammunition to those congressmen and representatives hostile to the program. Candidates, such as Agnew, Reagan, and Nixon were making deprecating comments about the war on poverty. After Sergeant Shriver left as director of the OEO, this position was not filled on a permanent basis. Many persons argued and feared that this symbolized the fate of the entire program.

Curious features of the war on poverty, e.g., the funding period of the program, were topics for concern and discussion. While the fiscal year of the federal government is from July 1 to June 30, the fiscal year for the war on poverty is from March 1 to February 28. This resulted in a hiatus between the time when war on poverty funds ran out and new permanent funds were allocated and is indicative of the way the war on poverty was never quite integrated into national policy and, though legal, never quite made legitimate. In order to keep the program operating local umbrella agencies, such as the EOC, had to borrow on its next year's funds on the assumption they would be refunded. There was concern that this curious funding period rendered the program especially vulnerable to being cut off and dropped.[6]

While these considerations may seem far removed from the issues in San Ysidro, they were real points of concern which inhibited certain actions and elicited others. Many community action programs that aimed at social and structural change in American society were stultified for fear of rocking the boat, and the trend toward services was amplified. As I noted, most people were not aware of all those considerations indicated above. All, however, were topics of concern among different people. The totality of their affect was to develop a suspicion among the poor regarding the intentions of the government. This was also compounded by factors which made for the precipitation of issues at the local level which were rooted in other structures and organizations intermediate to the federal government and the poverty habitat.

Integration generally signifies a meshing and articulation of parts of a system. The integration of the federal war on poverty agency with these intermediate structures, the state, city and county, always seemed less intense, and real, than its integration with the poverty habitat. Still, much of this presumed integration was, I think, a matter of a thin thread of rhetoric by which the government attempted to present a sense of affinity with the poor of the nation. There are other, less well known factors which indicate that the war on poverty was being undermined from its beginning by pressures which emanated from these intermediate sectors of American society and to which the federal government in a variety of ways conceded.[7] While a full study of the attrition rate of the war on poverty is not possible here, there are sufficient examples from my research to suggest the tack it followed and pressures to which it succumbed.

Much hostility against the war on poverty was generated by state officials. Many of the nation's governors feared the war on poverty and its political repercussions, e.g., an organized, voting minority. Governor Reagan of California was outspoken in his antagonism to the program.

Early in the war on poverty it was possible for a concerned community agency to develop a good antipoverty program and submit it directly to the national OEO for funding. While not a very common occurence, it certainly did take place, especially in the early days of the war on poverty when the "distance" between the federal government and the poverty habitat was least and there were frantic efforts to get the war on poverty activated. While this still exists as a possibility, increasingly there are prescribed bureaucratic channels and review boards through which any proposal must flow for evaluation prior to being funded. Each of the fifty states established a state OEO. This was explained rather innocuously as a means by which the states, which had been somewhat excluded from initial planning of the war on poverty, could participate. As a result of the establishment of state OEO offices one additional channel was implemented through which programs had to flow and a veto power by the state governor over antipoverty programs accompanied this participation.[8]

Of course, the regional OEO also had veto power over the program. If both vetoed the program it would be sent back for revision or further review at the local level. However, if the regional OEO office approved it and the state OEO office vetoed it, the program moved on to the national OEO office in Washington, D.C. Here the state OEO veto could be overridden, and most generally was. In Califfornia, Governor Reagan was reported to have vetoed some fourteen programs, all of which were overridden by the national OEO. Apparently, vetos at the national OEO level were rare.

However, relatively few persons from poverty habitats seemed aware of the existence of the state OEO. It is also quite difficult to find reference to the office and its function in the literature, either that which emanates from Washington or elsewhere. In San Diego those persons who had heard of it were not terribly familiar with its policy or operations, even at the level of the EOC. For example, no one could tell me exactly how many programs the state OEO office had vetoed; the figure of fourteen Reagan vetos was reported on a television news broadcast.

It was suggested by some persons that the state OEO was established in anticipation of the day when the war on poverty would become a local and not a federal program. This, or the demise of the total program, was often speculated upon as a real possibility should there be a change in federal administration, as happened in 1968. If the control of the war on poverty had fallen to a local state bureau it is probable that in some of the more conservative states the program would have died almost immediately. Concern over the fact that the directorship of the OEO was not filled permanently after Shriver left was associated with this concern. Many people saw the vacant directorship as a way of expediting the transfer of the program to a more local level, if not to kill it more easily. In this event, such policies as the development of San Ysidro in the service of a few vested interests would not have to confront opposition from organizations legally constituted and funded by the federal government.

City governments represent another intermediate structure out of which emerged inimical actions and attitudes which affected the political activity of the poverty habitats of the United States. Politicians in many areas were hostile to the war on poverty. The governments in many major American cities attempted either to ignore or more actively countereffect the war on poverty because mayors and city halls generally represent the traditional establishment and support traditional influentials and vested interest groups, such as the San Ysidro Planning and Development Group, and anything which threatened to abruptly alter this conceptualization was viewed as a threat. Many mayors apparently feared an uprising of the poor or a forced alteration, even relinquishment, of their control over city government to rabble from the streets.[9]

In a real sense, one feature of the specific evolution of American culture was an increase in space between what constituted the grass roots and other levels of political participation in American society. Poor people in poverty habitats after World War II and prior to the war on poverty never comprised a grass roots level of political participation. The grass roots of American politics had become increasingly relegated to individuals and groups who represented the middle-class urban and suburbanite statuses of American society. The poor, as political activists prior to the agitation of blacks for civil rights were quite invisible.[10] City politicians preferred it that way. The political ties local politicians maintained extended upward through the state and federal structures, not downward into the developing organizations of the poverty habitats. The about-face that many cities—Los Angeles, Chicago, Atlanta, San Francisco, San Diego, Boston, and others—had to make in order to recognize the black power emerging from the poverty habitat, suddenly legalized by federal law, was not an easy turn. The exact influence mayors had on the war on poverty which led to eventual neutralization of the war on poverty is an area of needed investigation in order to fully comprehend the articulation of urban politics to American national political culture, for it has been suggested the ties of city politicians to state and federal government has been more influential in the control of the war on poverty than generally known or expected.[11]

San Deigo was one city in which many of the above considerations were manifest and it came to recognize the war on poverty slowly and begrudgingly. In establishing and recognizing the EOC of San Diego County, the city first attempted to develop an organization manned by persons hand picked by the local politicians, none of whom represented the poverty habitats of San Diego. Although this problem was eventually resolved and the poor did become members of the EOC, the EOC and the City of San Diego, while existing together compatibly, rarely seemed to develop any really close working agreement.[12] For example, it took threats and near violence before the city of San Diego recognized the depth of the discontent in San Ysidro over the redevelopment of the area.

In San Diego the war of poverty was eventually tolerated. After it proved to be nonrevolutionary, it was even accepted. Still, some hostility to it in some circles persisted. Somehow it represented something anti-American—anti-Calvinistic; it was "new-dealish" and repugnant to conservatives. As one prominent San Diego business leader said: "I don't think most businesses can afford in this competitive day to put people on the payroll merely to get them off the streets. This isn't the American free enterprise way of doing things."[13]

After the EOC restructured its board of directors in accordance with the Green Amendment, one board member, a representative of the poor and a member of the EOC executive committee, told me that now the EOC would have to be careful not to offend the newly incorporated elected officials from the city and county: "They can do you a lot of damage," he said. "In (our area) we offended (one) just by not recognizing him enough in meetings—didn't feed his ego, in other words—and we found all kinds of doors that had been open to us closed, and we had to start a lot of things all over again."

Still, in defense of San Diego, it did initiate a series of programs by which the poor and their representatives could confront one another and attempt to talk out their problems. These "City-Community Dialogues" were held every two weeks in the city hall. They brought together the poor and the officials representing county and city law enforcement agencies, school districts, welfare agencies, politicians. At the time of this research they had been going on for approximately two years. While a lot of tensions were released, near the end of the summer of 1968 a counter tension was beginning to build. In one stormy session a Mexican-American representative from a CAC pointed out that there were very few minority policemen—twenty or so—on the San Diego police force, and none above the level of sergeant. Probing further, it was revealed that the review board which conducted final interviews with applicants, even though its members were chosen from outside San Diego so as to insure impartiality, had never had a representative of a minority sit on it. In anger and frustration a black stood up and said to the assembled city and county officials, "Man, we been talking shit here for two years and we still ain't seen no change, no improvement. That's all it's been, man, a lot of shit! You either do something and do it quick or you're going to have one hell of a hot time on your hands." Within the year there were riots and massive school walkouts by blacks and the presumed lethargic Mexican-Americans, and the black ghetto had rioted.

In San Ysidro in the fall of 1968 a series of public meetings were held to "cool off" the tempers which had emerged as a result of the proposed re-development of the community and the protracted struggle over the Community Action Council. They were initiated by the city in conjunction with the San Ysidro Planning and Development Group. A member of the development group chaired each session. Some good did emerge from them; a few extra street lights and an announcement that San Ysidro was going to be included in the Model Cities Program of San Diego. For the moment, under the attention of so many officials from city, county, state and federal offices, the people of San Ysidro were, to a degree, mollified. Most with whom I spoke, however, felt that the meetings were a waste of time. "They're just telling us what they're going to do to us," was one comment. "They're not asking us what we want done." To a great extent this was true. For example, a rent subsidy apartment

project was being constructed for the supposed purpose of accommodating
the families being displaced by the freeway. However, it was well known by city
officials and the San Ysidro Development Association that the Mexican-Americans of San Ysidro placed a high value on living in single family dwellings.
They categorically rejected the high density zoning and apartment complexes
planned for San Ysidro.

The effective neutralization of the war on poverty generally was, in
part at least, initially stimulated by the frustrations and suspicions caused by
the activities of these intermediate structures. While the people of the poverty
habitat were more aware of the tensions generated by those structures closest to
them, such as the city of San Diego as opposed to the more distant state OEO
of California, they all took their toll. Perhaps the hardest role of all was that
played by the EOC of San Diego County.

The EOC served as a brokerage house, a buffer, viable, obvious, most
generally misunderstood, between the traditional power structure of American
political culture and the grass roots political organizations of the poverty habitat.
The EOC was put into the uncomfortable position of having to accommodate
all participants in the war on poverty: The state, regional, and federal OEO,
city, county, state and federal politicians, private agencies, and their delegate
agencies and Community Action Councils within the poverty habitat. As a result
of its role it had the worst of two worlds and its personnel, policies, and structure
probably inadvertently did more to stimulate the issues in San Ysidro than any
other single factor or agency.

Problems at the local level, such as in San Ysidro, elicited negative
responses from other levels, such as the state and federal OEOs. These tended to
impair the efficiency of the war on poverty generally in San Diego and at times
seemed to threaten the existence of the antipoverty program itself. Many of
these problems stimulated insecurity at the level of the poverty habitat and, in
San Ysidro, were certainly significant in the precipitation of issues in that arena.

Although the war on poverty in San Diego started somewhat later
than it did in many other communities, there are factors which suggest that it
developed too quickly for the kind of conservative community San Diego
represents. For example, despite the composition of its board and staff, both of
which reflected a cross-section of the county, the EOC and the war on poverty
was never able to develop or command the kind of broad and viable constituency
that it should have. This meant that it lacked an essential resource of power, a
broad base of support. This was certainly rendered difficult by the political
character of San Diego, which is one of the five counties in California that has
more registered Republicans than Democrats and which along with Orange
County, its county neighbor to the north, represents a powerful conservative
block.

The leadership of the EOC, primarily as manifest in its director, was
also accused of being wish-washy. The leadership did not seek as actively as it

might the kind of broad support base that would render the program more effective. This leadership did not take firm stands on most issues, although it was very concerned with issues in the poverty habitat that might reflect unfavorably on the EOC.

At the heart of this consideration rested distinctly different ideas by the OEC and several of the Community Action Councils about what actually constituted social change. The leadership of the EOC was very oriented to services; the director was a welfare official prior to assuming his role in the EOC. Any attempt by Community Action Councils to stimulate structural change in the major institutions of America was regarded with apprehension; there also frequently seemed to be a lack of skill in manipulating the various forces with which it had to contend. CAC staff members frequently complained that the EOC bent over backwards to accommodate influential people and the "establishment" and all too frequently ignored the needs and problems of the CACs and the poverty habitats. Conversely, in almost the same breath, CACs would argue that the EOC dictated too much and forced the CACs to rubber stamp preconceived EOC policy. Obviously, the EOC was unable to please everyone.

Much of the Economic Opportunity Commission's difficulty was due to the fact that its policy was originally predicated upon an expanding war on poverty program. Instead it found itself in a holding action as funds and resources declined. Forces hostile to the war on poverty re-emerged as President Johnson's "mandate" slowly receded and the EOC increasingly was forced into compromises, lest itself and the whole war on poverty be scrapped. The national elections of 1968 and the possibility of a change in administration made political compromises a necessity. In short, policies and programs which may have seemed "like a good idea at the time," e.g., an ombudsman for San Diego, a citizen-police review board, certain programs to help the elderly, and others, were subverted by withdrawal of resources and other tactics by which the war on poverty generally was neutralized, and which will be discussed in Chapter 6.

One impediment which affected the relationship of the EOC to the CACs and augmented the conflict in the arena is a structural incongruity which resulted in an imprecise rapport between the two agencies. No one was able to explain satisfactorily its development. Some EOC authorities said the structural design was purposeful; others said it was a mistake due to the rapidity with which the CAC program was implemented. The EOC official who conceived and organized the CAC program, the director of the EOC Area Development, argued that the structural relationship which obtained was intended, although the problems it created were not anticipated. Others argued he was trying to save face.

The structural problem resulted in a kind of mutually dependent autonomy between the two agencies. Although they were linked together in a number of ways, the EOC expected the CACs to function with a high degree of autonomy. For example, the CACs, as the mechanisms which insured the maximum feasible participation of the poor, are linked by law to the EOC through the representative each CAC places upon the EOC board of directors. The EOC consultants are charged with assisting the CACs in assuming their role in the poverty habitat. There are regular and frequent meetings between CAC presidents and executive secretaries with EOC staff to discuss CAC problems. Frequent sessions are convened in which the OEO and EOC personnel attempt to train CAC staff and board members to their expected roles.

Beyond these functional links, the EOC had sole control over the funds the CAC and delegate agencies depended upon. This functional aspect was of critical importance, for regardless of how much the EOC stressed that CACs were autonomous from the EOC, it controlled the purse strings, and this affected the CACs in a variety of ways.

Programs could be diluted or excluded due to availability of funds. This led CACs to question the value of their efforts if programs they desired could not be implemented to the extent they felt necessary. Theoretically, the CACs could refuse to fund any delegate agency which they decided was not serving the needs of the poverty habitat. However, the EOC was ultimate arbitrator over any issue of this sort also. Theoretically, the CACs made the decision regarding what programs came into the habitat. This too was always subject to final EOC approval as determined by the availability of funds and the problems the EOC thought such a program might generate in the habitat.

All CACs were very aware that the EOC, as the funding agency for the war on poverty in San Diego, was also obligated to insure adherences of war on poverty agencies to federal guidelines. Should a CAC or a delegate agency, not adhere to guidelines, misuse funds, or become too strife ridden to carry out its obligations, the EOC has the right to step in and close it down, or assume its operation until its particular problem is resolved.

Community Action Council staff salaries were also paid by the EOC. For the individual this resulted in a cognitive as well as a structural and functional dependency of the CACs on the EOC because his livelihood and subsistence were linked to the EOC. Still, the EOC insisted that CAC boards have complete control over hiring and firing of staff. However, in the event a staff member was fired by the CAC board, he had recourse to a grievance committee composed of EOC board members which had the power to overturn any decision made by the CAC board.

The effect of these matters in San Ysidro was that the CAC board did not really believe they had power to fire a staff member. At the height of the conflict several board members complained of the structural relationship of the CACs to the EOC. As the retired Anglo board member put it, "No corporation I ever worked for was like this." He and others never understood this structural relationship, and in most times of crisis refused to move without EOC approval.

This incongruous structural relationship compounded other areas of potential and real misunderstanding between the EOC and the CACs. For example, there was never any clear understanding between these agencies over what constituted social change in the war on poverty. Several CACs interpreted change as referring to institutional change or change in the structures of institutions, e.g., schools, which they confronted in the arena. The EOC was always concerned about the affect the conflict involved in such confrontations would have on the total program as viewed from above. This became an increasing concern as funds for the war on poverty became tighter and more conservative elements began to emerge at the national level and frequently resulted in attempts by the EOC to "cool it" at the local level.

In short, although the CACs theoretically were expected to be autonomous from the EOC, in practice they were not. In San Ysidro the result was that the CAC board did not really believe they had any power. As the conflict expanded and grew more intense, the CAC board became less willing to take strong stands without EOC advice and approval. The one positive stand they did take when they fired a staff member and impeached members of the board was immediately regretted. After this the board became even more uncertain of its authority.

One of the major problems caused by this "gray area" was a fear in many of the CACs that the EOC had created this particular kind of articulation between the two agencies in anticipation of a time when it would divest itself of the CACs. This fear had its roots in a study commissioned by the EOC in 1967. It was a *Study of Management, Organization and Administrative Practices of the Economic Opportunity Commission of San Diego County (1968)*. This became known as the Birge Report, after the individual who compiled it. Among other recommendations it suggested that the CAC program as presently constituted be done away with. It suggested that the CACs be reorganized into one office because the decentralized nature of the program, the lack of coordination between EOC and CACs, and the overlap of functions at all levels hindered progress of the war on poverty.

The CACs regarded this as a threat to their existence and demanded a counter investigation. This was conducted by a committee representing the EOC and CACs. As might be expected it strongly advised that the present program be continued. Regardless, the Birge study did undermine the confidence of the CACs in the EOC and suspicions and fears which had been latent became manifest and affected almost all the CACs. This was expressed privately and in the meetings held between EOC personnel and executive secretaries of the CACs in San Diego County. The executive secretaries were fearful of being severed from the EOC because it was the source of their salary and because they viewed the EOC as a kind of buffer between the CACs and the establishment. Some of the CACs, as in San Ysidro, were having serious problems which involved the establishment. Without EOC backing, and the strength of the federal government this implied, the CACs feared they would lose whatever power and influence they had. This constant suspicion over the motives of the EOC tended to debilitate more positive actions by the CACs.

The EOC, on the other hand, argued that CACs were never intended to be permanent dependents of the EOC. The EOC hoped that the CACs would become self-sufficient and powerful enough to exist on their own, seek their own source of funds, and with community backing and support became viable and powerful political organizations in their own right. Some CACs, the EOC argued, were capable of doing this now; most CACs however did not feel that secure. This insecurity was amplified when, in the fall of 1968, the EOC did attempt to cut ties with the CACs.[14]

Justifiably, the EOC was concerned about the impending change in administration and the affect this might have upon their ability to fund the CACs. The CAC program was under fire from a number of sectors in the society; the events in San Ysidro did not help this matter. At least one other CAC in the county was having problems similar to San Ysidro's; others had gone through similar problems and the potential for their re-emergence existed; another was in a struggle with the schools in its area.

A congressional investigating team came into San Diego County in the fall of 1968 to look into some of these problems, and letters from Washington and the state OEO had come down to the EOC requesting clarification of and solutions to the problems manifest in some of the CACs. From the CAC point of view, this was an ill-advised time for the EOC to argue that CACs could now go it alone; most saw it as an attempt by the EOC to extirpate the CAC so the EOC could survive without the stigma of CAC radicalism and conflict.

The problems created by these inconsistencies in the real and ideal expectations of the role of the CAC did not stimulate conflict in all CACs. The extent to which problems developed seemed to depend upon the character of the CAC board and staff and its knowledge of the program. The board and staff of the Border Area CAC, as well as being riddled with dissent and plagued by conflict, was also quite indecisive, generally uninformed, and not willing to comprehend and assess the implications of this structural incongruity. This had profound implications for the efficiency of the CAC and the conflict in the arena.

The EOC made it clear that it wished to divert itself of any part in the conflict in the Border Area CAC. It hoped that a natural process of resolution followed by a development of CAC responsibility would effect itself. The EOC was also concerned that the intense conflict in the Border Area CAC and problems in a few other CACs and delegate agencies in the county would reflect unfavorably upon the whole program and impair its funding possibilities. The EOC was caught in a situation in which the Anglo and Mexican-American board and staff members of the Border Area CAC both wanted and expected EOC advice and assistance at the expense of the other. It was exactly the kind of ethnic struggle the EOC hoped at all cost to avoid. In the long run it could not avoid taking a stand and, as will be discussed, did so to the relief of all concerned.

Finally, satisfactory communication and coordination within the program has always been a problem. This is because of the widespread distrust of other's motives and actions at all levels in the war on poverty and because of the unclear and undefined lines by which the communications travel. For example, although the EOC denied that it would implement the suggestions of the Birge Report, CACs never accepted this. The attempts in 1968 to amputate the CACs from the EOC only justified the CAC's suspicion of the EOC. A massive and unmanageable amount of information flowed down to the CACs from the EOC, most of it rather worthless. On the other hand, on critical problems there frequently seemed to be a dearth of information and clarification of certain problems often went begging. One justified and major complaint in Spanish-speaking CACs was that most of the information was in English only. Also, the EOC consultants were regarded as of little help from the viewpoint of the CACs. Their actions were capricious and often unpredictable. Many of the CACs considered the consultants spies from the EOC. By and large, their help and assistance to the CACs was never satisfactory, primarily because they were poorly trained for those duties, [15] and in most cases their assistance deteriorated as the program persisted. A report by the chairman of the EOC Board of Directors issued on February 27, 1969 lamented that "The coordination, planning and development of programs . . . through a rational planning system has been lacking in San Diego as well as other communities." Problems of seeking funding to keep the program viable, governmental and bureaucratic red tape, and lack of coordination at all levels, all seemed to reduce meaningful communications and foster suspicion of agency's motives. This tended to impede action against poverty and foster issues at the level of the poverty habitat.

Finally, in conjunction with these more general factors which precipitated conflict there were others quite specific to the Border Area CAC and the social organization of San Ysidro. These were significant in keeping issues alive once they were born and fostering their expansion to a point which at times seemed to approach irrationality. These will be introduced here, but since they are such an essential warp in the fabric of the events they will be returned to in greater detail in the course of the analysis of the conflict. For example, the ethnic distinction between Anglos and Mexican-Americans mentioned previously also became a major point of dissension and conflict and emerged out of a long dormant hostility.[16] Even though individuals denied it, there were strong underlying feelings of hostility in San Ysidro that predated the conflict in the CAC.

For one thing, San Ysidro is, to a great extent, residentially segregated.[17] In some of the Anglo areas of San Ysidro Mexican-Americans were openly disliked and accused of being prejudiced toward Anglos. Among the population generally interethnic hostility was more prevalent among Anglos than

Mexican-Americans, though in the conflict in the arena the Mexican-Americans expressed it most virulently and intensely. Some individuals could point to particular instances in the past which smacked of ethnic hostility. For example, one woman pointed out that about twenty-five years ago the San Ysidro Women's Business Organization was integrated, but an Anglo woman made a disparaging remark about a Mexican-American and practically no Mexican-American woman has participated since. There are also two Voluntary Associations within the Catholic Church of some long ancestry: one Anglo and one Mexican-American, and they still compete in raising funds for the church. Another person pointed out that about fifteen years ago square dances were held regularly in San Ysidro. At one, a young Anglo told a still very prominent San Ysidro Mexican-American family that Mexicans were not welcome. This family has never participated in an Anglo organization or socialized with Anglos to any great extent since. The ethnic hostility became quite pronounced in the arena and was openly referred to. It also assumed the characteristics of a class struggle, for, as noted, the Mexican-American contestants made a clear distinction between the rich Anglos and poor Mexican-Americans of San Ysidro.

Of course, another primary factor alluded to previously which precipitated issues in the arena was the impending development of San Ysidro. The San Ysidro Planning and Development Group which was responsible for these activites added another dimension to the schisms and cleavages developing among the field in the arena. The blanket accusations made by the Mexican-American contestants that all the Anglos in town were rich was not true; it was, however, a useful propaganda device utilized by the leadership of the PFTA. The San Ysidro Planning and Development Group certainly was composed of higher status individuals than were most other contestants in the arena. The pattern of interstatus variation present in San Ysidro is simply one more variation on a theme that has been described in a variety of other community contests and which has an affect on local level politics.[18] The existence of the San Ysidro Planning and Development Group and the secondary contestants which entered the arena as a result of the conflict over the redevelopment of San Ysidro gave the arena a hierarchical character that otherwise would not have existed. This has implications for the kind of political activity which ensued, because it resulted in an unequal distribution of power and forced the emergence of a variety of tactics by the poorer contestants which otherwise might not have developed.

SUMMARY

The factors which precipitated conflict in the poverty habitat and CACs were rooted whether really or abstractly in the factors discussed above. The problems at the local levels were frequently caused by intangible pressures created by upper levels of organization within the war on poverty which were only articulated with the local levels through imprecise channels and techniques of communication. Many of the factors which precipitated conflict at the local level were built into the structure of the war on poverty as it developed in San Diego and have their roots in the initial founding of the program. In the Border Area CAC, it is possible to demonstrate that some of the factors which precipitated the conflict antedate by sometime the inception of the CAC. Some of the conflict in this particular CAC during the two years prior to my research was certainly as intense, perhaps in certain instances more so, as that which followed. In order to explicate the issues and conflict and factors which precipitated it in 1968, I will in the next chapter present a brief history of the Border Area Community Action Council and discuss the emergence of the issues over which the contestants fell into conflict.

Chapter Five

A Fight to the Finish

INTRODUCTION

In a discussion of the boundaries which delimit ethnic group identity Frederick Barth suggests that one criterion which forces the emergence of ethnic distinctions in an area is an "acceptance of the principle that standards applied to one such category can be different from those applied to another" (1969:17). San Ysidro represents a case in point; for ethnic distinctions and hostility were a significant part of all the events in San Ysidro. It was Mexican-American housing that was poor, Mexican-Americans who were to be displaced by the freeway, and Mexican-Americans who desired control of the Community Action Council at the expense of Anglo-Americans, so that poor Mexican-Americans might be better served by the war on poverty. The schools of San Ysidro became involved because it was Mexican-American children who were most affected by decisions made by Anglo administrators.

    Kramer pointed out that one pattern of conflict resolution in some of the struggles in the war on poverty that he analyzed can only be characterized as "a fight to the finish" (1969:174). The political conflict in San Ysidro exemplified this condition. This is largely because the ethnic hostility in San Ysidro and its political manifestation were very similar to the problems Kramer described. Kramer explains this by theorizing that:

> The extent to which power is concentrated and structured along
> partisan and ethnic lines heightens the stake of those in whom it is
> vested and increases the possibility of disagreement and opposition
> to any effort to disturb the current distribution or balance of power.
> Conversely, where power is decentralized and diffused with few
> discernable blocs, there may be less at stake for any group and less
> likelihood of a militant posture. (1969:165)

The San Ysidro case bears out this hypothesis. Prior to the war on poverty and the emergence of political issues, there were few discernable blocs of power and San Ysidro was known as a "quiet" little community. Once issues began to emerge and become structured along particular, and especially partisan lines, the conflict grew and expanded accordingly. I will demonstrate this by discussing and analyzing the process involved in each issue and the points of articulation between the issues and the variety of contestants in the arena. This discussion is based upon the principle that the events which take place in an encapsulated arena can only be understood in terms of the variety of forces both internal and external to the arena and which influence the events in complex and myriad ways. Hopefully, this discussion will reveal the intricacy of the conflict.

In order to put all the events into a perspective I will, however, first give a general history and overview of the events particular to the Border Area CAC. This covers the period from January 1966 to January 1969. This brief history is designed to demonstrate the continuity of conflict in the CAC and the reasons, both covert and overt, for it. The period in which the major events with which this work is concerned took place and which will be analyzed in the next three sections of this chapter takes up the year from January 1968 to January 1969.

THE HISTORY OF THE BORDER AREA CAC

Hughes (1966) has theorized that the effectiveness of a council is in direct proportion to the size of the political arena in which it functions; its effectiveness will decline should the arena expand beyond reasonable limits and the council will become divisive along other lines of potential cleavage within the society. Other lines of potential cleavage could, for example, develop between kinship groups or socioeconomic categories in the society. The arena of San Ysidro in which the Border Area CAC competed was too large from the outset and dissension developed almost immediately along intercommunity and, ultimately, interethnic lines. It was this latter cleavage line which generated the most intense conflict.

Early in the war on poverty in San Diego County enthusiasm among the participants was high. This enthusiasm at times affected the rationality of actions and good intentions frequently seemed to overshadow practicality. Such was the case with the founding of the Border Area CAC. The EOC official who was responsible for organizing the Border Area CAC was a past resident of San Ysidro and knew the general area. However, as he admitted, and subsequent events proved, his team erred in incorporating the three communities of Otay, Woodlawn Park, and San Ysidro into one CAC.

The area they encompass is fragmented with reference to land use and community organization and there are few factors that would provide any basis for intercommunity social, economic, or political cohesiveness. Each also had its own special problems and viewed its needs quite differently. For example,

Woodlawn Park wanted improved health services and a community center. Influential people in Otay were most concerned with obtaining a teen post for their youth. San Ysidro was faced with a severe housing problem. Also, as noted, each community was somewhat distinct politically, ethnically, and physically. All this had implications for the antipoverty programs that could be provided to the area, and the cost of implementing them would be high.

The Border Area CAC also incorporated a more heterogeneous ethnic mixture in a more narrowly circumscribed area than any other CAC. Due to this and other circumstances, the CAC was plagued with problems that were never resolved. For example, from the outset of the war on poverty in the area the Mexican-Americans of San Ysidro and the blacks of Woodlawn Park always felt their needs and problems, poor housing, poor transportation, and poor services to be special and demanding of attention at the expense of Otay and each other. The battle lines between San Ysidro and the other communities were drawn early in the program.

The Border Area CAC held its first meeting on January 25, 1966, with 300 people in attendance for the purpose of selecting a board of directors and developing a set of by-laws by which it might become a legal body. At this time the CAC had no staff, though the possibility of hiring a staff was discussed. This would depend upon the allocation of federal funds for a program which would provide staff to CACs and which was being written by the EOC. From the beginning the board of directors was too large. It ranged between twelve and seventeen members, including officers. Throughout the history of this CAC its board has been comprised of a variety of individuals, almost all good intentioned but very unequal in skills and abilities. The more astute members were in continual conflict with those less skilled and intraboard bickering was rampant. The obvious result was an inability to make decisions regarding war on poverty programs. Interest was diluted by petty bickering, personality conflicts, and a multitude of minor issues, such as the legality of a motion presented at a previous meeting, whether the previous minutes were in order, whether the problems of one community were relevant to another, and the like. A lack of a quorum for board meetings became the rule.

The office of president of the board became unpopular. In the first two years of the program changes in board personnel were common and there were eleven presidents or acting presidents, four in the first year and seven in the second. Several of the presidents tired of the bickering and hostilities they were unable to resolve; others, flushed with their first taste of authority, became petty dictators. One of the most dictatorial of the presidents, Mr. Brown, a black from Woodlawn Park, is still one of the most active and irritating participants in the CAC, although the people will not permit him to hold a position on any board or committee.

When Mr. Brown was president almost every event or issue required a special meeting of the board. In the absence of a quorum Mr. Brown would declare an emergency and hold a meeting which, according to the by-laws, was illegal. On occasions Mr. Brown would make unilateral decisions. His intemperate actions eventually threatened the existence of the CAC, and the EOC became concerned. Although Delia Garcia was assigned to the Border Area CAC as EOC consultant, during this tumultuous period one other EOC consultant became involved to support her. Delia and the other consultant began to politic behind the scenes and suggested to other CAC board members that the EOC would support any attempt to impeach the president. They increased their pressure, and finally, under duress, Mr. Brown resigned the office.

As a result of a lack of comprehension and understanding of the War on Poverty Program the Border Area CAC floundered. At a time when the CAC and other war on poverty institutions in the area, such as the service centers, Headstart, or Legal Aid, should have been coordinating their efforts and developing programs to attack poverty they were, in fact, not communicating. When they attempted to communicate they immediately fell into contention over who was doing the best job, or who even should do the job, who had ultimate control over programs, and so forth. The result was a disparate group of institutions which overlapped in their efforts and argued among themselves.

Programs that should have come before the CAC for review never developed. For example, the delegate agencies of the EOC, especially the MAAC service center in San Ysidro under Yolanda Chaca which should have worked closely with the CAC, became disillusioned and undertook programs and activities without CAC approval or involvement. The director of the local Headstart program refused to hand over reports to the CAC. This resulted in an autonomy of action and intense distrust between the war on poverty institutions. While the Border Area CAC floundered and bickered among itself the MAAC service center, as well as dispersing service, usurped the role of the CAC and carried out an active, if somewhat select, program of community organization and action and attempted to subvert and undermine the CAC at every turn. This general disenchantment with the CAC spread throughout the communities and effectively impeded not only CAC activities but also the war on poverty in the area.

Meetings of the CAC were supposed to alternate between Otay and San Ysidro. For half of the first year meetings attracted quorums. As the infighting grew and developed it became increasingly difficult to obtain a quorum for either board or general Community Action Council meetings. By the end of the first year the EOC was pressuring the CAC to have a legal meeting since it was far behind in its business regarding the development and execution of war on poverty programs. For a while after this, with the help of EOC consultants and staff who visited the area and advised board members and suggested techniques by which attendance might be increased, such as supplying coffee or providing entertainment before or after the meeting, quorums were more successfully obtained. However, near the end of the second year, for a variety of reasons, quorums again became difficult to obtain.

The board remained large, sixteen to eighteen members, and was hopelessly divided by community interest, ethnic identity and comprehension of the war on poverty generally. Members from San Ysidro complained that translation at meetings was inadequate for its Spanish-speaking residents. They complained that the people of Otay and Woodlawn Park had no interest in the problems of San Ysidro, and that compared to San Ysidro they had no problems. The San Ysidro representatives finally refused to serve on the CAC board and for all practical purposes San Ysidro withdrew from the CAC. Strife also increased between Otay and Woodlawn Park. Representatives from Woodlawn Park complained that Otay members ignored its needs and problems; two factions within Woodlawn Park, both represented on the CAC board, feuded among themselves.

The EOC became increasingly passive in offering assistance to the CAC, and seemed embarrassed by its activities. Delia Garcia and the other EOC consultant continued to attend, but their main involvement consisted of writing depressing reports on the activities of the CAC. If the consultants did attempt to offer suggestions one group or other took it as a threat by the EOC, or unnecessary involvement of the EOC in problems that were none of its business; when the consultants didn't speak out or offer suggestions the people complained that the EOC didn't care and was not giving the assistance it should. However, it was over the problems and conflict that developed between the board president and the executive secretary that the Community Action Council was first dissolved.

By August 1966 the Border Area CAC was ready to consider hiring a staff and obtaining office space for it. However, this was delayed due to procrastination by the CAC board in considering applications, the problems presented by dictatorial presidents, ineffective and conflicting board members, as well as a short period in November and December of 1966 in which the hiring of staff was frozen due to budget problems in the EOC. In January and February 1967, again under pressure from the EOC, it was decided to proceed with the hiring of staff. On March 16, 1967, Mrs. Parker, a black woman from Woodlawn Park and the mother of sixteen children, was hired as executive secretary. At this time, also, Esmerelda Hurtado from San Ysidro was hired as community aide. Sally Horton, a resident of Otay, was hired as clerk-typist shortly thereafter. Office space was procured in a small building in Woodlawn Park.

In July Mr. Amos Proud, a black man from Otay, began making himself heard in the CAC meetings. Mr. Proud pleaded for greater unity and increased efficiency within the CAC. While he understood the war on poverty and how it might be better implemented in the area, he was an intolerant man and expected too much too quickly for his efforts. In September 1967 he was elected the eleventh president of the Border Area CAC.

Once in office, realizing the urgency of the situation, Mr. Proud attempted to implement his ideas as rapidly as possible. One idea was to develop a program for the staff to follow, for throughout the four months during which a staff had been employed it is safe to say that nothing in the way of community organization, rapprochement between conflicting groups in the CAC, or any gain whatsoever on the problems the various communities faced had been accomplished. At best the staff had augmented services that were already being offered by the ACCESS service center in Otay and the MAAC service center in San Ysidro. Mr. Proud attempted to redefine the role of the CAC away from services and toward community organization. He attempted to create a better liaison between CAC and the EOC. He tried to implement reasonable evaluating procedures for the staff, since the six months probationary period for which staff is initially hired was at hand and the EOC was again concerned about the persistent lack of productive activity and general confusion within the CAC. He also attempted to force two elderly blacks who represented Woodlawn Park to retire from the board in order to reduce friction and improve parliamentary procedure. This aligned the CAC block from Woodlawn Park against him. In short, his changes were too fast and radical for the CAC to absorb.

In a meeting in October 1967 all issues came to a head. The president pleaded for unity and a cessation of bickering. Inadvertently he offended many people. He referred to the low education achievement of some individuals, personal problems of others, and the lack of ability of others as reasons for the CACs failures. Rather than reducing friction his actions caused the contending groups to realign into two factions: one in support of him and his attempts to effect change; the other quite hostile to his efforts. Disputes became sharper and the divisiveness crystalized between Otay members who supported him and Woodlawn Park representatives hostile to him.

In another October meeting the board attempted to replace the president but lost by a vote of six to five. He, in turn, recommended they fire Mrs. Parker, the executive secretary, since he blamed her for many of the CACs shortcomings. He won this vote by the same figure. This was the final straw for the people of Woodlawn Park and they united in hostility against the president. After this the angry residents of Woodlawn Park extended their hostility to the other CAC staff members, Esmerelda Hurtado and Sally Horton, and both became afraid to go to Woodlawn Park. There were even threats to burn the Community Action Council office.

The last confrontation took place at the last CAC board meeting in November 1967 at which time violence nearly erupted. The next day the EOC closed down the Border Area CAC office in Woodlawn Park. It did not function again until January 1968, at which time it underwent reorganization and began operating out of an office in San Ysidro.

In January 1968 the Border Area CAC reopened in San Ysidro. It shared an office with Mr. Flores, a local representative of the United Farm-

workers of California (UFWOC). Mr. Flores was also president of the Board of
Directors for the National City CAC and was vice president of the EOC Board
of Directors. Ideally, his presence and knowledge should have provided the
Border Area CAC with a tremendous resource. Although he was Mexican-
American and deeply concerned about his people's problems, and was influential,
especially in an advisory capacity to several of the contestants, he was unable
to alter the course of events.

The move to San Ysidro did very little to alleviate the old problems.
Insufficient time had passed for the old wounds to heal and old problems were
augmented by new ones. The program was no better understood, and no better
implemented by the old and newly-involved personnel. The staff, minus the
executive secretary, remained the same. Although two new CAC board members
were elected they represented essentially the same ethnic and community
interests of the members they replaced. Many able individuals who might have
been recruited to serve on the board would not because of the CAC's history.
Some of the old problem individuals, e.g., Mr. Brown, the dictatorial ex-
president, still made their presence felt. And now, in the arena of San Ysidro,
new actors and problems emerged, such as the severe housing problem and the
threat of the freeway.

Otay representation on the board was sporadic and most residents of
Otay refused to attend CAC meetings. Otay essentially did not participate in the
CAC for the next year. Representatives from Woodlawn Park continued to
participate though those persons who supported the discharged executive
secretary did not. The board of directors remained too large, about fourteen
persons, on paper, with about eight to ten members actively participating. It
was the newly involved members who represented San Ysidro who were to
dominate the CAC and represent the new focus of conflict.

Tex Stillman was elected the new president of the CAC. He considered participation in such organizations morally incumbent upon him; about
this time he also became a member of the San Ysidro Planning and Development
Group. However, once the housing issue emerged in San Ysidro he resigned the
presidency as a result of accusations from the Mexican-American community
and CAC board members that he was a trailer court land lord. He was replaced
in July 1968 by Mrs. Osmond from Otay, the thirteenth and last president of
the Border Area CAC as originally constituted. She held the job for six turbulent
months. The board at this time also included Mr. Von Lutz, the elderly and
retired "hippie," also a member of the San Ysidro Development Group, and the
Mexican-American contingent who eventually organized the PFTA: Ramon
Cervantes, Mercedes Paredes, and Pablo Guzman. Mexican-American CAC
representatives from San Ysidro had previously requested a separate CAC for San
Ysidro because, they argued with some justification, San Ysidro had special
problems. The EOC was not sympathetic to such a move because of the cost of
operating another CAC office, some $3,000 per month. The Anglo board

members from San Ysidro were not in favor of a separate CAC either. They argued, with some justification, that such a CAC would simply become a Mexican-American organization and not represent the total community.

In early June 1968 Jim Duran was hired as the new executive secretary of the CAC. He had attended a local junior college for one year and was considered by all concerned to be the person who could do the job and make the CAC work. Regretfully, he immediately fell into conflict with the Mexican-Americans of the emerging PFTA. His first effort, as his job dictated, was to gain a working relationship with Yolanda Chaca of the MAAC center. This antagonized the Mexican-Americans of the board who were hostile to her and were maneuvering to build up their support at her expense. They had dealt with Yolanda for the previous two years and argued that she did not do her job satisfactorily, that she was arrogant, supercilious, and generally hostile to the Mexican-American people of San Ysidro. Once Jim Duran fell under attack, he simply proved incapable of doing anything to resolve it. Within two months other qualities which registered his general incompetence became obvious and it was recognized that he could not do the job. This precipitated the question of who would succeed him and the succession became another major issue in San Ysidro.

From this point on the events and conflict in the arena spiraled and increasing numbers of contestants were sucked into the whirlwind's vortex. The fight over who would replace Jim Duran involved the PFTA and led ultimately to Esmerelda Hurtado being fired as Community Aide and the impeachment of the PFTA representatives from the CAC board of directors. Rather than resolve any problem this merely added fuel to the conflict.

The issue over the poor housing in San Ysidro and the displacement by the freeway of the Mexican-American families drew the PFTA and other city and EOC officials into a not always pleasant relationship. The EOC became increasingly embarrassed and resentful of the events in San Ysidro since they saw them as reflecting directly upon the integrity of its countywide organization.

As a result of the concern of the San Ysidro Planning and Development Group over the events in San Ysidro, and in conjunction with the Planning Department of the City of San Diego, the San Ysidro Planning Group commissioned a study of the community during the summer of 1968 in order to determine how to effect the development of San Ysidro more efficiently and in line with community expectations. They found this to be impossible. Also in conjunction with the San Ysidro Planning and Development Group, the city of San Diego decided to hold a series of public meetings in San Ysidro to explain the redevelopment of the community to its citizens in the hope of cooling things down. The meetings did not accomplish this end.

The hostilities in the CAC continued throughout the duration of these meetings. In September the elementary school district of San Ysidro was drawn into the conflict over its Special or Educationally Mentally Retarded

(EMR) Programs. By November the conflict had reached a point where violence was threatened daily and the EOC, fed up with it all and under pressure from a variety of sources, seriously began to consider splitting the Border Area CAC in two, one CAC for San Ysidro, another for Otay and Woodlawn Park. In January 1969 this was done.

HOUSING AND DEVELOPMENT

The issue which served as a catalyst for forces which ultimately were to rend the fabric of the CAC and San Ysidro generally developed very quickly. This issue was the poor condition of housing in San Ysidro. This condition had developed over a decade or so as landlords, knowledgeable of the impending freeway, permitted their rentals along its route to fall into disrepair. San Ysidro was also afflicted with a severe housing shortage, a condition general to San Diego, due to the rapid growth of the area. This resulted in a sellers' market and caused rents to escalate beyond reason.

One of the first CAC casualties of this issue was Tex Stillman. Even Mrs. Osmond, the thirteenth and last president of the CAC, who rented a small property in Otay, fell under attack as a landlord. However, the real slum land-lords of San Ysidro were not Anglo. Most of the very worst housing along the freeway route was owned by Mexican-American realtors, a phenomenon which bears out the argument made by Bodine (1968), Romano (1967) and others that the worst oppressors of poor ethnic peoples are persons of like ethnic background, especially if they are upwardly mobile and were once poor themselves.

The issue over the housing conditions and the freeway began to crystalize in February 1968. A committee to investigate the poor housing conditions was established by the CAC under the leadership of Ramon Cervantes, a CAC board member. This committee reported back to the CAC in March and reaffirmed what everyone knew, i.e., much of the housing was quite poor, a large number of families were going to be displaced by the freeway, and that plans for housing facilities to accommodate some of the displaced families were grossly inadequate. At the same time, plans for the freeway and relocation of people were progressing quickly.[1] The first families were scheduled to be displaced in October 1968. However, construction on the low-rent subsidy housing development on a hill behind San Ysidro,[2] about a mile from the center of San Ysidro and two miles from the border, a fair distance for any family without a car, was to begin the same month and end one year later. This was designed to coincide with the projection by the State Highway Department as to the point in time when the largest number of families were to be displaced. A segment of the Mexican-American population which later affiliated with the PFTA decided to fight because they were angered by the facts that: (1) a considerable number of families would be forced out prior to that time, ostensibly with no place to go; (2) that the only housing proposed to accommodate this population was a rent subsidy apartment project; and (3) that the units were not of sufficient size to accommodate many of the large Mexican-American families that were to be displaced.

The CAC, MAAC service center, and officials from the EOC contacted city, state, and federal officials concerned with the freeway and redevelopment program and urged them to attend a special CAC meeting on April 30 to discuss these problems. The meeting convened with approximately 200 people plus officials in attendance. The tenor of the meeting was set by the first speaker, John Thom, the city councilman who represented the area. He began by telling the people all that the city of San Diego had done for San Ysidro—city water, police protection, and sewage—and was immediately and soundly attacked over the issues of poor housing and high rents. Citizens complained they could not get housing inspectors to condemn the poor housing or force landlords to make repairs. If they complained to the landlord they faced eviction, for there was no problem finding another tenant in San Ysidro, even at the grossly inflated rents. Under severe attack and accusations that the city had in fact forgotten that San Ysidro existed, the city councilman was literally driven from the meeting. None of the other officials fared any better.

Representatives of the sanitation department were attacked as they claimed they didn't have time or personnel to examine all the complaints over poor housing in San Ysidro.[3] Under attack, other officials acknowledged the fact that renters had no legal recourse and could expect no help from the city should they be evicted as a result of complaining to landlords. It was pointed out to the federal officials representing the Department of Housing and Urban Development (HUD), which was responsible for the low-rent subsidy housing, that many of the families being displaced were too large to qualify for the proposed housing development.[4] The representatives of the state highway department were castigated for never having contacted the residents of San Ysidro regarding the freeway route, even though it had been on the drawing board for a decade. And the San Ysidro Planning and Development Group was attacked and criticized for representing not the citizens of San Ysidro but only the vested interests of its members, several of whom owned land and commercially zoned areas along the freeway route and who were instrumental in its routing and the subsequent zoning.

After the officials had left, the meeting continued. It was agreed by the participants that something had to be done. A protest march on the city council meeting in San Diego two days hence to display the depth of concern of the citizens of San Ysidro was suggested. The suggestion caught fire and the following day it was acted upon.

Early the next morning individuals from the Community Action Council, the service center, the EOC consultant for the area, and the director of EOC Area Development Program met and decided to organize a demonstration at city hall for the following day. The plan was to set up a picket line outside city hall with placards lamenting the problems of San Ysidro. Inside a delegation was to confront the city council during its meeting and demand to be heard. The intention was to catch the city off guard, make a dramatic display, and force the city into some action regarding the freeway and housing problems in San Ysidro.

The staff of the CAC and service center, with the aid of volunteer help, set to work at a frenzied pace. They began to contact the Mexican-American residents of San Ysidro, especially those threatened with displacement. There was a general consensus and excitement for the plan, and the community was organized. Placards were hastily put together. Transportation of a variety of sorts was arranged. Newspapers and television media were informed of the event.

Early the next morning, two days after the Community Action Council meeting, approximately 250 Mexican-Americans congregated at the San Ysidro Civic Center prepared to go to San Diego. Unexpectedly, Yolanda Chaca of the MAAC center, who had been one of the most outspoken at the special CAC meeting, and who had been very active in organizing the protest, decided this was an improper tactic. On the morning of the proposed march she contacted Mr. Hermann, superintendent of the San Ysidro Elementary School District, and informed him of the march. He, in turn, called the mayor's office and informed it of the impending march. The mayor was contacted and replied that should the people of San Ysidro attempt to disrupt the council meeting he would adjourn the meeting and have the lights turned off; however, if they wanted to talk with him he would try to make himself available in chambers after the council meeting.

Yolanda Chaca then returned to the civic center and informed the people of her action. The people were stunned, then disgruntled, and finally disillusioned. Over 200 people returned home. About forty went to the city hall. Yolanda accompanied them, although the hostility to her was open and vocal, and would have repercussions later. The people milled around outside the council chambers, uncertain of what to do. After a few confused interviews, the press and television personnel left. Just prior to the adjournment of the city council meeting, one Mexican-American woman ran up to the podium and began to address the mayor. The lights were turned off.

Word was passed out to the gathering, however, that the mayor would meet with them in his chambers. The people filed in slowly, awkard in the presence of stuffed leather chairs and a polished walnut conference table. The mayor appeared aided and supported by a battery of officials. After a few hectic and awkward moments during which the mayor threatened to walk out if the people were not orderly, Yolanda informed the mayor of some of the problems in San Ysidro and complained about the activities of the San Ysidro Planning and Development Group. The mayor told the people that he "had no idea San Ysidro had any such problem," and that the San Ysidro Planning and

Development Group was indeed representative of the community. He did, however, promise the people that he would look into their complaints and issued a series of directives to his aides. In ninety minutes the entire incident was finished. After that the vast majority of the Mexican-American citizenry of San Ysidro sunk into a resigned apathy regarding the ultimate fate of its community's development.

This incident has been described in detail because it represents the high point of community action, interest and involvement for the war on poverty institutions in San Ysidro. After this a new phase of activity began. Yolanda Chaca was never forgiven by the people of San Ysidro for informing the city of the intended march.[5] Much of the latent hostility held for her by the people suddenly became overt. The CAC was also blamed for the failure. Ramon Cervantes and other members of the committee established to investigate the housing conditions organized into the PFTA which, through its membership in the CAC, began to attack the CAC and service center with the intention of taking them over.

However, the demonstration, a failure in the eyes of the people of San Ysidro, was not entirely wasted on the city and the San Ysidro Planning Group. After the meeting with the citizens of San Ysidro the mayor called the Federal Housing Authority (FHA), which is the ultimate authority over low-rent housing projects such as the one proposed for San Ysidro, and obtained changes which more nearly accommodated the needs of the people of San Ysidro. Of the 400 units originally proposed none were to be four-bedroom. The FHA agreed to change their plans so that the unit would accommodate 270 three-bedroom units, 90 to 100 two-bedroom units, and 30 to 40 four-bedroom apartments.[6] To some extent this mollified the people of San Ysidro, especially Yolanda Chaca who took credit for obtaining the concession. She argued that had she not warned the city of the impending demonstration there would have been no concessions. Her argument did little, however, to win her favor with the people of San Ysidro.

The San Ysidro Planning Group was also forced into action by the demonstration. Disturbed by the events, and with the assistance and agreement of the City of San Diego Planning Department, they decided to sponsor a survey of San Ysidro in order to assess the mood of the people, discover what they wanted with respect to the development of the community, and how the development might be better and more efficiently expedited. The aim of the survey was to interview each household in San Ysidro if possible and to make the report available to the community and interested agencies, such as the CAC and service center, when it was completed. Three Spanish-speaking college students were hired as enumerators by the San Diego Planning Department during the summer of 1968 to conduct the survey.

The city and the San Ysidro Planning Group gave more credit to the CAC for the demonstration than did the people of San Ysidro. Upon advice of the CAC members who were active in the San Ysidro Planning Group, the CAC was invited to participate in the survey. By this time the CAC had hired Jim Duran as executive secretary and he agreed to develop a questionnaire by which the CAC could obtain pertinent information on the community. This was, however, beyond his ability. Instead he borrowed a questionnaire used by another CAC. It was irrelevant to San Ysidro and the city enumerators and other CAC staff, especially Esmerelda Hurtado, the community aide, considered it a waste of time. The survey proved to be the primary stimulus for conflict between Duran and Mrs. Hurtado and eventually the PFTA. It was also instrumental in revealing Duran's incompetence and was a significant factor in his downfall.

By the time the results of the survey were compiled and ready for distribution in the fall, the conflict within the CAC had reached proportions of near violence. The San Ysidro Planning Group was continuously apprised of the events by Tex Stillman and Mr. Von Lutz and was openly disdainful of the CAC and PFTA in its meetings with the San Diego Planning Department at city hall. On one accasion Mr. Von Lutz contemptuously referred to the PFTA as "a bunch of Castros."

A preliminary version of the San Ysidro Community Survey was finally discussed in a meeting at city hall in early December of 1968. The San Diego Planning Department claimed it was a good report and referred to such points as the poor transportation of the area, the overwhelming desire of the people to live in single family dwellings rather than apartments, the high unemployment, and so forth as relevant matters to be considered in the development of San Ysidro. Several members of the San Ysidro Planning Group agreed. Then Tex Stillman unexpectedly announced that the survey was rife with errors, as well as being biased, because the student enumerators were pro-Mexican and anti-Anglo radicals, and that if it were released it would create further confusion and hostility in San Ysidro. Although there was no disagreement prior to this, almost all other members of the San Ysidro Planning Group immediately supported him. At a special and private meeting of the San Ysidro Planning Group in San Ysidro a few days later it was decided to suppress the survey and limit its distribution to the members of the city and San Ysidro Planning Group only. At a later meeting of the Development Group and City Planners in city hall, Mr. Hermann pointed out that even though the survey was erroneous they should use its statistics where necessary and feasible to bolster their case for development and other funds. This was agreed upon.[7]

Throughout the summer and fall the city and the San Ysidro Planning Group were also involved in other activities in San Ysidro. In early August the San Ysidro Planning Group organized a bus tour of San Ysidro to explain to a variety of officials the proposed redevelopment of the community. The tour was by invitation and was attended by American and Mexican officials and businessmen who would profit by the redevelopment. Approximately fifty people participated; among them bankers from the area, realtors, developers, members of the San Ysidro Planning Group, Congressman Van Deerlin, and the owner of Caliente Racetrack in Tijuana. No attempt was made to contact the people of the community and the appearance of myself, the city survey enumerators, and CAC staff members was a surprise, We were not warmly received. The tour ended with Margarita cocktails and snacks in the unfinished rectory next to the church which was being built near the new housing development on the hill overlooking San Ysidro. The gathering was addressed by the local priest who thanked them for the wondrous things they were doing for San Ysidro, and by Congressman Van Deerlin who spoke glowingly of the development and increased economic potential of the area. In November he won his race for re-election.

The tour and the events surrounding the San Ysidro Survey are significant for several reasons. They demonstrate the forces in control of the development of San Ysidro and the lack of involvement of the community as a whole in their plans. The extent to which land speculators were becoming involved in the area was demonstrated, and there was much hope expressed that San Ysidro would change from a low-incentive profit area to one of high profit potential as the development and growth of the area accelerated. These events made it clear that the area was beginning to boom, and that any changes other than those desired by this group of influential men were going to be hard to implement.[8]

The mayor also reacted to the demonstration and to an increasing number of letters from the PFTA protesting conditions in San Ysidro and the ineffectiveness of agencies, e.g., the CAC, in coping with them. In August, again in agreement with the San Ysidro Planning Group, a series of public meetings, each two to three hours long, were scheduled to be held in San Ysidro. These became known as the Mayor's Meetings.[9] The CAC and the service center were informed of these meetings and agreed to assist in implementing them. However, by this time the San Ysidro Planning Group and the city had become aware of the degree to which conflict in the area was debilitating the CAC and the service center. In effect, their participation in these meetings was relegated to that of messenger boys charged with the task of putting up posters around the area advertising the meetings.

The actual planning and organization of each of the eight meetings was in the hands of the city and the San Ysidro Planning Group. The first meeting was held in mid-September and was informational in nature. The mayor addressed the people and informed them of the proposed redevelopment of San Ysidro and the benefits the community would derive from this. About two hundred people attended. Consensus in city hall was that the meeting was a success, although it was felt more people should have attended. It was pointed out that many people did not know of the meeting and the CAC was blamed for not putting up the advertisements supplied by the city. In fact, the CAC had

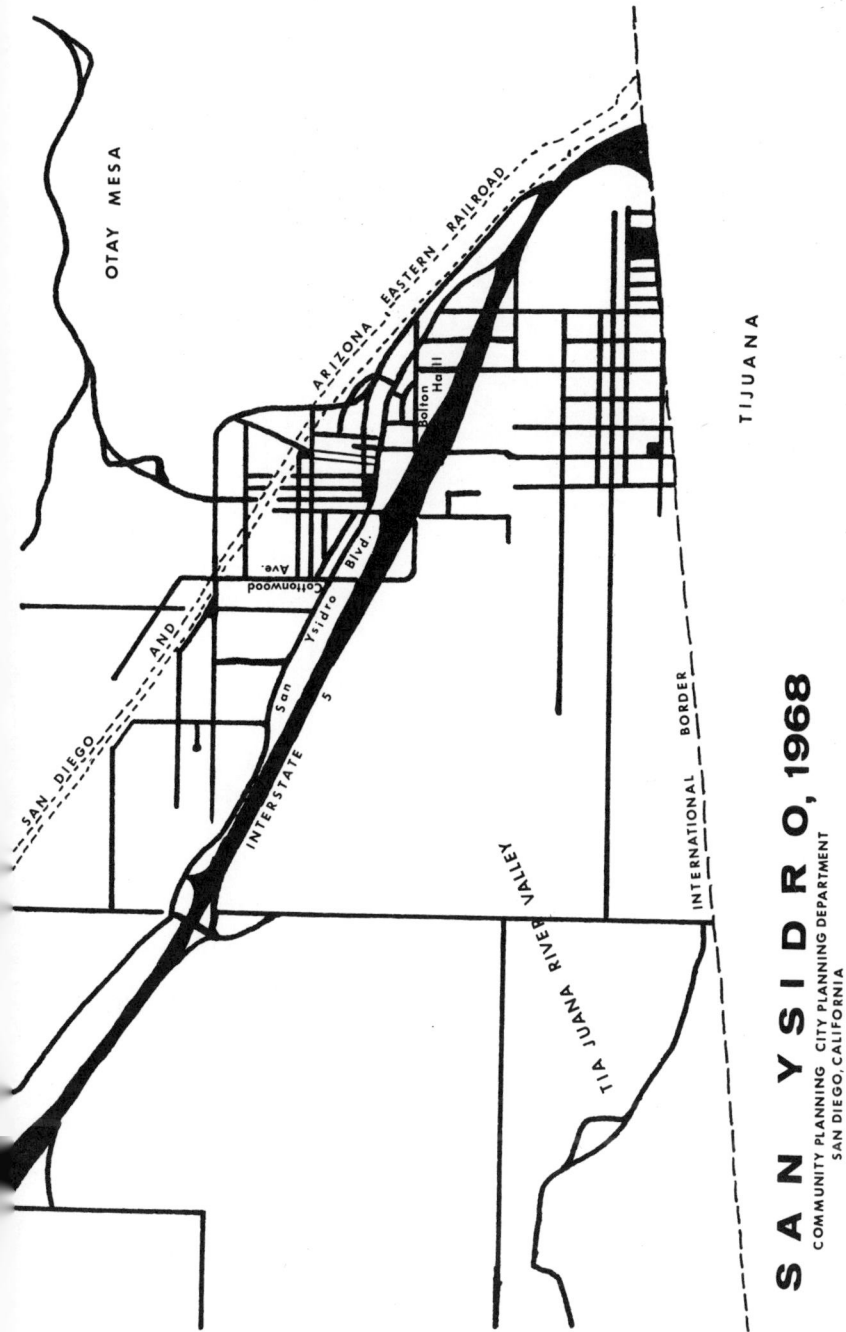

SAN YSIDRO, 1968
COMMUNITY PLANNING CITY PLANNING DEPARTMENT
SAN DIEGO, CALIFORNIA

Figure 5.1. Major Highways and Streets: San Ysidro, 1968.

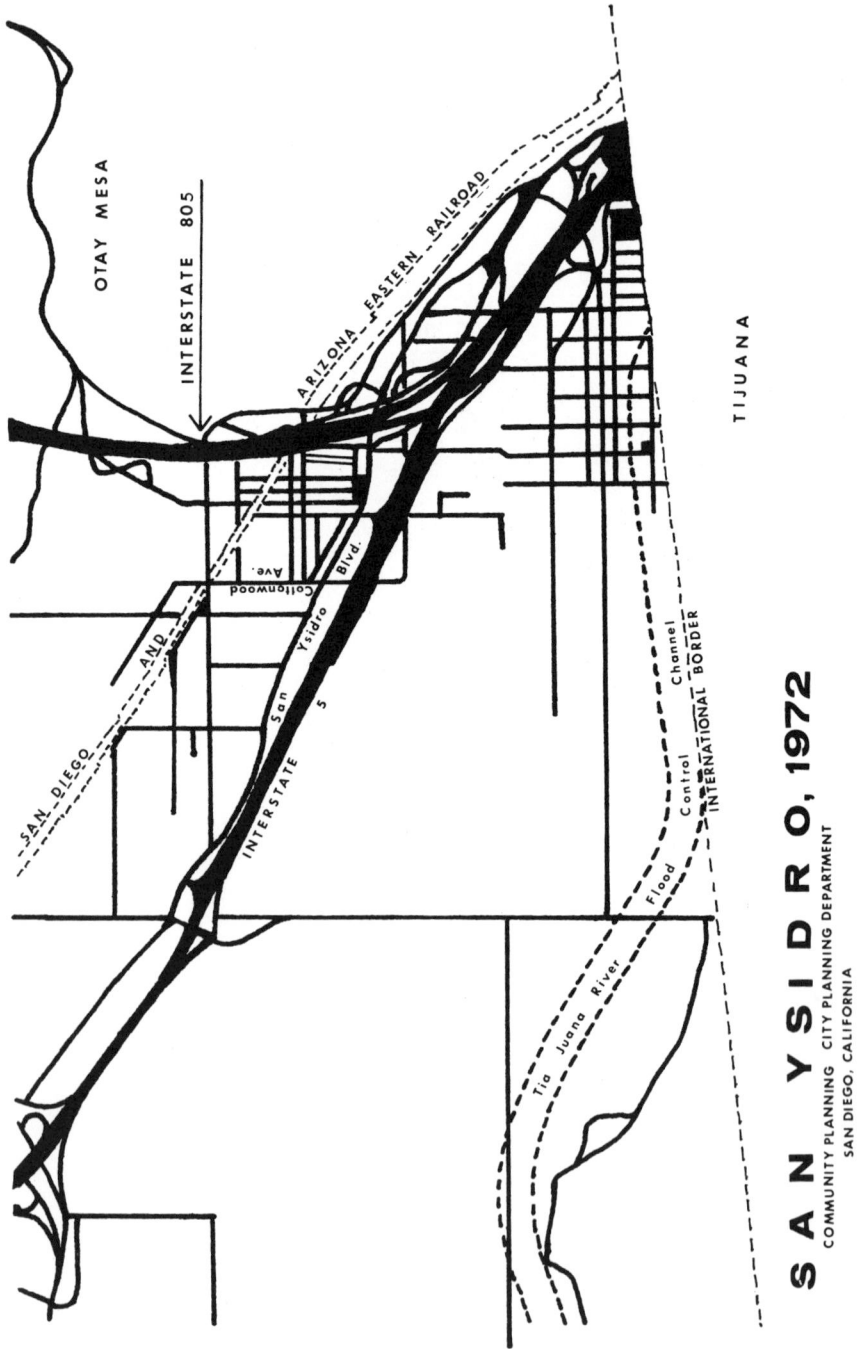

Figure 5.2. Major Highway and Streets: San Ysidro, 1972.

produced and distributed throughout the area over 2,000 notices of the meeting. The conflict between the CAC and PFTA was becoming worse, and when the criticism and lack of acknowledgment of their efforts by the city filtered down to the CAC, the staff after that gave minimal assistance to the remainder of the meetings. Except for the housing meeting, which was packed due largely to efforts of the PFTA, the rest of the meetings were far less well attended, and after the intermission of each meeting there was a depletion in attendance of between 30 and 60 percent.

Lack of community interest in the meetings was due to several factors. The meetings often dragged on interminably and speakers frequently were unable to convey to the people any interest in what they were doing; in short, they often did a poor selling job. Translation for the Spanish-speakers was also often uninspired, and the language used by the participants was generally over the heads of the people. The people of San Ysidro also saw little in the meetings that was immediately going to improve their condition; most of the meetings spoke of future plans for the area while the people felt their current problems required immediate attention. They did not really believe that the development of San Ysidro was truly to their benefit. For example, an announcement by the mayor of an expenditure of almost $100,000 on renovating the San Ysidro park and installing shuffleboard and tennis courts was greeted coldly. Most of the people expressed a desire for a swimming pool and improved bus service. The city argued they could not provide these.[10]

There was also some hostility to the chairman of the meetings. He was the member of the San Ysidro Planning Group and an immigration counselor and was disliked and distrusted by many Mexican-Americans. Perhaps the most serious failing of the meetings was due to the fact that they provided by and large only a one-way communication channel: from the city officials to the people. Time for questions was generally quite short and an exchange of ideas between the officials and the people were not encouraged. One city official suggested in a meeting at city hall that 90 percent of the time of each meeting should be devoted to questions from the floor. A member of the San Ysidro Planning Group insisted that no more than 40 percent be devoted to questions. Frequently it was much less.

In planning the meeting concerned with educational development, consideration was given by the mayor's office and the San Ysidro Development Group, especially Mr. Hermann, that no questions be accepted from the floor because of the potential protests of a variety of Mexican-American ad hoc groups regarding the quality of the education Mexican-American children were receiving. By this time the San Ysidro Elementary School District was under fire from the CAC over its EMR classes. However, at the meeting, as a result of shouts from the floor, the chairman was forced to recognize questions for a much longer period than originally prescribed. They proved to be quite innocuous and not nearly as devastating as had been expected.

In general, the people of San Ysidro did not expect that the meetings would resolve any of the problems the community was confronting, and they did not. The most significant result of the meetings was an announcement that because of an excess of funds for the Model Cities Program scheduled for San Diego, San Ysidro, which was not initially considered for participation, would now be considered. Otay and Woodlawn Park were not considered eligible for Model Cities funds and this was one factor in the eventual splitting of its Border Area CAC.

The Model Cities Program gave one final dimension to the involvement of the San Ysidro Planning Group in San Ysidro. The boundaries of the Model Cities Program adhered to those of the CACs in the city of San Diego. As a result CACs were supposed to participate in the Model Cities Program planning and the EOC worked vigorously to accomplish this. However, the initial representatives to the Model Cities Planning Committee from the Border Area CAC were Tex Stillman and Mr. Von Lutz; they also unofficially represented the San Ysidro Planning Group. Due to the conflict in the arena, the CAC was tardy in appointing these representatives, and for several weeks these two had been reporting back to the San Ysidro Planning Group. Eventually the PFTA also placed members on the Model Cities Program Planning Committee, arguing that only they represented the Mexican-Americans of San Ysidro.

As soon as the Model Cities Program became a reality for the area the San Ysidro Planning Group became actively involved in it and in conjunction with the city decided to "spearhead this program" for the border area. A major concern of the San Ysidro Planning Group was the ways in which the Model Cities Program might affect their plans for the development of San Ysidro. As a result the San Ysidro Planning Group decided they would make the fundamental decisions for the area, even though the EOC was attempting to obtain this for the poor through their CACs. One reason the Border Area CAC was split in two was to facilitate this involvement.

The ultimate result of the participation by the CAC, PFTA, and the San Ysidro Planning Group cannot be commented on since my research terminated at this point. However, it was clear that the San Ysidro Planning Group had decided to become involved in this program and that they, not the poor of the area, intended to speak for the Model Cities Program in San Ysidro.

The issue over the housing problems and redevelopment of San Ysidro demonstrates the role of relatively powerful persons in processes of change and development at the local level. However, the role of these influential people in these processes was obfuscated by other events in San Ysidro, especially the conflict in the CAC. This conflict was the result of a kind of feedback; it was generated by the initial attempt to cope with processes of change and development stimulated by these powerful people, and resulted in political conflict at another level in the arena.

FROM CONTENTION TO CONTRADICTION:
THE CAC

In a discussion of the maintenance of order in stateless societies Gluckman establishes a typology by which the terminological problems concerned with "oppositions compelled by the very structure of social organization" may be clarified (1965:109). It also has application in arenas other than those associated with stateless societies. Gluckman states:

> For surface disturbances of social life, depending on their nature, we can use use competition, dispute, argument, quarrel, strife, dissension, contention, fight, etc. I like to reserve "struggle" for events with deeper and more fundamental roots, and "conflict" for discrepancies at the heart of the system. But I reserve "conflict" for the relation between discrepancies that sets in train processes which produce alterations in the personnel of social positions, but not alteration in the pattern of positions. I prefer the already established term "contradiction" for those relations between discrepant principles and processes in the social structure which must inevitably lead to radical changes in the pattern. (1965:109)

The evolution of political activity and events in San Ysidro was, in large measure, the result of contradictions built into the structure of the CAC. In the arena of San Ysidro, ethnic identity served as one contradiction and was exacerbated by the ethnic hostilities which carried over from the previous tenure of the CAC in Woodlawn Park. All the original ethnic groups continued to be involved in the CAC; there was, however, a shift from conflict in which the blacks of Woodlawn Park confronted Anglos and Mexican-Americans from Otay to one in which the Mexican-Americans of San Ysidro confronted Anglos from San Ysidro and Otay and blacks from Woodlawn Park.

While the Anglos involved in the arena of San Ysidro tended to be intolerant of Mexican-American political activity, claiming that their tactics were crude and unnecessary, the Mexican-Americans, especially members of the PFTA, were acutely aware of the significance of ethnic differences and the implications of this for politics in the arena. The Mexican-Americans saw their ethnic affiliation and Spanish language as differences which established an idiom of identity and reflected and maintained their social and political boundaries. They argued that no non-Spanish-speaker could understand the problems of the poor Mexican-American of San Ysidro and in this way affirmed the significance of their language as a boundary-maintaining mechanism.

Furthermore, within the context of a social boundary system, language also structures the cultural values, symbols, ideologies, and cognitive patterns of ethnic groups. In San Ysidro, in the struggle over control of the

CAC, the Spanish language provided a primary symbol system for and served as the basis of ethnic identification and values. While the conflict was a direct result of the failure of the housing march and the seeming inability of anyone to do anything about the housing problem and redevelopment of San Ysidro, the issue of who would control the CAC, Mexico-Americans or Anglos, and a sharpening of ethnic lines of cleavage began almost as soon as the CAC opened its office in San Ysidro.

The Mexican-Americans believed that the move of the office to San Ysidro would give them an organization by which they could come to grips with the problems of San Ysidro. They were, however, sensitive to the fact that the present structure of the Border Area CAC had not appreciably changed and the continued participation of Otay and Woodlawn Park would dilute energies needed for San Ysidro. The new board of directors contained members from all these communities although only two Anglo representatives from Otay and one black from Woodlawn Park made any pretense at regular attendance. Among others, the San Ysidro representatives included Tex Stillman and Mr. Von Lutz of the San Ysidro Planning Group and those individuals who were to develop into the leadership of the PFTA.

The first note of contention to rattle the CAC was the election of Tex Stillman to the presidency of the CAC Board of Directors. He was attacked by the Mexican-American board members openly and covertly over the slum-like state of his trailer park and sufficient complaints were lodged with the city by persons unknown so that he was ordered by the sanitation department to make repairs or face closure. He later complained of the great expense this entailed and of the hardship he was forced to endure as a result. He argued that he had intended to make repairs all along and complained of the ignorance of the Mexican-Americans regarding the problems and expenses of running a business. He was, he argued, a victim of Mexican-American racism.

Although he attempted to resign his office in April, the Anglo board members delayed this, refusing to accept his resignation for some six weeks. They were afraid this would reflect poorly on the CAC and simply carry the turmoil of the past into the present situation. Delays of this sort were to become common over the next several months. It was after Tex's resignation and before the appointment of Mrs. Osmond as the new president that the city hall demonstration took place and the PFTA began to emerge as a significant force in San Ysidro.

In July Mrs. Osmond was elected thirteenth president of the CAC and Jim Duran was hired as secretary. They were old friends and hopes were high that through them, especially Jim Duran, the CAC would be able to regain whatever momentum and prestige it had prior to the city hall demonstration and that it would finally begin to function in organizing the community for social action.

By this time Mexican-American individuals on the CAC board and in the membership had gone a long way toward establishing the support network which was to become the PFTA. As far as they were concerned if one was going to be involved in the issues in San Ysidro, one was either with them or against them. For a while in July they hoped Jim Duran would work with them, especially since he too was Mexican-American. However, Jim's first actions brought him into conflict with the PFTA. Mrs. Osmond became embroiled shortly thereafter. The CAC fell into a struggle from which it was not to recover.

For sometime the EOC had been concerned over the lack of cooperation between the MAAC service center in San Ysidro and the CAC. They were aware and disturbed by MAAC's policy to undercut the CAC. Sensitive to the fact that community was being poorly served by both agencies and that more problems were being created than were being resolved, the EOC directed Jim Duran to undertake as his first task a reconciliation with Yolanda and to develop a working relationship with the MAAC Center. He attempted to comply and it proved his undoing.

Duran's initial contacts with the service center director infuriated the PFTA. They considered Duran's attempt to develop a working relationship with the service center a betrayal to them and the CAC; they also feared that a rapprochement between the two agencies would be detrimental to their interests by somehow selling them out to the developers and other antagonists as the PFTA was beginning to define them. Yolanda was not well liked by many people in San Ysidro, especially members of the PFTA. She was accused of dispensing services to a small group of friends only and not to the community at large. Her stature in San Ysidro fell even farther after her part in sabotaging the protest march on city hall. That action firmly identified her as a member of the establishment and in collusion with the "rich" anglos. "She don't even speak good English," one PFTA member said bitterly. "Who the hell does she think she is?" The PFTA determined to get rid of her and take over the service center.

One morning about a month after he'd been on the job, as Jim arrived at the CAC office, he was confronted by Ramon Cervantes, Esmerelda Hurtado, the CAC community aide and his subordinate, and others of the PFTA leadership. The delegation bluntly demanded to know whose side he was on, their's or Yolanda's. Jim Duran was already beginning to feel unsure of himself; he was overwhelmed by the mass of information he was expected to master and the multitude of diverse tasks he was expected to undertake. In the ensuing argument the PFTA found that they could intimidate him and sufficiently confuse his loyalties and efforts so that he was ineffective in almost everything he attempted. From that point on they never ceased to do so and contributed to the undermining of his authority and destruction of his confidence.

After this incident the relationship between Duran and Esmerelda Hurtado deteriorated rapidly. Mrs. Hurtado began to defy his orders, especially when he insisted that she conduct a survey on the forms he had borrowed from another CAC in order to attempt to elicit the problems in San Ysidro to which the CAC should address itself. She argued that these problems were quite obvious. She became furious when Duran instructed her to help the enumerators hired by the city planning department and the San Ysidro Development Association with their survey of San Ysidro. She considered this an intrusion into the time she could spend helping the people. In fact, during the several weeks she spent playing around with the surveys, the sign in sheet in the CAC registered a notable decline because she was unavailable to people who had come to depend upon her. It soon became evident that Mrs. Hurtado had stopped taking the survey and was openly defying Jim Duran at every turn.

Duran was bewildered. He could not grasp the principle and concept of community organization and action. He sat through several EOC/OEO-sponsored training sessions without absorbing a thing. Bimonthly meetings were held at which time the executive secretaries of all the CACs, and sometimes board presidents, would gather and discuss their problems with the head of the EOC Area Development Department and the consultants. Invariably Duran became lost in these meetings. While his general incompetence was due to his lack of familiarity with the war on poverty in general and especially the intricacies of the program in San Diego, it was accentuated by the struggle developing in his own office.

Mr. Flores, the vice president of the EOC Board of Directors, whose union office in San Ysidro the Border Area CAC shared, had frequent discussions with Duran about his duties, the program, and what he should do about his increasing struggle with the community aide. For several weeks Mr. Flores and others kept insisting the Duran only needed time to comprehend the program, that his confidence would develop and he would master the situation. However, the struggle between Duran and Mrs. Hurtado was rapidly developing into a conflict which one or the other could not survive. By early August Duran was quite confused and disillusioned. He was beginning to rationalize his predicament by attacking the program and the people involved. Eventually he too became derelict in his duties and began to disappear from his job for hours on end. The final disaster of his career had tragic consequences for several other individuals.

Duran was informed by the EOC of fifteen openings in a job training program. Several people in a number of agencies had worked very hard to develop these Mexican-American slots and involve San Ysidro in the program. Duran informed Yolanda Chaca of the openings and told her the training program paid $1.75 per hour. Almost immediately the service center, through its files, had fifteen men ready to undertake training. Five of them, family men, quit their jobs to enter the program. However, when the men appeared at the training center they discovered that this particular program did not offer a wage. Furious, the men returned to San Ysidro. Yolanda sent them to the CAC office. Duran was not in the office. He was finally located in another part of San Diego and informed by Sally Horton, the clerk-typist, of his error. When Mrs. Horton asked what was to be done, he hung up and did not report to the CAC office for two days. The burden of resolving this fell upon Mrs. Horton. Through her efforts several of the men did get into other training programs. Of the five men who had quit their jobs to accept the training, three could not regain their jobs. Eventually, through efforts of Mrs. Horton and the service center, they did obtain others. The incident, however, further impaired the image of the CAC.

Throughout most of this period Sally Horton had been in solid support of Duran and, through her knowledge of the program, attempted to guide and inform him as best she could. Gradually she began making his decisions and slowly began to run the office and the program in San Ysidro. After the incident with the training program she literally gave up hope for Duran and quietly began to marshall support among the board members in order to have him discharged. Her aim was to replace him. This was not an easy task.

Most of the board members were somewhat aware of the events that were transpiring. Those from Otay and Woodlawn Park, however, were generally disinterested; they had been through it before. Mrs. Osmond, the president, and the Anglo members of San Ysidro were becoming sensitive to their increasing struggle with the PFTA and generally believed that under the circumstances Duran was doing the job quite well. This was largely because they were even more ignorant of their role and the purpose of the CAC than was Duran.

Mrs. Horton attempted in a near emotional fit to explain to Mrs. Osmond Duran's gross incompetence in the incident of the job training program. After she finished, Mrs. Osmond reminisced at great length about how Jim Duran and her son used to play together, and about the time Duran took her daughter to a high school prom, and really what a nice young man he was. To the consternation of the clerk-typist and others she left without acknowledging the fiasco. Another Anglo board member, Mr. Von Lutz when informed of the incident, remarked, "It could happen to anyone. Jim's doing a good job." More than once the events in San Ysidro assumed a surrealistic quality. Mrs. Horton became quite depressed and complained that with such a board of directors the CAC would be better off closed.

Throughout July the dissension within the CAC grew rapidly, encompassing more and more people, board, staff, and general membership. By early August a real struggle had developed between the PFTA and the executive secretary and other board members. The service center was not excluded from this struggle and the first real conflict in which the PFTA engaged was concerned with the service center and resulted in a victory for them. This gave them additional support from contestants outside San Ysidro and increased confidence in their power.

In mid-August Yolanda Chaca unexpectedly requested a meeting with the CAC staff. The purpose, she explained, was to discuss how they might better work together. The service center and CAC staff plus Delia Garcia, EOC consultant, and myself attended. After an initial statement regarding the potential accomplishments of the agencies if they would work together, Yolanda broached the real intent of the meeting. She wanted the CAC staff to cooperate with her in having John Diaz, the director of the MAAC project, dismissed; since the delegate agencies of the EOC were supposed to work through the CAC this was theoretically within the power of the CAC.

John Diaz was a shrewd manipulator and had been involved in problems previously with the accounting office of the EOC regarding the use of certain funds. He also did not get along well with Yolanda. Immediately after the meeting the CAC staff and consultant concluded that this was Yolanda's attempt at revenge. At the meeting Delia Garcia strongly advised against such a move and the CAC staff refused to cooperate.

However, Esmerelda Hurtado immediately contacted Ramon Cervantes of the PFTA. Cervantes and other PFTA members went to see John Diaz and informed him of the attempted conspiracy and agreed to support him in filing charges on insubordination with his board of directors against Yolanda. Diaz checked this matter out with Jim Duran who confirmed the attempted conspiracy. A week or two later the charges were brought before the MAAC board and Yolanda was asked to submit her resignation.

The PFTA now hoped to have one of their people hired as director of the service center. After a several week interval another appointment was made, but not from among the ranks of the PFTA. During this interval the PFTA turned its attention and energies upon the CAC. John Diaz reciprocated their support against Yolanda and proved a significant ally of the PFTA in the struggles that were about to emerge.

For some time now Esmerelda Hurtado had been in open defiance of Jim Duran's authority. She was also marshalling support among the board members for the showdown that had to come eventually. By early August the board members were aware that they were going to have to make adjustments to the emerging conflict. Mrs. Hurtado obviously had the support of the PFTA and a few other board members. While others did not give unequivocal support to her, they were increasingly aware of Jim Duran's incompetence.

Duran was also communicating with board members. He wanted to have Mrs. Hurtado fired and argued that if she were to leave he would be able to do his job. Many persons were not convinced of this, but he was advised to draw up a list of charges against Mrs. Hurtado by which she might be fired and present them for consideration at the board meeting. With the assistance of Sally Horton he did this. In early August a special board meeting was held to discuss the matter.

By this time the board was quite confused. The PFTA members were demanding that Duran be fired. They hoped to replace him with Mrs. Hurtado; this was common knowledge. The Anglo board members were afraid this would appear as another defeat for the CAC and incur repercussions from the EOC. The EOC consultant, Delia Garcia, had been active in the area and helped stimulate and maintain the confusion as a means of validating her position, since her other CACs had dispensed with her services.

Delia had convinced the Border Area CAC that they could not act without her advice, which was not true. The Anglo members were stymied. They were uncomfortable in the structural incongruity that existed between the CAC and EOC. They were either not interested or not knowledgeable enough with the EOC and CAC guidelines to question the advice of the consultant. Above all, they were becoming increasingly frightened of the militancy of the PFTA and were concerned about the hostilities that would develop if they did fire Mrs. Hurtado. They argued instead that since the EOC paid the salaries of the staff they should resolve this problem. Delia took advantage of this concern to make her services increasingly indispensable to the CAC. The board, except for the PFTA members, became quite confused over the extent of their jurisdiction and power and relied increasingly on Delia's advice which was not always free from imperfection.

Only the PFTA seemed to have a coherent program, centering about their hostility to all the war on poverty agencies. They accused the CAC and the service center of wasting funds and not helping the people and the EOC of aiding and abetting this through the actions of the consultant. The Anglo CAC board and staff members were accused of being "los ricos" and not sympathetic to the problems of San Ysidro. They demanded that Jim Duran be fired and replaced by Esmerelda Hurtado.

At a special board meeting called to deal with the problem Duran read off a list of charges against the community aide. Mrs. Hurtado countered with a list of her own. The meeting broke down into a tirade of charges and countercharges. Finally, the board voted by a narrow margin to call a one-month moratorium on the struggle. The executive secretary was instructed to draw up an explicit list of duties for Mrs. Hurtado to follow. In one month her performance would be reviewed by the board and a final decision would be made regarding her status.

In effect, this was a victory for Mrs. Hurtado. The board had failed to support the executive secretary against her. Duran's confidence was shattered. He drew up the list of duties to which Mrs. Hurtado was supposed to adhere and posted them. She pointedly ignored them and set out to build up a broad base of support in the community for the showdown. Duran was totally bewildered by all the events. It was during this period that he perpetrated the faux pas of the training program. This, coupled with the board's refusal to support him, further destroyed his confidence in himself. He withdrew further from the program and absented himself on one pretext or other for days on end. In the interim the office was run by Sally Horton, the clerk-typist, who so far, due to her subordinate and generally inconspicuous position, had not been attacked. However, behind the scenes she was quietly working very hard to gain support from the board in order to become the next executive secretary.

Duran talked increasingly of resigning. John Diaz had offered him the directorship of the service center for the support he had given Diaz in having Yolanda discharged, and he thoughtfully considered this. He was, however, aware that this would simply initiate a new point of dissension between himself and the PFTA. Then, a couple of weeks after the board meeting, he announced one morning that Ramon Cervantes had phoned him and threatened him if he didn't resign as executive secretary. The police were contacted, but could do nothing on such evidence. Besides the PFTA leader denied the call.

A week or so later, in early September, another board meeting was called at the request of Duran. Seven board members attended, four Anglos and the three PFTA members. Duran resigned. The Anglo board members debated whether or not to accept the resignation. The PFTA attacked them viciously, threatening to picket their houses, their jobs, contact the EOC, even the president of the United States if they did not accept it. Duran insisted they accept his resignation and left.

The Anglos were now furious at the PFTA for their attack. In one of their more positive actions, another board meeting was called a week later and the same board members attended. Amid a storm and furor Mrs. Horton was made temporary executive secretary by a vote of four Anglos to three Mexican-Americans. By the same vote another woman of Mexican descent, Mrs. Dominguez, was appointed temporary clerk-typist.

Mrs. Dominguez's appointment was an exceptionally unfortunate choice by the Anglos. She has worked in a poverty program in Otay previously and had on occasion volunteered her services to the CAC. She also knew Mr. Flores and Delia Garcia quite well and was acquainted with persons in other antipoverty programs in the area. However, she was not well liked in the community, especially by the PFTA. She considered herself an upper-class Mexican, was proud and arrogant, and also had close associations with many Anglos. The PFTA was furious at her appointment and threatened to close the CAC. By this time many people were beginning to believe it was the only tactic possible to avoid violence.

The new executive secretary, Mrs. Horton, who previously had been immune to most of the conflict, now found herself in the center of it. She had been fired originally at the same time as Mrs. Hurtado and they had been close friends for almost two years. She hoped that she could work with the PFTA and Mrs. Hurtado. She knew the War on Poverty Program better than anyone in the area and believed that she could convince the PFTA to work with her through the CAC and its resources. Her appointment as executive secretary, however, infuriated Esmerelda, and Mrs. Horton became "just another Anglo." Mrs. Hurtado's determination to become executive secretary was greater than ever and through her, the PFTA expressed no interest whatever in working with the CAC board, staff, or membership so long as it was controlled by Anglos. As with the previous executive secretary, Mrs. Hurtado refused to work with Mrs.

Horton. The Anglo members of the CAC board became increasingly disturbed and increasingly demanded help and advice from the EOC staff.

The EOC was afraid of what these events and others like them across the country would do to the war on poverty, for a national election was pending and the period during which the national antipoverty program was considered for refunding for the next fiscal year was at hand. Also, while the Border Area CAC was the most chaotic in the county, other CACs were also having problems. Hostilities such as this could only be detrimental to the local program. Still, to the chagrin of the Anglo board members, the EOC tried not to become involved. By this time the EOC was having problems of its own.

The EOC was becoming involved in organizing the Model Cities Program scheduled for the city of San Diego. The period of refunding local war on poverty projects was at hand and it was deeply involved in developing a method to make this procedure more efficient than it had been in the past.

Also, the head of Area Development who had been responsible for establishing the CAC Program had just recently suggested that the CACs be separated totally from the EOC and most of the CACs in the county were frightened and angry over this. Finally, the head of Area Development decided to resign and accept the directorship of the Neighborhood House, one of the EOC delegate agencies. He was thoroughly fed up with the CACs and increasingly believed they would not work and that service policies were a more significant answer to the war on poverty. He was tired of constantly being under CAC attack for not doing his job and helping them as they expected. Some of this was justified, for as he became increasingly discouraged with the CACs he withdrew farther from involvement with them. One unfortunate result of this was that Delia Garcia, the consultant, received no directives from the EOC regarding how to handle the situation in San Ysidro. She also feared that after the resignation of the Area Development director they might cut the CACs off and dispense with her services. Her attempts to justify her job by keeping the CAC dependent upon her created more problems than she resolved.

In effect the dependence of the board members upon Delia precluded their learning anything about their role, and to a great extent they were at the mercy of her capriciousness. As a Mexican-American she sometimes sided with the PFTA, at other times with the Anglos. Eventually, the PFTA tired of this and disavowed her; she became just one more representative of an agency they were out to destroy.

It was also revealed later that Delia had not been keeping the EOC fully informed of the events in San Ysidro. Eventually, this caught up with her and in the final stages of the conflict she was blamed for having permitted the CAC to fall into such a state of chaos. She was relieved as consultant and assigned to another program. The affect of all this was that the Border Area CAC became isolated in the arena. Its leadership remained confused and the conflict grew.

The PFTA did not relinquish their attacks. It was doubly painful to them that Mrs. Hurtado had not been elected executive secretary because about this time the MAAC board of directors rejected the person they selected to replace Yolanda Chaca as the project director of the San Ysidro service center. They explained that the job demanded someone more proficiently bilingual. Without PFTA knowledge, the CAC also had complained to MAAC board members that if a PFTA member was placed in the service center there would never be rapprochement between the two agencies. The young man who was eventually appointed did in fact develop a rather good working relationship with both the CAC and the PFTA. This did not resolve the intent of the PFTA to gain control of the CAC.

Under Ramon Cervantes guidance the PFTA launched a letter writing campaign which they carried on with intermittent intensity for over three months. They also acquired the attention and interest of a small South Bay newspaper. In their letters and in reports printed in the newspaper they complained about Anglo domination and injustice in San Ysidro and made scatter-gun attacks against Sally Horton, Mrs. Domingues, Mrs. Osmond (the board president), the Anglo board members, the San Ysidro Planning Group, Delia Garcia, and the EOC. They deliberately arranged meetings which conflicted with scheduled CAC meetings and then announced that the CAC was sabotaging their meetings by drawing off attendance. This, in fact, rarely happened.

Mrs. Horton attempted to establish an understanding with the PFTA. The struggle, however, was rapidly developing into a conflict and resolution of the problem was already beyond her control. Mrs. Horton attempted to re-organize the dissident elements in the CAC by evoking changes in the school district's EMR program. For a while she had Mrs. Hurtado's support in this endeavor because one of her children was in the EMR program. This support proved to be ephemeral. She then tried to organize the Anglo board members into a united faction against the PFTA. This proved impossible. The board was increasingly intimidated by the PFTA. Each Anglo member responded in his own way to the intimidation and no united front developed. It became increasingly impossible for Mrs. Horton to accomplish anything. On the twenty-fifth of September a crisis was reached and the conflict entered its final phase.

According to guidelines developed by the EOC the CAC at this time called a meeting to discuss procedures concerned with refunding the war on poverty for the coming fiscal year. In accord with their policy of alternating meetings between San Ysidro and Otay, the meeting was scheduled in Otay. The PFTA vigorously objected and argued that the meeting should be held in San Ysidro. Attendance at the meeting was surprisingly quite large. Among others it included Delia Garcia, PFTA members (who had not been expected), and representatives from the delegate agencies in the area who were to present preliminary programs to the CAC. As soon as the meeting was convened Ramon

Cervates stood up and announced that it was an illegal meeting and that the people of San Ysidro were going to boycott it. "People of San Ysidro," he called, "Vamonos!" Twenty-two people walked out. Mrs. Hurtado had brought some of the people in her car and as they walked out, she did also. Then, at the insistence of Delia Garcia, she returned and did remain for the rest of the meeting.

John Diaz was also in attendance at this meeting and was supposed to introduce the MAAC proposal for San Ysidro. He, too, walked out with the PFTA, conferred with them for awhile, and then returned. When the time came to present his proposal Diaz refused and argued that it was an illegal meeting because the people of San Ysidro were not represented. After this point he became visibly involved in the activities of the PFTA in San Ysidro.

The CAC board of directors at this meeting was composed of one Mexican-American from Otay, three Anglos from Otay and San Ysidro, including Mrs. Osmond and Mr. Von Lutz, and two blacks from Woodlawn Park. The Anglo and black members were furious. In consultation with the EOC consultant they decided to fire Esmerelda Hurtado and impeach Ramon Cervantes and the other PFTA members on the CAC board. They agreed to fire Mrs. Hurtado at a board meeting scheduled one week later and to initiate impeachment proceedings at the next regular CAC meeting, about two weeks hence.

The board determined to hold the impeachment proceedings in Woodlawn Park rather than San Ysidro for several reasons. It was fairly certain the Mexican-Americans of San Ysidro would not attend a meeting there because they now insisted that all meetings of the CAC be held in San Ysidro. A quorum and a two-thirds vote of the members in attendance was needed for impeachment and this would not be guaranteed in San Ysidro. Finally, the black representatives argued that this would be a good way to re-involve the people of Woodlawn Park and Otay in the CAC. Although the board hoped to keep their moves as secret as possible to avoid trouble, the Mexican-American representative from Otay informed the PFTA of the decision.

A week later a board meeting was convened. The Anglos and blacks outvoted the PFTA members five to three and Mrs. Hurtado was fired. The PFTA had, however, brought to the meeting about a dozen supporters. They sat through the proceedings in violation of CAC bylaws which dictate that meetings concerned with personnel problems be closed. Tempers flared and violence almost erupted. The PFTA vowed to destroy the organization of the CAC and close the office.

Two weeks later at a quiet CAC meeting in Woodlawn Park, the impeachment took place. The meeting was packed with blacks from the community, a few people from Otay and a couple of PFTA members, who later made only a mild complaint to the EOC that the meeting had not been translated into Spanish. It was really anticlimactic because a couple of days after their walkout in Otay, the PFTA launched a campaign against the CAC which carried on through October and November and which resulted in the final conflict phase of events in San Ysidro. Previous actions of the PFTA suggested how vicious these attacks were to become.

It had been common knowledge for some time that Mrs. Domingues, the woman appointed as temporary clerk-typist, was going to take her test for American citizenship in September. She was quite proud of this and confident of passing, and, in the way that made her unpopular in the community, arrogant about it. Not only were the PFTA members quite hostile to her prior to her assuming the temporary position on the CAC staff, she now represented one more impasse on their way to control of the CAC. The PFTA capitalized on her citizenship test in a most malicious way. They informed the naturalization officials that she had an illegitimate child.

In a manner that seems sadistic from later comments by the persons who accompanied Mrs. Dominguez to her hearing, the naturalization officials put her through the battery of questions, all of which she passed. At the end of the questioning she was confronted with a letter which pointed out that her youngest child was illegitimate and the officials asked if this was so. Shocked, she admitted it was, and her citizenship was refused.

Even then the PFTA did not relinquish their attacks on her. Individual members were rude to her face. The gossip about her became extreme in the community. Many people in the community stopped talking to her. In the letter writing campaign the PFTA launched with increased vigor, her immoral conduct and the fact that the CAC had a person of such low character working for it was reiterated to the mayor of San Diego, the EOC, and the federal OEO. In early December Mrs. Dominguez left San Ysidro and moved to Sacramento.

As noted the PFTA had been writing letters to a variety of officials protesting conditions in San Ysidro for some time. The firing of Esmerelda Hurtado and impeachment of Ramon Cervantes and the other PFTA board members gave new ammunition for their attack and they launched it with gusto. There was also a sudden change in the quality of the letters. Compared to previous letters they now became quite literate, and many of the facts they exposed were quite precise. This suggested that the PFTA now had access to information not available to it previously. The letters also began to go to a new order of officials beyond the mayor of San Diego and EOC officials.

John Diaz began to appear increasingly in San Ysidro and at meetings held by the PFTA. It was suddenly obvious that he was making available to the PFTA his resources and services. For example, the letters became pointed regarding facts about funding and expenditures of war on poverty funds. These were used to argue that considering what the Border Area CAC was accomplishing for San Ysidro, it was a waste of money to keep it open. The letters also were directed to the proper persons in the proper offices. Letters were sent to: local newspapers; the director of the EOC; the director of Area Development in the EOC; the mayor of San Diego; the governor of California and the governor's advisor on Mexican-American Affairs; the state OEO; Bertrand Harding, the interim director of the OEO in Washington, D.C.; the Department of Justice and Naturalization regarding the immorality of the CAC clerk-typist; Ambassador Telles of the Mexico-United States Border Commission; the president of the United States; and the president of Mexico.

Various letters claimed that the PFTA represented between 800 and 4,000 citizens of San Ysidro, and on one occasion, 99 percent of the community. They argued that the Border Area CAC squandered funds and did not serve the people of San Ysidro. They claimed the executive secretary could not speak Spanish, and was immoral. In November a letter was sent anonymously to Mrs. Horton's husband. He was in the Navy doing submarine duty off Vietnam. The letter accused her of having an affair with me and with Mr. Flores.[11] In other letters they attacked Mrs. Osmond, the president of the CAC; they accused the EOC of doing nothing for the community, and so forth. Most of them complained in detail about the unfair treatment of Esmerelda Hurtado. They argued that she alone in the CAC worked for and with the community and demanded that these agencies and individuals do all they could to reinstate her, this time as executive secretary.

Jim Duran, who had continued attending CAC meetings since his resignation, reported that another telephone call had been made to him threatening him and his family's lives if he persisted in this attendance. He did not attend after this. Mrs. Osmond was called and her life was threatened if she did not resign. Her employer, the San Ysidro post office, was called on numerous occasions and informed that the PFTA was going to begin picketing the post office. For a while Mrs. Osmond was afraid of losing her job. The PFTA also threatened to picket the CAC office. Despite the threats, the picketing never materialized.

PFTA members did begin to watch the CAC office and record the time of entry and departure of CAC staff and other persons. After this Sally Horton was accused in letters to officials and in stories in the local press which was capitalizing upon these events and which seemed sympathetic to the PTFA, of taking two hours for lunch, drinking on the job, taking five coffee breaks a day, and so forth. The local newspapers ran a story in which Ramon Cervantes claimed in a letter to Governor Reagan that someone had attempted "to kill him with a car (in San Ysidro) on the night of October 30."[12] The PFTA also claimed that the action of the CAC in firing Esmerelda Hurtado and impeaching the board members was going to cause riots and violence in town and that "carloads of Negroes were seen in San Ysidro and that violence might soon erupt."[13] This angered the blacks of Woodlawn Park, to whom the remark was directed, and for over a month their representatives boycotted the CAC.

These tactics led to anger, fear, and debilitation of the CAC. Mrs. Horton, for example, after the letter to her husband, was also slandered in a meeting between the PFTA and the EOC officials at which time splitting the

CAC was discussed. She became afraid to remain in the community. Mrs. Osmond seriously considered resigning, but then decided to remain and fight the PFTA. Tex Stillman and Mr. Lutz kept the San Ysidro Planning Group informed of much of what was happening. This was instrumental in the suppression of the San Ysidro Community Survey in early December. Other CAC board members simply dropped out, and for a while during October and November, no business was conducted and, for all practical purposes, the CAC simply did not operate.

The individuals who were under attack by the PFTA were not idle during this period. For a while they did attempt to counter the PFTA with rebuttals to the press and in letters of their own. Most of their efforts, however, went through traditional channels available to the contestants, e.g., the police, Legal Aid Society, and other agency officials to whom they had access. Mr. Flores of the EOC board argued that the PFTA would wither if it was left alone and ignored. The Legal Aid Society gave the same advice, and also advised the CAC not to reply in the press to the PFTA charges because they would only enhance the ego and prestige of the PFTA.

Mrs. Osmond and Mrs. Horton did contact the MAAC project board of directors and informed them of the actions of John Diaz. At first the MAAC board was unwilling to reprimand their director. Pressure, however, was also exerted upon the board by other MAAC staff personnel who were concerned about the effect of the conflict on the reputation and efficacy of the MAAC project, and by the EOC which was becoming increasingly disturbed over the events in San Ysidro and the affect they might have on the future of the war on poverty in San Diego. The EOC director was reported to have lamented that the Border Area CAC "hung like an albatross around his neck and wished the whole thing would just disappear." It did not. Eventually, under these pressures, which ultimately resulted in a threat from Mrs. Osmond and Mrs. Horton that they would implement CAC prerogatives and attempt to curtail funding for the MAAC project if the board did not stop the actions of its director, Diaz was ordered to stay out of San Ysidro. It remained evident, however, that he did continue to advise the PFTA clandestinely.

Police were also alerted to the PFTA and Ramon Cervantes was questioned about his treats and actions. He and others were kept under police surveillance. Mr. Cervantes complained vociferously in the community that he was being harassed by the police and that this was just one other aspect of the plot of the rich against the poor. His constant barrage of such propaganda elicited much support and sympathy from the community and helped maintain his following.

Members of the San Ysidro Planning Group were informed of the events by their liaisons Tex Stillman and Mr. Von Lutz, and by Mrs. Osmond. The immigration consultant of the San Ysidro Planning Group suggested that since the leader of the PFTA, Ramon Cervantes, was not an American citizen, it might be possible to have him deported, at least detained in Mexico, should he cross the border. This rumor spread throughout San Ysidro and Mr. Cervantes did not cross the border, nor was he deported. Another member of the San Ysidro Planning Group attempted to have the PFTA leader picked up for a psychological examination to test his sanity. Nothing came of this either.

Another factor which fed into this conflict in a most significant way was the unionization of the staffs of the war on poverty agencies in San Diego in the early fall of 1968. This was the result of efforts by Mr. Flores, the UFWOC representative in San Ysidro. One feature of the union contract was the development of other channels in addition to the EOC by which various agency staff who might be fired could appeal their case. A discharged person had twenty days to appeal.

Mrs. Hurtado and the PFTA were unaware of this, and Mrs. Horton, Delia Garcia, and others who were aware of this decided not to inform her. However, a similar case was pending in another CAC. The EOC consultant to that area supported this particular individual and requested assistance in this case from Delia Garcia. She refused. The other consultant then informed Mrs. Hurtado of her rights and arbitration of her case was set into motion. At this point, other CACs became involved.

Both Mrs. Hurtado and Mrs. Horton informed friends in other CACs of what was transpiring and requested their assistance. Several Mexican-Americans from other CACs sided with the PFTA, primarily due to their common ethnic identity, and argued with EOC representatives that the Border Area CAC should be split and San Ysidro made a separate Mexican-American Community Action Council. The Anglos generally sided with Mrs. Horton, who still hoped to exclude or at least neutralize the PFTA so that the CAC could work for the community at large. In the long run none of this support was of any avail.

Despite these efforts, which were quite intermittent, by and large the CAC board and staff adhered to a policy of "benign neglect" regarding the PFTA. For a while it seemed to be working. The viciousness of the attacks of the PFTA offended as many members of the community as other tactics attracted. By late October, support for the PFTA in the community seemed to be waning. Housing meetings called by the PFTA were poorly attended. In the Mayor's Meeting the PFTA leadership seemed increasingly isolated. Even the visible consultations the PFTA held with the governor's advisor on Mexican-American Affairs at the Mayor's Meetings did not seem to spark more interest in their efforts. John Diaz was no longer visible in the community. Mr. Hermann of the San Ysidro Elementary School District and the local priest formally withdrew their honorary status from the PFTA because they believed it had gone beyond its original aims of helping the poor and was now discrediting the community.

Other contestants in the arena were aware of this. However, as the PFTA influence waned, Ramon Cervantes and his supporters attacked more vigorously. Letters increased to officials outside the arena, and the local press, anxious for news, printed all the PFTA had to say. The PFTA also drew some sustenance from the fact that Mexican-American families were beginning to be evicted along the freeway route and the housing development to accommodate them was behind schedule. At the same time a few contestants were attempting to ignore the PFTA, and others, such as Mrs. Horton and Mrs. Osmond, were taking actions against the PFTA; still others outside the arena, influenced by letters, press, and rumor, were becoming increasingly alarmed. The result of this was quite beneficial to the PFTA cause.

It would have been difficult to predict the future of the PFTA had it been left alone as Mr. Flores and others suggested. Contradiction was so imbedded in the structure of the Border Area CAC and so compounded by outside events that it is probable that the struggles would have continued in one form or another. Regardless, a series of actions and events led to an eventual PFTA victory in the struggle for control of the CAC.

Very shortly after the strong stand the CAC board took after the PFTA walkout of the September meeting, board members began to have second thoughts about its actions. Delia Garcia did also, although the only predictable thing about her actions was that they would be unpredictable. After the firing and impeachment proceedings Delia gradually swung back to support the PFTA, although she also continued to assert her support of Mrs. Horton and the CAC board. Delia's actions were predicated upon her philosophy of keeping the contestants off balance and of being ready to take advantage of any situation that would serve her job security. As the PFTA attacks mounted, many of them directed against her, she quietly began a campaign in support of Mrs. Hurtado and the PFTA generally. She also kept control of the CAC board, having generally convinced its membership that they could not act without her approval. They viewed this as an EOC sanction to their actions. This was the very kind of dependence the EOC hoped to eliminate.

Eventually the CAC began to select new board members to replace those impeached. By the end of November this was complete. They included Tex Stillman again, a black woman from Woodlawn Park, and a Mexican-American from San Ysidro. Delia Garcia argued that these members would placate the Mexican-Americans of San Ysidro and the blacks of Woodlawn Park. In fact, about this time the black representatives from Woodlawn Park did begin again to attend board meetings. The inclusion of Tex Stillman had been decided upon earlier by Mrs. Osmond and Mr. Von Lutz in order to bolster their position against the PFTA.

The EOC was also increasingly distressed. It knew it was not getting the true facts of the situation in San Ysidro. The refunding procedures of the new fiscal year were in operation, and it was reported that they had received letters from OEO in Washington, D.C., and other officials inquiring into the furor in San Ysidro. The EOC feared this scandal would jeopardize the program.

Originally it had argued that it could not afford to split the Border Area CAC and set up another CAC office.

Then it was announced at one of the Mayor's Meetings that due to a sudden availability of funds, San Ysidro was going to participate in the Model Cities Program. At least one EOC official suggested privately that if the CAC was split, eventually the Model Cities Program would take over all the CAC and war on poverty functions in the area, therefore why not split it and bear the expense of another CAC for a short period of time; it was certainly better than the options of closing it completely or continuing to bear with the conflict, both of which gave the war on poverty in San Diego an undesirable notoriety.

By this time, the director of Area Development who had founded the CAC was preparing to resign his office, and it was strongly rumored that the director of the EOC was also going to resign. Both were disillusioned by the CAC program and both were increasingly pessimistic regarding the war on poverty in San Diego. Richard Nixon had been elected president and there was deep concern for the future of the war on poverty. Spiro Agnew was making strong statements questioning the ability of the poor to participate meaningfully in the war on poverty. The antipoverty program in San Diego was one among others in the nation scheduled to be investigated for its efficiency and use of funds. More frequently now the EOC talked of splitting the CAC in two: one CAC for Otay and Woodlawn Park and one for San Ysidro.

In early December, the new CAC board of directors took a decisive step. They voted to rehire Mrs. Hurtado. Only Mrs. Osmond voted no. She was still hostile to the PFTA for the insults and pain they had caused her and saw this action as a concession to it. Sally Horton was despondent. Again, the CAC board had refused to support their executive secretary, and she knew she could not work with Mrs. Hurtado or the PFTA members. The board itself was fairly certain the CAC would be split by actions of the EOC and they were anxious to avoid any further conflict. The PFTA was jubilant.

About this time the EOC decided to hold hearings in each of the three communities involved in the Border Area CAC to poll and assess the wishes of the people. Everyone was now agreed that the best thing to do was split the Border Area CAC. On January 16, 1970, one year from the time it began its turbulent history in San Ysidro, the Border Area CAC was split in two.

The conflict stimulated by the contradictions in the Border Area CAC had finally resulted in an attempt to change its structure and thus resolve the conflict. The Border Area Community Action Council now became a Mexican-American organization, representing only the Mexican-Americans of San Ysidro and not the total community. Most people were relieved the conflict has been terminated,[14] and no one seemed to mind that the aim of the war on poverty, which was to serve all the people of a poverty habitat, would not be achieved. Since, in fact, this aim had never been achieved, the community at large was little affected by the split. Esmerelda Hurtado was elected executive secretary and the board of directors of the CAC was reorganized and made up exclusively of PFTA members. The PFTA now became the Border Area CAC.

THE SAN YSIDRO ELEMENTARY SCHOOL DISTRICT: EMR

Whether we like it or not, the educational system is one of society's most powerful mechanisms for sorting out children to assume different roles in the educational hierarchy and for allocating them later in life based upon this sorting out process to status and occupational slots which the society makes available in its class structure. The problems Mexican-American children confront in the American educational system and the implications of that education for their future in American society has been documented very well.[15] It is a history which details the result of a self-fulfilling prophecy regarding cultural and biological attributes arbitrarily assigned to Mexican-Americans in the United States; Mexican-Americans are not specially equiped for agricultural stoop labor because they are built closer to the ground as Senator George Murphy of California argued in the early 1960s, nor has it been demonstrated that they have inherited genes which make them especially good with their hands or intellectually dull because their parents have worked all their lives in the fields. Even where cactus is available—and this is not frequent in urban barrios—they are not often found napping under them. Still, this represents the prejudiced image of Mexican-Americans and their children that is widespread among educators and in the society at large.

Several of the school districts of the South San Diego Bay Area were notorious for their intransigence in responding to the linguistic and cultural characteristics Mexican-American children bring into American schools. If not given special attention these characteristics become translated by the society into problems which become overwhelming inhibitors to Mexican-American integration into American national culture. Prior to my research, several of the South Bay school districts had been under attack for some time by concerned Mexican-Americans regarding their prejudicial and bigoted attitudes concerning the education of Mexican-American children.

The San Ysidro Elementary School District was not one of these districts, primarily because it was a somewhat more progressive district. However, 84 percent of the children in its three schools were of Mexican descent, and approximately 50 percent of these spoke Spanish as their first language.[16] Although the district had its problems, they were overshadowed by the magnitude of those in other school districts of the area. Still, it became ensnared in the conflict in San Ysidro in the fall of 1968. It became involved as the result of an incident regarding its most vulnerable area, the Special Educational or EMR (Educationally Mentally Retarded) program, which it operated under guidelines established by the county of San Diego. Mrs. Horton, as the conflict in the arena escalated, saw this incident as the last chance for the CAC as constituted to prove that it could do the job and not be forced to succumb to the attacks of the PFTA.

The Special Educational Program, better known as EMR classes, was initiated in San Ysidro in 1958 by the San Diego County Department of Education as a means of tracking children who were educationally mentally retarded and distractions in regular classes into a program which would, presumably, facilitate their learning abilities. Approximately forty-seven children were in the Special Educational Program in San Ysidro at the time of this research.

The tracking procedure was simple. In the third grade the teacher may request that a child who is not achieving satisfactorily be administered an I.Q. test. If the test results in a quotient below eighty, the child is then interviewed by a psychologist appointed by the county. If his findings verify the teacher's suggestion and the result of the I.Q. test, the parents are informed and their permission is requested to place the child in a special class program. It was explained to the parents that this is for the child's own benefit. Apparently very few parents ever disputed this decision.

The attitude of some of the teachers of EMR classes is that these children are culturally deprived. Although EMR children are supposed to receive a standard elementary curriculum, in fact EMR classes stress craft activities. Underlying this is the widespread assumption among educators and members of the larger community that "these kids are so good with their hand." A teacher who had taught in the program since its inception told me that over the last few years about half of her students came from the Bolton Hall district, the very poorest area of San Ysidro, and in which Spanish was the predominant language. One of the principals argued that EMR children are genetically predisposed to low educational achievement because their parents represent the lowest class of Mexican society; farmworkers and indigents.

Over the years, EMR classes have tended to become catchalls for a variety of dispositions. Children who are slow learners, who are socially maladjusted, who are discipline problems, who do not speak English, who are hyperkinetic, as well as a very few who are genuinely mentally retarded, all may find themselves in EMR classes. Once a child is placed in an EMR track, he generally remains there until he drops out or graduates with a diploma indicating he is the product of a Special Educational Program. As a result of this program it is highly probable that a child who does graduate with a Special Educational Program diploma will not be able to read, write, or speak English. However, far less than half of those tracked into EMR classes finish school. As a result of either circumstance, the educational product is poorly fitted to most of the role options available in American culture.

The issue over the EMR classes developed in early September 1968, shortly after Sally Horton had been appointed temporary executive secretary. A

Mexican-American woman who spoke no English, a friend of Mrs. Hurtado, came to the CAC office and complained that the third of her four children was about to be placed in EMR class. In tears and quite distraught, she complained that her child did not belong in the class and that the EMR classes were a great waste of time. The community aide was sympathetic. One of her children was also in EMR class. Mrs. Horton and Mrs. Hurtado agreed to look into the matter.

Although relations between Mrs. Hurtado and Mrs. Horton were strained, with the importance of this immediate problem, they agreed to work together and confront the school district over the matter. Their motivations, however, were quite distinct. Mrs. Hurtado, true to her caretaker proclivity, saw the problem only in terms of resolving the dilemma of the unhappy parent and of perhaps having her own child withdrawn from the program. Mrs. Horton, on the other hand, quickly decided that this could become a major issue around which the CAC could demonstrate the value of community organization in effecting meaningful changes in an institution which affects the lives of the community's children. She was optimistic that this would prove to be a way to muster community support and effectively undermine the growing influence of the PFTA. Toward this end she made preparations. She spoke of tactics at length with Mr. Flores, who was also deeply involved in confrontations with other South Bay schools. She informed Delia Garcia and invited her to assist. With the help of the offended parent, four other mothers whose children were in EMR classes were contacted. Then a meeting was scheduled with school officials.

In mid-September the meeting took place, It was attended by the assistant superintendent of schools, the principal of the school, the EMR teacher, Sally Horton, Mrs. Hurtado, Delia Garcia, five parents of children in the school's EMR classes, and myself. The school officials were confident they could explain and justify the program to the assembled persons. They were totally unprepared for what they confronted.

After Mrs. Horton stated the complaint that the CAC had received, the school officials explained the EMR program and spoke of its value to the child and community. Mrs. Horton responded and on many points embarrassed, and eventually angered, the officials. She questioned the EMR curriculum, the nature and validity of the tests by which children were tracked into EMR, the reasons other than mental retardation for which children were placed in EMR, the possibilities of a child ever being tracked out of EMR once committed to it, the attitudes of the teachers, administrators, and psychologists who tracked children into EMR classes, and the like. The officials admitted that the program was not perfect. However, they pointed out, they only administered it for the county of San Diego. After being quizzed on this point, the officials admitted they had more or less complete control of the program. However, they argued, beginning the next school year the San Ysidro Elementary School District was going to assume full responsibility for the program and then changes would be made. They argued with increasing exasperation that the people should be patient until then.

When Mrs. Hurtado argued that Mexican-American parents really were not aware of the implications of the program, the officials responded that parents were fully apprised of the implications and purpose of the Special Educational Program and that their consent was always obtained prior to tracking a child into EMR. All the parents and the community aide disagreed with this and pointed out that they had merely been informed that their children were going to be placed in a special class and that nothing was said regarding the nature of that class. The woman who registered the original complaint argued that she never gave her consent, and only through her other two children discovered the real content and quality of special classes; in the case of her third child she protested vigorously before going to the CAC office and the school ignored her protests.

Actually, according to the principal with whom I spoke just prior to this meeting, the principal had called the child's father and obtained his consent for the placement of the child in the EMR class. Somewhat smugly he told me that the school had been expecting trouble from this woman and that when he contacted the father, "I had a secretary on an extension to verify all this, so she doesn't have a leg to stand on!"

Mrs. Horton finally suggested that the parents of EMR placed children should come to the school and observe the classes. She also suggested that the CAC organize groups of parents and transport them to the school. The officials became immediately defensive, reluctant, and eventually angry. They suggested that the parents make individual appointments. The executive secretary argued that this would permit the school to intimidate each parent and insisted that the parents come in groups. By this time the conversation was becoming heated and the meeting broke up without this point being resolved.

The school district officials were quite unprepared for this confrontation. The principal of the school argued that the whole EMR issue was a plot inspired by radicals from outside the community. Mr. Hermann, the superintendent, argued that Mrs. Horton was a new arrival in the community and a troublemaker. He was surprised to learn that she had been involved in the Border Area CAC for almost three years. He also lamented the intrusion of these nebulous activist elements into San Ysidro and the loss to the community of Yolanda Chaca and Jim Duran, both of whom the school district got along with quite well. The school staffs were warned about Mrs. Horton and she was typed as a troublemaker. The principals in the districts three schools were instructed to withhold from her the names of parents whose children were in EMR classes. Although the San Ysidro Elementary School Dsitrict attempted to isolate the CAC, this proved impossible and the school district was forced to develop liaisons with it.

About a week after the meetings, with the help of Mrs. Hurtado's child, several of the thirteen children from this child's EMR class were persuaded to come each afternoon after school to the CAC office for what was announced to the school officials as special tutoring sessions. Mrs. Horton informed the school that they had professional help and were prepared to continue the tutoring until the school did something about the EMR program. In fact, there was no professional help and the children were induced with cookies and soft drinks and for a while enjoyed the informal atmosphere and game orientation of the CAC office. The local press was alerted to the tutoring sessions and a short article was run in the newspaper regarding the situation. It was far less than Mrs. Horton hoped for, but the school officials did respond. The assistant superintendent threatened to close down the EMR program if the attacks against it weren't stopped. Mrs. Horton replied that that was a good idea, because then the children would have to be put back into regular classes where they belonged. After that the school officials became more reasonable. Had they known of the problems she was beginning to have with the PFTA perhaps they would not have been.

Mrs. Horton also informed other Mexican-American ad hoc committees in the area who were confronting other school districts over educational issues of her actions and requested assistance. They were too involved with their own problems to offer more than moral support. She contacted Mexican-American educators in the area and officials involved in the English as a Second Language Program in San Diego and requested their advice and assistance. Their advice was to play it cool. They assured her that changes in the education of Mexican-American children were coming and that there was little they could do immediately.

The EOC was disturbed by the entire situation. Another South Bay CAC had been in conflict with the schools of its district. The state of California was concerned over this and investigators from the state Department of Education had been in the area. The EOC viewed all these attacks on and problems with institutions, such as the schools, as threats to the continued viability of the program, especially as the national elections approached. Nor was the CAC president, Mrs. Osmond, in favor of this action. Schools were, to her, a sacred institution and not subject to attack. Her children had done well in the South Bay schools, and so could any other child who applied himself. When Mrs. Horton attempted to explain the problems of Mexican-American children in Anglo schools the CAC president referred to Jim Duran as a Mexican-American who had done quite well in the San Ysidro schools; if he could, she reasoned, so could others. Community organization and institutional change were alien concepts to her. As her personal struggle with the PFTA grew, little was ever again said about the involvement of the CAC in the EMR program.

Mrs. Horton was disappointed in the response and reactions she received. There were radical elements in the area which she could have contacted and who would have made a large fight out of the issue. Despite the allegations of the school district that she was a radical because of her attempt to organize community support under the CAC for this local problem, she pointedly refused to involve these elements. In a short time other events in the arena effectively undermined her efforts.

Had the school district officials been more aware of the nature of the problems she and the CAC began to confront they would have realized that the issue, from the executive secretary's point of view, was dead. However, they were not aware of this and continued to respond as though they were being threatened. The result of this was the initiation of some desirable changes in the San Ysidro schools. Over the next couple of months the school district officials promised Mrs. Horton that they would obtain new books, bilingual readers, a bilingual-bicultural section in the library and perhaps even a total bilingual educational program, as well as make adjustments in the EMR classes. A tentative bargain was struck; if the school attempted these changes, the CAC would assist them in obtaining a year-round Headstart program. Currently the school district had only a summer Headstart program which served only a few children.

The day after the tutoring of the EMR children began in the CAC office, the PFTA walked out of the CAC meeting. This and the subsequent events, already described, also affected the school issue. After that the attacks mounted quickly against the CAC. Mrs. Horton and Mrs. Dominguez, her clerk-typist who was refused citizenship, lost interest in the tutoring sessions. The lack of support from other agencies also undermined their interest. Mrs. Hurtado, when fired, dropped out of the school issue.

In early October the school district apprised Mrs. Horton of the fact that they were going to begin retesting EMR children with tests more accommodating to Mexican-American culture and the Spanish language. [17] As the PFTA attacks mounted, Mrs. Horton became increasingly fearful of coming to San Ysidro, especially for meetings at night. In early November the public meeting concerned with education was held. Prior to this the superintendent, at a meeting of the San Ysidro Planning Group in city hall, expressed concern about problems and hostility at the meeting against the educators. It was suggested that questions from the floor be kept to a minimum. The meeting, in fact, went quite smoothly. Questions of some hostility were leveled against school officials present at the meeting, but the EMR issue never was raised. Sally Horton was too afraid and tired of the conflict now to care about the EMR.

Events had determined that the CAC would never function as originally constituted and most of the people involved were resigned to it being closed or split. Still, the school district officials kept Mrs. Horton informed and she maintained a facade of interest. In mid-December she was invited to attend a meeting of school officials at which time it was announced that San Ysidro was going to participate in a bilingual education program and that positive changes were going to be forthcoming in their EMR program. By this time it was certain that the Border Area CAC was going to be split. Mrs. Hurtado had been rehired, and Mrs. Horton was no longer active in San Ysidro.

The issue over the EMR program did result in positive gains for San Ysidro and its school district. It did not, however, serve the cause of the CAC. The parents of children in EMR classes, as well as the community at large, were never organized. In fact, most members of the community probably would not have supported Mrs. Horton in her attacks on the school. As pointed out in Chapter 2, in the survey conducted by the CAC in conjunction with the city planning department survey, of some 516 responses to the question, "Are you satisfied with the schools in San Ysidro?" Only sixteen persons expressed any dissatisfaction. As was the case with the president of the board of the CAC, most citizens in San Ysidro considered schools sacrosanct institutions, significant mechanisms by which their children might achieve better than the parents had. Even though in many cases their children were not succeeding in them, and throughout San Diego generally schools were under severe attack from ethnic minorities regarding the education their children received in them, all too frequently the parents blamed the children themselves for their persistent failures.

It might be speculated that it would have proven more beneficial to the Border Area CAC had it attacked the housing issue in some more positive fashion in order to swing support away from the PFTA. It's doubtful the CAC could have obtained any legitimacy in the community at that time over this issue. Although the attack upon the school may have been a futile effort from the start with reference to regenerating any CAC support in the community, nevertheless, in defense of the effort by the executive secretary in service of the ideology of the CAC, it must be said that given the available options, it did seem like the best thing to do at the time.

SUMMARY

Factors which generated conflict in the arena emanate from a variety of sources and interact in a variety of ways. The emergence of the issues in the arena and the conflict in which the contestants participated has been described in some detail to demonstrate the nature of the conflict and the intricacies by which it fed into a variety of issues. Added insight is offered into the war on poverty in San Diego County and special attention is paid to the history of the Border Area Community Action Council as a means of explicating the critical role of this organization in the conflict. In the next chapter I will discuss the tactics and strategies employed by the contestants in the pursuit of their goals and their significance for the contestants and the character of the conflict in the arena of San Ysidro.

Chapter Six

Tactics and Strategies

INTRODUCTION

Several authors have developed models to explain the sociopolitical process by suggesting the phases through which such a process progresses. Most of these models begin by suggesting some breach in sociopolitical relationships of contestants and culminate in a resolution of the resulting conflict.[1] Through the intermediate phases of this process emerge the strategies and tactics by which contestants attempt to achieve their goals.

Strategy refers to the plans and political decisions made in the service of long-range goals; tactics refer to the means by which and the ways in which the various resources available to the contestants, such as the personal support one is able to muster, are applied in the fight toward these ends. While strategies and tactics in a political arena may not always be as calculated and forthright as in a military campaign, all wars are characterized by them; the war on poverty is no exception.

There are those who would argue that the war on poverty has a planned strategy. For example, the Cahns state:

> The strategy of (the war on poverty) appears to have been shaped by awareness of the interrelatedness of the social, economic, legal, educational, and psychological problems which beset the poor and by a recognition of the necessity to involve all segments of society in a many-pronged attack on these problems. (1964:1317)

Others would argue that very little thought was put into the war on poverty and that any plan or strategy for this war was fortuitous and a matter of on-the-spot expediency.[2] Regardless, all the contestants in the war on poverty in San Diego and San Ysidro undertook activities and formulated policies and plans

121

which may be characterized as the tactics and strategies they employed in
attempting to achieve their goals.

In general, tactics and strategies employed by institutions and agents
representative of the national culture were more calculated and planned in
greater detail and depth than those utilized by contestants in the poverty
habitats; they were in large measure also a response to the activities and anticipation of actions of the poor in the arena. Tactics and strategies by contestants
from poverty habitats of San Diego more frequently appear somewhat ill-planned
and poorly calculated. To a great extent, they were expedient responses to
events and policies which emanated from the institutions of the national culture,
and as a result of this expediency no long-range strategies developed within
the poverty habitat.

However, the agents of the national culture, as a result of the
informational flow upward regarding events in the poverty habitat and the
resources they controlled, were generally quite able to develop long-range
strategies and tactics by which to cope with the events in the poverty habitat.
One result of this was that contestants in the poverty habitat were continually
kept off balance by national policies and their problems in understanding
them. This certainly inhibited the development of more efficient strategies and
tactics on their part.

Perhaps most significant in this process were those subtle and
covert factors which influenced events at the level of the poverty habitat but
which were unplanned and undetermined by any of the contestants. They
manifest a "superorganic" quality that represents the outcome of cultural forces
which contestants are unable to perceive or control once they are initiated. They
represent natural emanations resulting from the institutionalization process by
which governmentally supported beaucracies were augmented with additional
personnel and affiliate organizations developed. In large measure, this process had
an enervating and neutralizing effect on the war on poverty.

The tactics and strategies which contestants attempted to implement,
especially those by agents of the poverty habitats, also have to be understood as
adaptations to the power and influence the various contestants controlled. In
a sweeping generalization, one feature of this adaptation is that persons in
poverty undertake activities to achieve their goals with a minimal amount of
planning; among more powerful contestants their actions are planned in detail
and supported by contingency plans in the event something goes awry. The less
power and influence possessed by a contestant, the more erratic and less
calculated his political activity will be; the more power and influence a contestant has the more predictable his tactics and strategies will be.

Contestants such as the EOC of San Diego County, which served as
a political broker intermediate to the national culture and the poverty habitat,
pursued strategies and employed tactics which were both calculated and precise
as well as erratic and expedient depending upon which contestants were being

served at the time. The strategy the EOC followed in pursuit of its goal to eliminate poverty in San Diego County constantly needed to be adjusted to the realities and demands of both the national culture and the poverty habitat. As noted previously, the EOC was in a difficult position. Because of this, particular features of its strategy and tactics were most difficult to ascertain. The EOC did, however, serve primarily as an agent of the national culture and was a significant force in the subtle neutralization of the war on poverty and at the same time it served as a force in attempts to obliterate poverty. In order to exemplify some of these allegations, I will now turn to the tactics and employed by the contestants and their ultimate significance in the integration of poverty habitats into American national culture.

BATTLE PLANS OF THE CONTESTANTS

Expectations of the Brokers

The CAC Staffs and boards charged with organizing communities for action on behalf of the residents of poverty habitats were not without potential resources by which they might have more effectively developed strategies and implemented tactics to achieve their goals. For example, they did have available to them sources of knowledge and training regarding the tactics they could have utilized to accomplish community organization and action. Resource individuals were made available to CAC and delegate agency personnel by the EOC and the federal OEO. They were paid or funded by these offices and held frequent training sessions in San Diego in order to explain the purpose of community organization, the means by which it might be developed, and the tactics which might be used in community action. Many of these individuals were drawn from the ranks of university and college faculties. They most frequently represented establishment-oriented organization men and were of questionable value to the poor. "They just don't speak our language," was a theme reiterated by persons in the poverty habitat.

An organization known as the Western Center for Community Education and Development was funded by the OEO. It distributed personnel throughout the Western OEO region to inform and train people in the skills of community organization, planned war on poverty projects, and developed leadership. Other similar kinds of agencies also supplied personnel for training and informational purposes to members of the community action programs in San Diego. The regional OEO in San Francisco supplied trainers. Such a trainer accompanied Jim Duran in San Ysidro for about a week in order to familiarize him with his duties and to educate him in tactics of community organization.

EOC personnel, such as the director of Area Development, met officially and regularly with CAC personnel and among other things discussed tactics by which their efforts could be made more efficient. Other EOC personnel, such as Mr. Flores with whom the Border Area CAC shared their office, lent their talents on political and community organization and action which were derived from the School of Hard Knocks unofficially to a variety of personnel involved in the community action program. A massive, almost unmanageable, amount of literature was made available to CAC personnel on these matters. Most of it was suggestive and information regarding tactics and strategies had to be gleaned from a tremendous amount of verbiage. Other literature was, however, quite to the point regarding tactics and strategies by which community action might be developed.[3]

In the more successful CACs of San Diego County a case could be made attesting to their success in implementing tactics by which community organization was achieved. However, success of a CAC most frequently was equated with the degree to which its operations in the community resulted in the least amount of problems for the EOC. Successful CACs were conceived of as those which developed programs and undertook activities concerned with problems of local improvement, such as new street lights, paved streets, and area beautification.

In San Diego and elsewhere most such programs mobilize persons around a single issue and then dissolve as soon as the problem is solved.[4] This is not intended to denigrate the value of such activities, but they do not get at the heart of the problem of poverty. At the heart of the problem lies the resistance to change in the basic institutions and structures which have imposed barriers to the participation and integration of persons in poverty habitats into the dominant culture of American society.

Within the war on poverty in San Diego, most attempts to employ tactics to change this condition resulted in conflict within CACs and other agencies, and become an anathema to the EOC and the war on poverty generally. A "safe" strategy for a CAC to follow was to administer services and augment service center functions. This at least did not challenge the basic institutions of American culture.

In San Diego I made phone calls to several of the CACs and explained that I was new in the area and would like information on their program so that I might consider becoming a CAC member. All those that I called indicated that their primary role was in administering services to the community; almost all others with which I was familiar echoed this. Hallman (1968) reports that a poll of the community action program in thirty-five communities revealed that only three were committed to a strategy of giving power to the poor complete with confrontation of and conflict with the establishment; the remainder emphasized improving services to the poor. Apparently this is a national condition.

The tactics and strategies suggested to the CAC staffs by the various trainers followed a few basic themes and these were iterated over and over to them. For a variety of reasons, the CACs were unable to implement these tactics. The reasons for this can be explained in two ways. First, by pointing out

the inapplicability of the tactic suggested as they applied to the CACs generally
and San Ysidro specifically; and, second, by pointing out the factors inherent in
the CAC's strategy of adaptation to the politics of the poverty habitat which
precluded adherence to such tactics and strategies.

Communication: We Talk, You Try to Understand

The strategy the trainers mapped out was basically simple: attack
poverty on a broad front and utilize any realistic means available to accomplish
the goal. In terms of logistics, all the tacticians stressed the need for communications at all levels of the war on poverty agencies and between these agencies and
the private sectors of American society. This always remained a problem in
San Diego, for realistic channels of communication within the war on poverty
agencies as well as between various agencies never developed as they should
have. This was due to many factors.

The English-speakers did not communicate well with the Spanish-
speakers. Language generally becomes the means by which an individual molds
the way in which he conceives of the environment in which he exists. The
objective reality of individuals adapted to conditions in a poverty habitat is, I
submit, different from that of individuals who represent other statuses and
adaptations to American society. [5] This frequently results in people talking
past each other. As one very articulate black put it in a meeting discussing
problems of communication within community action programs in San Diego,
"We hear the words we're all speaking, but we don't listen to the music to which
the words are written; unless we do this, we're in trouble." This problem
plagued the program in San Diego.

For example, the resource individuals who represented training
groups such as the Western Center for Community Education and Development
frequently spoke over the heads of many of the individuals they were expected
to train for community action. The few trainers I met were university faculty
either retired or on leave. All too frequently their major problem was one of
university trained personnel attempting to explain complex problems to people
who, as among many of the war on poverty personnel in San Ysidro, had
considerably less than a high school education. A trainer could, as one did in
attempting to gain rapport with a group of CAC personnel, tell them to "call me
Bob, not Mister Smith," and in the very next breath begin to talk about the
symbols to which influentials representative of the establishment respond and
how persons involved in community organization should learn to manipulate
these symbols to their own advantage! Even on more easily comprehended
practical matters, such as the necessity of rapping on doors in order to talk about
the issues with the people of the arena, there existed an infinite hiatus between
telling people how to do it and the reality of actually doing it. After listening
to one very lucid discussion on these matters, one Border Area CAC staff
member turned to me and whispered, "He don't know what he's talking about."

The war on poverty represents an American middle-class institutional structure by which persons with no skills or background for participating within such a structure were expected to implement revolutionary changes in American society. My observations in San Diego support the argument that there is little evidence to suggest that middle-class people and lower-class people can work effectively together over a long period of time in a citizen organization.[6]

Follow the Leadership: If You Find It

Establishment tacticians spoke at great length of the need to discover the real leaders and influential people of their particular community and involve them in the war on poverty. This, too, is much easier said than done and is conditioned by the cultural perception of who a leader is. From the vantage point of the establishment, officials who, for example, represented the city and county of San Diego or the state of California local leaders were those individuals who shared the value orientation and ideological commitments of the officials themselves. In San Ysidro many such influential Mexican-Americans and Anglos were either participating in or in support of the activities of the San Ysidro Planning Group. Others were busy in party politics for the upcoming election.

The notion that Ramon Cervantes, for example, might be one of the *real* community leaders was alien to them; he was a noisy Mexican who at best had to be placated until such time as a means could be found to short circuit him. Other potential influentials who had been involved in previous issues in San Ysidro, e.g., the annexation to San Diego and the debate which resulted in the rerouting of U.S. Route 5 in 1953 past San Ysidro, simply were not interested in the Border Area CAC or the problems of poverty; they categorically refused to participate and support "lazy bums." A representative from another Mexican-American Community Action Council insisted the Border Area CAC should involve the local priest, because this had been successful in their CAC. When informed that the local priest was not interested, he argued that the Border Area CAC was not trying. When he was invited by the CAC to talk to the local priest on their behalf, he refused. Potential local level influentials in Otay would have nothing to do with the CAC; the blacks of Woodlawn Park had no real influential community members or leaders who could speak for the area as a whole. Even in San Ysidro there was no consensus among the population regarding who the real community leaders were. Ramon Cervantes who had the largest and most cohesive following in the arena certainly did not speak for the community at large, despite his extravagant claims. However, just as the activities of the San Ysidro Planning Group filled a vacuum in the arena, so too did the lack of any real indigenous community leadership promote the emergence of the PFTA and the degree of power that Ramon Cervantes acquired.

Oscar Lewis has suggested that the culture of poverty is a shallow culture. Without engaging in a polemic over the value of the concept of a culture

of poverty, his reference to the shallowness of the culture of peoples who exist
in poverty habitats is not totally without foundation, although much of the
argument must center around how the term "culture" is defined in this context.
Still, one feature of the culture concept is the organization of human relationships by which persons interact, relate to each other and come to grips with the
problems that have to be solved in order for the culture of their society to
persist. Such organization may be said to be composed of the status slots and
role activities actors undertake in their culture. With reference to the status and
role of leaders, one has to be impressed with the depth and magnitude of such
actors in all of the institutions which constitute the complexity of American
national culture. However, it is easy to overlook the fact that this role depth
characteristic of the dominant culture is lacking in poverty habitats. It is
not only difficult to find individuals who will play leadership roles; frequently
they don't exist. And if they do the shallowness of this aspect of the culture
of persons in poverty habitats is manifest in the fact that only one or two
individuals would have to be eliminated in order to create chaos and disunity
and the possible demise of the particular poverty organization itself.

In San Ysidro some people hostile to the development of the
community spoke openly against the San Ysidro Planning Group and many
knew the powerful figures who were involved in it. Several of these individuals
could have been eliminated and the Planning Group would have continued;
some had already dropped out after their particular goals were achieved.
However, those hostile to the PFTA spoke only of disposing of the one individual, Ramon Cervantes, in order to destroy the organization itself: had this
happened I have no doubt that the organization would have crumbled. Also,
there was the problem of obtaining a good executive secretary for the CAC from
among poverty peoples. Due to a history of racism, social and other types of
segregation, a variety of barriers to participation in educational, economic, and
political institutions of American national culture, role depth anywhere near
comparable to that characteristic of the national culture is simple nonexistent in
poverty habitats. It is in this one respect, at least, that the culture of a poverty
habitat may be considered "shallow."

Tacticians argued that leadership in the poverty habitat can be
developed as a concomitant result of community organization. Trainers representing the EOC, OEO, and other groups suggested very simple procedures
by which this could be achieved. Implementing these procedures was an entirely
different matter.

A major procedure was that one person, interested in and concerned
over the community's problems, should begin by involving a couple of friends,
for example, and charge each of them to contact a few of his friends and attempt
to interest them in the community's problems. This nucleus should then
organize community block parties in which they explain the problems and
attempt to elicit support for them and in this way expand their base of power.

It is also very important to contact influential local people and enlist their support in solving these problems. Obviously there will be people who disagree or are not interested.

More than one problem and objective should be available to the organization at all times. In this way varying interests represented by the growing organization may be stimulated and support obtained. The variety of interests represented in the community will permit larger coalitions of groups acting in support of each other over their various mutual as well as discrete problems. In the event of a large, communitywide problem the organization is there to cope with it.

Also, small easily achieved objectives, e.g., installing a stop sign, should not be overlooked. In this way results of community action will always be visible and serve as attractions to others as yet uninvolved. Accomplishing a few "easy" goals will eventually result in the development of a sense of community power and increasingly larger problems may be confronted. A natural outgrowth of this program will be a knowledgeable and powerful indigenous leadership in control of a viable community organization; presumably, in this case, a CAC.

People in the Border Area CAC understood this tactical process and strategy, but many factors militated against its implementation and success. There was no rapport between the communities which made up the Border Area CAC. There were too many specific and vested interests represented in it. To undertake such a program demanded strong commitment. Very few had this, and those that did all too often were considered dissidents within their community. It meant that individuals would have to take risks which might cost them their status and prestige in the community.

Sally Horton, the last executive secretary of the Border Area CAC, was aware of this in her confrontation with the San Ysidro Elementary School District over the EMR program. When the dangers and problems of attacking the school district were suggested to her—possible hostility from the community, the EOC, and other agencies; lack of board support; perhsps even the loss of her job—she argued it really didn't make much difference; the CAC was worthless as it existed at the time and this issue couldn't make things any worse for her or the CAC, and it might possibly do some good.

Community organization offered the people nothing that was immediately tangible, and a commitment to it was a commitment to the frustration of a long, arduous task against which odds for success were not favorable.

Services and Support: The Easy Road

Administering services, on the other hand, was immediate and practical and became an important means of marshalling political support in the arena. Esmerelda Hurtado, the CAC aide in San Ysidro, was aware of this. Her altruistic arguments about helping the poor were always couched in the reality of the credit she was storing away and which could be cashed in at an opportune time.[7] Many of those who supported the PFTA and the struggle of Mrs. Hurtado to become executive secretary were recruited as a result of the services she rendered to them. The trainers also recommended this strategy and argued that services were good bargaining points; in exchange for them, persons could be pressured to join a community organization. However, the pitfall of service delivery becoming an end in itself was too great to be easily avoided. Mrs. Hurtado managed this more skillfully than most others in the arena and stole the thunder of the CAC by bargaining her services for support of herself and the PFTA at the expense of the CAC.

Administering a service can prove to be a viable tactic for marshalling political support, but there are also fragile characteristics inherent in the strategy. Personality is an important factor. Yolanda Chaca, the director of the MAAC service center in San Ysidro, believed that she had the support of the community in her struggle with John Diaz, especially the San Ysidro Mothers' Club to whom she extended services at the expense of the community at large. However, she discovered that the services were accepted by the mothers, but she was not. They disliked her as a person. Mrs. Hurtado, on the other hand, was "of the people" and support for her, even beyond the membership of the PFTA, was widespread.

Still, in the adaptations people make to a poverty habitat, support itself is derived from relationships which are personal, face to face, and reciprocal.[8] They also proved to be fragile, capricious and rather shallow. Relationships and alliances sever easily because so many issues and activities directly affect one's job, the services he could expect from agencies, and his livelihood generally.

In San Ysidro and other poverty habitats people were quick to rally to a cause, but just as quickly such support dissolved under the problem of surviving each day. The city hall demonstration is indicative of the mushrooming of support and its rapid demise in San Ysidro. Even the PFTA leadership had to generate a series of issues and maintain a barrage of propaganda in order to maintain support. As Coleman (1957) has pointed out, one characteristic of contests for power in communities is an escalation of conflict in which issues become generalized and attacks personalized. In San Ysidro this was one means by which the PFTA honed the conflict to a point where a nucleus of support always existed. As the more general issue over improving the housing conditions in San Ysidro and taking over the CAC seemed to wane as persons again had to confront the realities of living in a poverty habitat, the PFTA launched personal attacks against specific individuals who were typed and became known as enemies of the community. Even this personalization of attacks began to lose its effect on the community for the PFTA and it was the spray of other tactics it used—letters, threats, exaggerations, rumors—not any massive community support, which forced the EOC to capitulate and which ultimately split the CAC.

Support for political actions among the Anglos and other contestants in the arena were different than for the Mexican-Americans and the PFTA. Allegiance was given generally by the Anglos to institutions more representative of American national culture, such as the San Ysidro Planning Group, or the city government of San Diego, and the ideologies which gave meaning and value to these institutions. During the conflict over the CAC, when support from Anglo board members for individuals such as the community aide or executive secretary was critical, such support proved capricious and ephemeral in contrast to that given by the PFTA.

In comparison to the Mexican-Americans, it seemed as though the Anglos found the whole conflict personally degrading. To the Anglos local level, politics operated most sensibly not within the poverty habitat but at the level of city hall, the corporate government. Support for a party candidate was comprehensible to them. They did not seem to understand that support for individuals in the politics in which they were involved in the poverty habitat was equally essential.

Adaptation and Reality: Who's Got the Resources

Other strategies were suggested to the community action personnel that were equally difficult to implement. Trainers argued that the CAC should appeal to the self-interests of various groups of the community, regardless of their attitude to the war on poverty, and in this way attempt to win them over to their side. Some CACs were successful in this, but only to the extent, it appeared to me, that the interest group was already committed to the war on poverty or stood to gain from participation. In San Ysidro the few groups that did exist which potentially might work with the CAC in some community action were generally hostile to the CAC.

The San Ysidro Planning Group, for example, was not willing to involve itself in such programs. The values of most of its members were antithetically opposed to such involvement. Their commitment to serving the poor of the community was to develop the community and relocate the poor in apartment complexes which the poor of the community made clear, as revealed in the San Ysidro Report, they did not want. Rather than try to work with the community to solve this problem, the San Ysidro Planning Group seemed to withdraw even farther from the community. For example, they rejected and suppressed the very study which they had commissioned in order to understand better the desires of the community regarding the redevelopment. To win over such a group to the concept of community action through an antipoverty agency was virtually impossible, even though members of it also served on the CAC. The gulf in terms of the cultural patterns, values, beliefs, ideologies, and organizational allegiances to which these various groups were committed effectively precluded a rapprochement for any real community action.

Trainers also suggested that the representatives of the poor infiltrate such groups by joining them or making themselves heard at their meetings. Over a hundred years ago de Tocqueville spoke of the propensity of Americans to "constantly form associations." This is still generally true today. However, such organization does not seem to be especially characteristic of poor people, nor are Mexican-Americans especially prone to organize or infiltrate such associations.[9] The suggestions of the trainers often indicated their middle-class status in American society.

A strategy has to be relevant to those expected to implement it and, with reference to the advice of the trainers, this was not the case in the Border Area CAC. The war on poverty did stimulate the development of ethnic and poverty organizations such as CACs. Even in these, however, participation was low. There seemed to be even greater reluctance among poor contestants in San Ysidro to participate in such associations outside the context of the war on poverty institutions. The identity of the poor is with the poverty habitat. The adaptations they make are in accord with its realities. The world beyond that habitat for many of the poor is vast, threatening, unknown, and unknowable.

The tactics and strategies spelled out in detail by the trainers did not work for a variety of complex and intermeshed reasons in San Ysidro. As a blanket statement their advice could be considered too middle class and as such it did not fit the reality of the poverty habitat. Poverty contestants in the arena were forced to adapt their tactics and strategy to the resources they had at hand and upon which their power was founded. In this light, many of the tactics which seemed "dirty" and strategies which seemed ill-conceived are made comprehensible.

Yolanda Chaca frequently spoke of the people involved in the CAC as being "unsophisticated." In private she also said they were "stupid." After these "unsophisticated" and "stupid" people had achieved their goal of having her fired from the MAAC center she accused them of playing "dirty." In one of my early meetings with some CAC staff personnel, I referred in a similar fashion to how unsophisticated the people seemed to me at the meetings and discussions I had attended. My research very nearly terminated at that point.

"They're not stupid and they're not unsophisticated," one of the staff said to me angrily. "They're resource poor, that's all. And they don't know how to get any resources. And neither do we," he added sadly, "short of revolution."

Resources and Ethnic Identity: Who Are We?

The paucity of resources available to the Mexican-Americans in the poverty habitat conditioned all the political tactics in the arena. It may be postulated that this resource paucity was instrumental in ethnic alignments of the arena. The opposing contestants were most clearly delimited in ethnic terms. The "rich Anglos," however, were attacked no more viciously, frequently less so, than other Mexican-Americans, e.g., Mr. De La Torre and Mr. De Leon, of the

San Ysidro Planning Group; Mrs. Dominguez, the CAC clerk-typist; the director of Area Development; Delia Garcia; and others who stood outside the cultural identity prescribed by the ethnicity which underwrote the PFTA. The ethnic identity to which the PFTA adhered provided a culturally standardized rhetoric for their propaganda, an easily definable set of values, a symbol system, and an ideology expressed in terms of the denial of the rights of the poor Mexican-American of San Ysidro. A relatively powerful resource base was founded upon this ethnic identity and, as such, the stress placed upon this factor by the PFTA may be considered a kind of covert strategy by which they attempted to develop a power base which might otherwise not be possible. Once this base was established, all other tactics utilized by the Mexican-Americans were based upon the reality of their ethnic identity.

One man, Ramon Cervantes, and six to eight hard-core followers held the PFTA organization together and, at times, composed its total active membership. In terms of role differentiation and specialization it was truly a shallow organization. It maintained and obtained support for its activities by the only tactic available to it; it gave services coupled with effective propaganda at the expense of the service center and CAC which should have utilized the same tactics to develop their following. On more than one occasion the PFTA discredited the service offered by these agencies in order that they might offer the service to the individual.

For example, they confused the times at which people were promised by the CAC or service center to have things done, or of meetings at which some problem was to be discussed, and then attacked the efficiency of these agencies and their value to the community. Their leader's demanded impossible tasks of the CAC and service center, such as having a member's husband repatriated after deportation. While they could also do nothing, they were able as Mexican-Americans with pipelines into the community (which neither the CAC nor service center had) to again point out the other agencies' ineffectiveness.

Tactics of the Poor: A Bluff Hand

Even prior to my research, the Mexican-Americans, many of whom eventually joined the PFTA, were notorious for initiating petitions over a variety of community problems. They requested that the CAC be closed, that the service center director be removed, that certain school officials be replaced, that more street lights be added to the community, that more efficient bus service be implemented, etc. Their requests were to no avail. At the first Mayor's Meeting held in San Ysidro, the mayor pointed out that petitions are regarded as suspect by the city because of the ease with which signatures may be obtained. It may be coincidental, but very few petitions originated in San Ysidro after this and a new tactic emerged; letters complaining about a number of problems, often exaggerated in a number of ways, began to flow to officials at all levels of American government, to the office of the war on poverty and to the president of Mexico.

In the absence of resources, such as political skill, prestige, and money, a well-planned letter campaign of the sort initiated in San Ysidro can be effective. The letters which the PFTA distributed so widely and prolifically ranged over a variety of topics, from hard and real facts to vicious and slanderous attacks on individuals and groups, to extravagant claims regarding the power of the PFTA. They questioned the legitimacy and value of the CAC, the federal funds used to support it, and the morality of its staff. The quantity of letters and the intensity of their propaganda and rhetoric resulted in officials at a variety of levels paying attention to San Ysidro. Even though by late fall of 1968 the power and influence of the PFTA was waning in the community as people tired of its abusive tactics, probably no other PFTA tactic was as significant in forcing the EOC to split the CAC and turn it over to Mexican-American control.

Threats and accusations were also an important PFTA tactic, and since they succeeded in preventing Mrs. Dominguez from obtaining citizenship, they acquired a certain degree of validity. Despite its questionable virtue, the attack upon Mrs. Dominguez was actually a shrewd move on their part. Persons such as Jim Duran, Sally Horton, Mrs. Osmond, and others were more than a little concerned by the seeming irrationality of the PFTA.

However, irrationality is also culturally defined. In their bold and overt attack on Mrs. Dominguez, one of the most vulverable persons in the community and one that not many people in the community would miss or feel terribly sorry for, the PFTA risked very little of its prestige. Ramon Cervantes stressed and reiterated as a propaganda technique that a person who was despised by the community and was refused American citizenship had no business being employed by a federal agency, the CAC. This gave some validity to their argument that rather than serving the people, this public agency was actually demonstrating its disdain for the people by employing such a person.

These arguments served their long-range goals against the CAC and proved to be a skillful way of rallying support among certain members of the community as well as turning many against the CAC. The effects the charges in the letters over this issue had on individuals in upper echelon agencies can only be guessed. It was known that the EOC was under pressure to do something as a result of the quantity of letters. Most significantly, in this incident the PFTA demonstrated its power and established its reputation as a force in the arena. The PFTA demonstrates that they could destroy a person, and the accompanying implicit threat was that they could also destroy the CAC. After this, threats became a daily tactic. Threats were made on persons' lives, threats were made to picket the post office where the CAC board president was employed, to close the CAC, and so forth. None of these proposed events materialized, but the threats caused considerable personal stress and eventually undermined the ability of the Border Area CAC to function.

Letter writing campaigns, demonstrations, exaggerated propaganda, threats, and walkouts are not the tactics of stupid, unsophisticated people. They are, rather, examples of the adaptations in political activity that persons in a poverty habitat have to make given the resources available to them. To the agents of the national culture whose politics are certainly no less "clean" but who are more likely to practice their assassinations with a smile, a handshake, and stereotyped manners, they may seem crude and gross. They also were disturbing to the establishment because they often smacked of potential violence. However, there is little evidence that the poor are revolutionary, despite the way the dominant culture may view them.[10] Their problems are immediate and their immediate interest is in solving them.

How to Draw to an Inside Straight—And Make It
This is not meant to imply that the poor cannot become revolutionary. The dearth of their resources has, in most cases outside of black ghettos, impeded any meaningful confrontation with the dominant culture. Despite its many failures, one success of the war on poverty is the increased cognizance of many poor persons of their political potential. They are developing a constituency, a support base for future political action. Increasing numbers are being trained in political tactics and strategies. As they gather resources and power, they well may become a significant force in American culture.

For example, the political activities of the Mexican-American in the arena of San Ysidro are in some ways a microcosmic representation of the re-emergence of Mexican-American politics in the Southwest generally. Mexican-Americans have been notorious for their lack of political initiative, but it has not always been this way and an exaggerated myth regarding their political complacency has developed. Mexican-Americans may not yet be willing to riot and burn to obtain their goals, but there has been a significant rebirth of Mexican-American political activity to which relatively little attention has been paid by the establishment.[11]

In San Diego County there has been a significant emergence of Mexican-American political organization. Most importantly, they are not fighting each other but are cooperating in attempts to solve the variety of problems Mexican-Americans, especially those in poverty, confront. Despite the disclaimers of young Chicano radicals, much of this Mexican-American political resurgence has been due to the sitmulus provided by the war on poverty. Although Mexican-Americans, such as those in San Ysidro, are still forced to improvise political tactics due to a lack of resources, they have more resources now than in the past, plus additional expertise in utilizing them and developing others. It is doubtful they will be willing to relinquish what they have achieved.

It is also worth pointing out the role of women in Mexican-American politics in San Ysidro and San Diego as a significant element. As suggested throughout this work, Mexican-American women are involved in a variety of political activities. They are not passive. They do not meekly bow to male authorities in the Anti-Poverty Program. In fact, women of all ethnic categories are significant participants in the politics of the poverty habitats in San Diego County. Several factors account for this phenomenon.

The female activists were either single, i.e., had no consorts for a variety of reasons such as voluntary and involuntary estrangement, divorce, death; or were attempting to supplement their husbands' income. Career options open to Mexican-American women in poverty habitats are severely restricted. Menial domestic positions are a common form of employment. Welfare provides a solution for some. The war on poverty offered respectable employment with no discrimination according to ethnicity, religion, or sex, and women were quick to take advantage of this. Wages for many positions were also quite low and this attracted females rather than aspiring males. Females also fitted quite well into the "caretaker" relationships which many of the war on poverty institutions fostered. Finally, in post-World War II United States, as traditional sex roles became blurred in the adaptations the population made to career specializations in an industrial society, an increasing number of women have infiltrated traditional male employment categories. Women in policy-making and power positions in the war on poverty may be considered one more manifestation of the increased comingling of sex roles in occupational categories in the complex industrial society the United States currently represents.

Anglos in the Arena: The Hollow Men

The other contestants in the arena contrasted sharply to the PFTA in terms of their strategy and tactics. The blacks from Woodlawn Park and the Mexican-Americans from Otay, except for a few members of the CAC board, were only marginally involved in the conflict. Only Mrs. Osmond from Otay carried on the conflict with the PFTA to the end. After the blacks of Woodlawn Park were accused by the PFTA of coming into San Ysidro by the carload, they participated very little. When it became obvious that the Border Area CAC was going to be split, they again became interested, but only regarding what they might obtain for Woodlawn Park as a result of the split.

The overriding factor which mediated Anglo participation in the arena was that few of them were poor; almost all shared a middle-class status in American society and maintained values and beliefs congruent with that status. They happened to live within the boundaries of the poverty habitat, largely because of the agreeable climate, and they participated in the community action program primarily because it was their civic duty. Some of them simply had nothing better to do with their time. Others adhered strongly to the best—and worst—traditions of a caretaker ideology regarding the poor.

In the arena, the Anglos as an aggregate developed no real strategy or tactic to cope with the emerging conflict. With the "sophistication" due their status they identified strongly with the corporate organizations of the EOC, the city government, of the San Ysidro Planning Group, all of which fitted more precisely than the CAC their particular value and cultural systems. They were oriented to the kind of corporate identity these organizations provided and functioned more securely within it.

For those on the CAC Board of Directors the gray area, the structural incongruity as they perceived it between the CAC and the EOC was a worrisome problem. Although they had the power of independent action in a variety of problem areas, in times of crisis they refused to take action without EOC approval. When the EOC held back, this was interpreted as desertion and they floundered, wondering what next to do. Delia Garcia played this to her advantage, giving advice to them or withholding it or information to the EOC or withholding it as this best suited her ends at the moment. The EOC was often in the position of responding to problems in the Border Area CAC with insufficient knowledge at hand. The result was confusion and increased distrust of the EOC by the CAC. This uneven relationship between the CAC and EOC precluded the development of any Anglo leadership. In comparison, the PFTA whose leadership and membership was largely unfamiliar with American corporate institutions was unencumbered by a concern for any real or imagined gray area in some abstract structural entity. They attacked as fitted their immediate purpose. Only after the CAC was split did their lack of familiarity with the EOC and the war on poverty generally become a matter of concern to them.

The Anglos were appalled at the tactics of the PFTA. It was quite beneath them to consider such tactics on their own behalf. For example, the night the PFTA membership walked out of the CAC meeting, the board members present caucused and decided to fire Mrs. Hurtado and impeach Ramon Cervantes and the PFTA members. Delia Garcia suggested that they would avoid problems and aid the cuase of the CAC if they impeached the PFTA members first and fired Mrs. Hurtado some time after that. In this way, Delia argued, because of the wide community support Mrs. Hurtado had, they would be able to obtain more easily the two-third majority necessary to impeach the PFTA members at a general meeting. Also, with the proper rumor and gossip, they might be able to convince the PFTA that Mrs. Hurtado, one of their stalwarts, had in fact conspired against them. This, Delia Garcia argued, would split and weaken the general membership of the PFTA because many of its members were quite sympathetic to Mrs. Hurtado for the services she provided. Later, after the break up of the PFTA and at their convenience, they could fire her. Only one black from Woodlawn Park thought this was a good idea. All the others rejected it as a "dirty" way of doing things.[12] The tactic they finally employed, firing the community aide first, resulted in the period of intense conflict in the arena.

The primary tactic employed by the Anglos in the conflict was to attempt to enlist the aid and support of organizations with which they were most familiar. Few of these agencies served the beleaguered Anglos very well. Until its decision to split the CAC, the EOC gave little support or solace to them. The police were contacted regarding the actions of the PFTA, but could do nothing unless there was a crime committed, which there was not. The threatening phone calls to Jim Duran and Mrs. Osmond were denied by the PFTA. Beyond that, most threats, such as picketing the CAC office, were not illegal.

The Anglos received sympathy from members of the San Ysidro Planning Group, but little else. The CAC members who were in the planning group were angry at the PFTA, but other members of the planning group frequently seemed to see the whole affair as a kind of joke and not really worthy of their interest. After firing Mrs. Hurtado and impeaching the PFTA members, the only positive strategy the Anglos developed, and it was covert and by default, was to refuse, upon advice from the Legal Aid Society, to answer the charges made by the PFTA in the hope that everything would eventually die down. Obviously, it did not.

Networks of support among the Anglo contestants were almost non-existent, and attempts to develop them rarely materialized. In the struggle between Sally Horton and Esmerelda Hurtado over succession to the office of executive secretary the PFTA firmly supported Mrs. Hurtado; although the Anglos voted Mrs. Horton into office, she was not certain of their support until the vote was taken. She later argued that if the Anglos had not become so mad at the PFTA at that meeting they probably would have supported Mrs. Hurtado merely to avoid further struggles with them. After assuming office, Mrs. Horton never fully enjoyed the support of her board, and it was the Anglo board members, bolstered by the selection of Tex Stillman as a replacement for one of the impeached PFTA members, who forced the vote by which Mrs. Hurtado was rehired. As I have discussed, this victory for the PFTA effectively destroyed Sally Horton's authority and placed her in an impossible position.

Other than the demonstration planned before city hall, the only other strategy with any potential of making the CAC work was the confrontation Mrs. Horton generated with the San Ysidro Elementary School District. This became her own personal, one-woman crusade in the name of the CAC due to the lack of Anglo support. This same lack of support was significant in undermining her efforts. Had she been supported, it is conceivable that she would have been able to withstand the PFTA attacks and possibly develop a base of support for the CAC. Alone, without support, this was impossible. The Anglos again gave allegiance to a familiar institution. The superintendent of the school district was respected by the Anglo board members. Two, Mr. Von Lutz and Tex Stillman, served with him on the San Ysidro Planning Group. The schools generally, as well as representing sacred institutions, were doing an excellent job from the Anglos' point of view.[13]

Support is an important resource. As money in a bank account, it may be built up as credit among persons to whom favors or services are given and drawn upon when needed. The PFTA built credit by giving services. There was little the Anglos needed and thus no way for those who needed Anglo support, such as Mrs. Horton, to build up anything other than moral support, one of the least effective and satisfying kinds of support. The executive secretary could only appeal to their values and honest intentions and attempt to sway them to her side by word and deed. The actions of the PFTA undercut her at every turn by keeping the Anglos off balance and frequently afraid. As the conflict heightened, the Anglos reacted by identifying even more strongly with those institutions and organizations representative of the dominant American culture whose values and ideologies they represented and understood.

INTEGRATION

The Pious Wish

The strategies and tactics employed by the contestants representative of the mainstream of American culture are most critical in the process by which poverty habitats may be integrated into the nation. Ultimately this process is contingent upon the actions of contestants whose ideologies, beliefs, and value systems are congruent with those of the national culture. They are most significant as a force in this process because, from the sanctity of the national institutions with which they are affiliated, they control the access of persons in poverty habitats to these institutions and the national culture generally. The insulation from the reality of poverty afforded mainstream agents of the national culture by these institutional havens imbues their strategies with confidence. In poverty habitats such confidence has to develop over time as minor victories over inequities in the system dispel disillusionment and very slowly build into more major achievements. In competition with persons in poverty habitats contestants representative of the national culture seem to be aware that their actions will generate some static. This was so with the San Ysidro Planning Group. They are also confident that they will persevere and achieve their ends because, as members of the San Ysidro Planning Group believed, what they are doing is good and right for the community.

The vast majority of the population in American society has made a successful adaptation to the industrial level of sociocultural integration that the national culture represents. The structure of cultural patterns abstracted from the behavior of persons in poverty habitats is a result of their lack of integration into the national culture and may be considered as an adaptation to a pre-industrial level of sociotechnological integration. Schatzman and Strauss (1966) argue that there are cultural and cognitive differences between social classes and that lower-class persons who are given the opportunity to absorb middle-class culture cannot do so without at least attempting to begin the social climb upward. To begin the route upward through the stratification system is one aspect of what the politics of persons in poverty habitats is all about.

Valentine (1968) argues that one characteristic of persons in poverty is that they aspire to middle-class American values and desiderata. It seems, however, that before they can achieve these their political power has to grow in order that the structural and institutional changes in the national culture that so many persons saw promised by the war on poverty may be effected. Until then the nation's "urban peasants" who are marginally involved in the means of production and share minimally in the rewards of distribution, such as the Mexican-Americans of San Ysidro, will manifest in their kinship relationships, peer group influences, techniques for social control, and intragroup interaction patterns adapted to a level of culture more or less distinct from mainstream American national culture.

Even though persons adapted to different levels of social integration may exist within the same national environment, one important concomitant of these adaptions is the kind and degree of political power they will control. There are simply more, as well as different, resources available to contestants who represent the dominant national culture. As such, the political tactics and strategies of the contestants will vary. This is demonstrable in an innovation such as the war on poverty which, although grounded in and predicated upon the values of the national culture, demanded a confrontation of contestants representative of these different adaptations.

The uneven balance of power, however, results in the fact that the terms by which a poverty habitat will be integrated will be those dictated by agents of the national culture. The only way these terms may be negotiated will be when sufficient pressure emanates from the poverty habitat and is applied in such a way to agents of the national culture that it cannot be ignored.

However, there are several critical factors which tend to limit the amount of power poor ethnic populations may achieve. One is based upon the restricted access the poor have to the rewards which may be derived from participation in America's national institutions. This results in a concomitant disenfranchisement which perpetuates a strata in the society which is ill-equipped socially, economically, educationally, and cognitively to participate meaningfully in the American sociocultural system. Another more subtle factor derives from a demographic consideration and which will increasingly stabilize the political efficacy of America's ethnic poor.

Although a few American cities have either elected or come close to electing black mayors, and a few blacks and Mexican-Americans have been elected to state and national political office, these populations are not strategically dispersed in sufficient number to alter the traditional power alignments in the United States. Nor does it appear that ethnic minority representatives can become significant agents in promoting change in their constituent's social and economic conditions, because in order to survive themselves they have to become skilled bargainers and compromisers and give as much if not more to the establishment then they receive in return. It is likely that as voter strength increases blacks and possibly Mexican-Americans may for a while elect mayors of some fairly large city and increase their state and federal representation. However, this has limited potential for political change. First, they are numerically inferior in the society. Second, they will find themselves increasingly in control of large urban poverty habitats whose ethnic poor will have limited resources and power, restricted potential to increase these, and thus limited means by which to effect their own destiny within the traditional American sociopolitical and cultural system.

There is one final factor which will influence their ability to alter their socioeconomic plight. Ethnic political activity is also to some extent distinct from that of poor persons and actually may not serve the poor. For one thing, ethnic politicians are susceptible to the good life American has to offer and as such frequently and quickly lose their affiliation with their poor ethnic counterparts. Politicians also tend to serve their constituents, their voting public, and people in a state of hard core poverty do not vote. It is very likely then that segments of ethnic categories within the nation may be more quickly integrated into American national culture—or achieve successful adaptations outside of it, but in a nonpoverty condition—than will those populations—blacks, Mexican-Americans, Indians, Anglo-Americans, and others—who exist in a condition of hard core poverty.

Although there has then been some change, persons in poverty still are largely powerless. However, it appears that the nation's ethnic minorities, especially blacks, are beginning to apply such pressures that most politicians today do not feel that they can ignore with the disdain of the past current ethnic minority demands. It is perhaps not so much a fear of ethnic political power but rather of their potential social explosiveness that prompts this deference.

In short, although one important attribute of the ideology of American national culture is a desirable state of national sociocultural unity, and one important means of obtaining this end is ideologically thought to be the realization of ethnic minority integration, the factors seem to suggest that there will be some integration of the nation's ethnic poor, but only so much and no more. Certain categories of persons from more inclusive ethnic categories may be integrated, but not all will be, and for good reasons. This I think, can be demonstrated in the interplay between the strategies and tactics of the poverty habitat and other levels of the national political system and the implications of this interplay for integration of the poverty habitat into the nation.

A number of social scientists present evidence from a variety of situations in support of the premise presented above. Their data suggests that the strategy of adaptation of persons in poverty habitats is a result of a variety of forces and conditions beyond their control. Warren (1956) argues that many aspects of community living are determined in whole or partly by decisions made outside the community by policies and procedures of state or national organizations, by state and federal laws and by developments in national economy. In actual fact this determination of community life may begin much closer to the local community through groups and agencies which in terms of their value and ideologies may be considered agents of the national culture. The San Ysidro Planning Group is one such agent.

Gans argues that because of the power influential people exert through strong interest and lobby groups, they have undue representation at top levels of government where decisions are made; "as a result legislation tends to favor the interests of the organized; of businessmen, not consumers; doctors, not patients" (1969:11). From the outset the poverty habitats were regarded by the agents of the national culture as patients whose ills should be cured for some vague national ideal; really the cure was for the interests of the "doctors" and "caretakers." For example, Harrington (1968) argues that despite claims of the federal government in adherence to the national ideology of the Protestant ethic, private industry will not alleviate the problems of poverty habitats simply because there is no profit in such ventures.

Captains of industry in various parts of the United States have attested to the fact that an altruistic concern for poverty is not an ethic of the business-profit motive. The manager of LTV Aerospace Corporation's Vought Aeronautics Division in San Antonio said, "LTV doesn't just open plants for altruistic purposes." A Vice president of a control data corporation plant in a Minneapolis slum argued that this is "not an example of do-goodism, but the result of a business decision by CDC executive council." And, as noted previously, a San Diego businessman strongly suggested that giving jobs to the poor "to get them off the streets . . . isn't the American free enterprise way of doing things."[14]

In specifically discussing the economic exploitation of Mexican-Americans as a strategy of industry in the Southwest and elsewhere, Carey McWilliams point out that in the late 1940s industries in the Southwest "consistently pursued a policy of isolating Mexicans as a means of holding them to certain limited categories of work. Systematically discouraging all 'outside contacts", they have kept Mexicans segregated by occupation and by residence" (1968:187). If the total budget of the war on poverty, which was always less than two billion dollars, is considered, it can be argued that even the government which initiated the program was not about to invest too much or anywhere near enough, to combat and cure the ills of poverty and meaningfully effect an integration of poverty habitats into the nation's social structure. As one anti-poverty worker remarked to me, "The war on poverty budget may be considered the drop that hit the bucket."

Similar activities, I am certain, could be documented for other ethnic groups in other parts of the United States. One result of these activities has been the perpetuation of poverty habitats.[15] Such exploitations are in violation of laws, morals, and ethics, but seem more frequently than not to be sanctioned, or ignored, by the national culture. As Blouner argues:

> . . . . various processes and practices of exclusion, rejection and sub-jugation based on color (and ethnicity) are built into the major public institutions (labor market, education, political, and law enforcement) with the effect of maintaining special privileges, power and values for the benefit of the white majority. (1970:355)

Several authors in Bloomberg and Schmandt (1968) echo this charge. And Walinsky perhaps get to the roots of the matter when he argues:

> . . . the poor are, by definition, without economic power; except for the Negroes, they are without effective leaders; they are only one fifth of a nation, *and the rest of the country is roughly satisfied with things as they are* (emphasis added). (1965:159)

Why should the other four-fifths of the nation not be satisfied? They have achieved a successful adaptation within habitats in the national environment of the United States through the daily roles they play as they participate in the institutions within which American national culture has its roots. The effects of the decisions made by the heads of economic, political, religious, educational, communication media, and other institutions upon populations who represent the national culture, on the one hand, and the poverty habitats, on the other, are quite different. Such decisions represent national cultural policies which, by and large, benefit and merely reaffirm the integration and identity of the majority population of the society with the nation as a whole. Those decisions may also result in the sudden unemployment of thousands of persons within poverty habitats across the nation in response to economic or political imperatives that are for the good of the nation as a whole.

As Cohen (1968a) suggests, processes of adaptation serve the majority population and are always, biologically or culturally, disadvantageous to a few members of the population. The disadvantaged in the national environment of the United States are those populations which reside in its poverty habitats. The strategy which underlies these national cultural policies becomes distinct and obvious when, through their implementation by agents of American culture, they are revealed in contrast to the culture and society adapted to the nation's poverty habitats. This can be demonstrated within the context of the poverty habitat of San Ysidro and the political oppositions which were manifest in its arena.

As noted, the San Ysidro Planning Group may be considered an agent of American national culture. Their activities and goals, though unkown to many of the people of San Ysidro, indirectly stimulated more conflict in the arena than any other single factor. While the interest and concern of the planning group was indisputably over San Ysidro's future, it was San Ysidro as an abstraction as they conceived it at some future time and not in terms of the real ingredient which gives any cultural habitat its character—the people. Prior to this proposed development, San Ysidro had been victimized, although to a lesser extent, by an earlier development program.

In 1953 the State of California planned to run U.S. Interstate 5 through San Ysidro and dissect it on an east-west axis, just as the current freeway will dissect it on a north-south axis. At that time the citizens fought the issue and were successful in having the freeway rerouted farther west. Although this dissected the community less equally, it did cut through the poorest area of San Ysidro. For example, children from the Bolton Hall area have to go to school via an underpass beneath the freeway and in the winters this is frequently flooded. The currently proposed freeway will eliminate this problem in two ways: First, an elevated walk ramp over the freeway will replace the underpass and, second, the Bolton Hall district and the other poorer areas of San Ysidro will simply be obliterated.

One of the arguments used in favor of running U.S. 5 through San Ysidro was that it would stimulate community growth. In fact, it tended to isolate San Ysidro. Travelers who previously had to go through the community on their way to Mexico now simply went by San Ysidro faster and a severe economic slump afflicted the community. All the road signs now point either to Tijuana or San Diego; none to San Ysidro.

The currently planned freeway will cut up San Ysidro even more. This time urban growth will follow in its wake, because the current plan is to develop the entire area.[16] As we have seen, the San Ysidro Planning Group is not only instrumental in this, but their past actions indicate that they will attempt to avoid any confrontation with the community which would alter this redevelopment, largely because of the deep economic interests they have in the area. The threat of controversy certainly affects their decisions. For example, their suppression of the San Ysidro Community Survey exemplified the lengths to which they would attempt to avoid conflict with the community and protect their interests. In their terms this is justified because they are regarded as a legitimate agency by the established power structure and their actions are supported by value and life styles which are derivatives of American national culture. They act without public or community support, involvement, or knowledge because they represent a legitimate power in the arena and their actions are sanctioned by the national cultural ideology of the United States.

The people of San Ysidro and those in other poverty habitats of the United States do not have these cultural advantages. Marris (1963) points out in assessing redevelopment in five American cities—Chicago, Philadelphia, Baltimore, Minneapolis, and San Francisco—that approximately 80 percent of the families who are relocated are nonwhite, and the remainder represent minority cultures, e.g., immigrants from Appalachia. He also points out that the accommodations made for those relocated has provided only marginally better housing, in very similar neighborhoods, at higher rents, and generally tends to worsen the social problems of the displaced families. In short, the poverty habitat is simply temporarily displaced and the forces which cause its emergence are not eliminated because they receive positive sanction from and have sanctuary in the national culture of the society.[17]

In order to avoid a fight, the San Ysidro Planning Group attempted to work without community participation. Had the community participated it is at least likely that a struggle would have developed between the San Ysidro

Planning Group and the PFTA rather than between the PFTA and the CAC, for, as Wilson (1963) points out, it is difficult for the poor to participate in community planning projects because, as the inevitable victims of the redevelopment, they are simply unable to work within the established power structure.

Many of the people of San Ysidro, especially those of Mexican descent, felt victimized by the power structure, but due to the covert nature of the activities of the San Ysidro Planning Group, it was an intangible oppression. Yet, tensions had to be released. As well as being aware that the CAC offered a basic power resource by which the people might confront this intangible pressure, it may be postulated that the viciousness of the conflict over control of the CAC was the result of its being the only visible manifestation of the "establishment" in the arena. Much of this conflict was to the benefit of the agents of the national culture who represented the real forces of change in the poverty habitat.

The degree to which a poverty habitat then is integrated into the national culture often is relinquished by default to the decisions and actions of those agents; as such, integration of a poverty habitat will be effected only to the extent that it serves the immediate ends of these agents.

Insidious Strategies and the Neutralization Process

It seems, in fact, that there are a variety of insidious strategies which, in the name of altruism or some vague antipoverty goal, do in fact serve the ends of the national culture at the expense of the poverty habitat. They are subtle and some of them absorb the energies of persons originally dedicated to the alleviation of poverty without their being aware of it. The neutralization of their commitment to eliminating poverty undermines the community action programs and results in an emergence of a traditional caretaker- and service-oriented program. These strategies all nominally dedicated to the abolition of poverty, actually serve to neutralize the entire antipoverty program and inhibit any meaningful integration of ethnic poor into American national culture.

Community action programs seem to have become caught up in an inexorable process by which they are becoming increasingly bureaucratized and rapidly absorbed into the national sociopolitical system.[18] The potential for this absorption was evident from the outset of the program, for the war on poverty bureaucracy was merely a replication of other bureaucracies in American society and thus subject to many of the same adaptive pressures and strategies. The main difference in these structures was that, perhaps for the first time in American history, political organizations were established at the real grass roots level of American society, the poverty habitats, and put under the control of their inhabitants.

Much of the furor in the early days of the war on poverty resulted from the confrontations between untrained and unskilled poor persons who, previously powerless, suddenly became chiefs with authority and power sanc-

tioned by the federal government. Without dispute, in a few of the Community
Action Councils in San Diego County, a viable leadership did evolve. In a few
others, as in San Ysidro, such leadership was lacking. In most others this problem
was resolved as middle-class persons took over and assumed authority positions
on the boards and staffs.

In San Ysidro and at least one other CAC which had real problems,
one important area of conflict was between, as the PFTA put it, "the rich"
and "the poor" attempting to work together. There are four strategies by which
this problem may be resolved; one is to close the CAC. Another strategy is to
wait for leadership to evolve, and a third is to permit middle-class individuals to
assume all the responsible positions. A final one is to fulfill the aspirations of
potential leaders of the poor for middle-class status and values and thereby undermine and neutralize any action on their part which might jeopardize their
respectability and salary. Although all these strategies took their toll of the war
on poverty activists, the final strategy was the most covert and perhaps the
most significant.

1. Unionization. With the best of intentions underlying the tactic,
the salaried staff positions of the war on poverty agencies in San Diego County
were unionized by agreement with a Teamsters local. As noted, even prior to this
there was a tendency toward job stability and security in the community action
programs of San Diego County. A pattern had developed in which persons who
quit one war on poverty agency tended to assume an equal, and on occasion
a better, position in another agency within the program. More frequently than
not, individuals who were fired fought the decision vigorously through the
levels of arbitration available within the war on poverty. Unionization of community action program staff not only reinforced this tendency toward job
security and further weakened the job training feature the war on poverty was
supposed to offer its employees, but it also resulted in salary increases which
further stimulated the tendency to job security and stability. As a result of
the unionization, a great amount of energy was expended by staff in attempts to
obtain a variety of adjustment in their salaries. In many CACs the already
prevalent drift toward services and community action programs that would not
offend the establishment and jeopardize the funding of the war on poverty
was expanded, and this tended to subvert the program in a way described by
Gladwin in a more general context:

> Community development has enjoyed widespread popularity through-
> out the world as a device for mobilizing . . . . workers with some
> special training and responsibility for organizing community
> activities. Unfortunately, experience has shown that these workers
> frequently become more responsive to the mandates of administra-
> tors at higher levels of government than the desires of the people
> they are supposed to serve. This substitution of direction from above

for the local initiative which originally guides newly organized community activities is seen as a dilution of the principle of community development, but it has undoubtedly contributed mightily to the widespread popularity of this strategy, (because) . . . (it) provides a ready-made device for relatively inexperienced government administrators to use in enlisting the participation of (persons) in complex programs of social and economic development. (1967:64)

"This substitution of direction from above" may not only dilute the principle of community development; it well may neutralize it. One criticism of the war on poverty is that it never really touched the hard core poor.[19] It is my impression that in San Diego County the unionization of the staff members of the war on poverty institutions certainly enhanced the basis for this criticism.

The unionization of the community action programs' staffs, initiated with the best of intentions in adherence to an accepted principle of American culture, placed a halo of respectability and middle-class sanctity around a program which at its inception was expected by many to revolutionize the structure of American society. Persons who were disillusioned with the war on poverty suddenly became secure in their jobs, received a higher salary, and assumed a kind of professional civil service status. Under these circumstances many could neither afford, nor really desired, to quit. It was, however, detrimental to the momentum of the war on poverty. It not only shifted the community action programs farther away from their already meager constituency; it forced them into an increasing dependency upon professional administrators, another strategy which helped to neutralize the war on poverty.

2. Divide and Rule.   Application by national agents and institutions of the principle of divide and rule among community action groups represents another tactic which aggravated the neutralization of the war on poverty. The real "sophistication" of persons in poverty habitats as well as the tragedy of their condition, is perhaps best suggested by the widespread extent to which they are not only knowledgeable of the degree to which they are victims of this principle but, given the resources they have available, they are unable to counteract it effectively. This became quickly obvious in this research as meeting after meeting concerned with war on poverty programs and policies broke down as poor Mexican-Americans, blacks, and whites began to bicker and then fight among themselves over the "crumbs" made available to them through the war on poverty. As one angry community organizer put it with reference to San Diego County, "What good are 900 job slots in Manpower training programs in a population of one million of which six percent are unemployed?" Invariably, some astute individual at the meeting would temper the growing anger and frustration with the advice, "Man, we got to stop fighting among ourselves; we got to start working together." On the occasions when this would cool things down, it was only until the next meeting.

"Divide and rule" was built into several of the war on poverty programs and goals. To place a blame for this on any particular individual, group, or political party is to beg the issue. This factor has to be seen as an integral part and manisfestation of the forces at work within the national culture and which are beyond the immediate control or direction of any particular segment of that culture.

To be sure, some forces at work within the institutions of the national culture tended to enforce this principle more than others. Basically, it was a concomitant of the bureaucratization and institutionalization processes of the war on poverty; that is the continuous tendency to absorb individuals into the variety of organizations which were expanding throughout the society in the service of the presumed war on poverty. This process proceeded despite the interests of the various groups which determined or implemented policy at the level of the national culture at any specific time. Much of the thrust of this principle seemed to be based upon the resources available to the national culture.

While federal resources are vast in comparison to the resources available to contestants within the poverty habitats of America, in all societies, despite their real or potential wealth, resources exist in finite supply. However, national resources are organized and mobilized and can be strategically deployed with greater facility and efficiency than can those of the poverty habitats. Part of the national cultural policy, in fact, seems bent upon precluding a similar mobilization within or among the nation's poverty habitats. The reality of available resources not only buttressed the principle of divide and rule but, couched in rhetoric regarding the importance of other national commitments and priorities, e.g., Vietnam, justified the excuses by which the principle was made acceptable to the American public and persons within the poverty habitats. In San Diego County, the result was an increased disillusionment with the war on poverty among many of its participants.

Built into such a policy is the risk that the poverty habitat might reject the excuses and demonstrate violently. Blacks especially have been prone to this in recent years. Although their agitation is increasing, Mexican-Americans and poor whites have not. Because of this, much of the risk was mitigated by focusing the service of the war on poverty primarily on blacks. In San Diego County, the Mexican-Americans were especially sensitive to this, and it served as one more divisive element between the ethnic groups involved in the war on poverty.

A potential divisiveness among the poor was also built into the strategy to attack poverty on a broad front. Every antipoverty organization had programs that were vital to their area—ombudsman, recreation, housing, jobs, programs for the elderly, community beautification, education. In San Diego County, certain programs were for the blacks, others for Mexican-Americans. Some served the county, others the city of San Diego. Areas had special needs and developed special programs. Some projects, such as programs for the elderly, could have served all areas. In funding these programs, they were categorized under broad headings, such as housing, recreation, manpower training, and then the $4.5 million dollars allocated to San Diego County was divided among them, as well as among general overhead and administrative costs. By their very multitude and discreteness, few were ever funded adequately; many not at all. This condition became worse as the war on poverty matured. Representatives from the poverty habitats pleaded and exaggerated their programs at refunding sessions in order to obtain funds. Factions and interest groups within the poverty habitats clawed and scratched at each other in order to get their program through.

For example, in the Border Area CAC the blacks of Woodlawn Park complained that the ACCESS service center in Otay did not serve them as it was supposed to. The ACCESS center complained they were understaffed and underfunded. The blacks attempted to get their own center for Woodlawn Park. Two factions emerged, each dating back to the early days of the war on poverty in the area, each with specific programs regarding what the center should include and how it should function. Mexican-Americans from San Ysidro were angry because they argued that Woodlawn Park had no problems compared to San Ysidro and funds to Woodlawn Park would drain off money needed for San Ysidro. In the end, neither program was funded and the hostility between the two factions and San Ysidro remained intense.

Each of the three communities which made up the Border Area CAC had severe housing problems. No federal housing programs were available which could satisfactorily serve each of these areas. Attempts to find ways to contend with this problem broke down in frustration and were compounded by the continued conflict within the Border Area CAC. One result was the emergence of the PFTA outside the context of the war on poverty. Another was general disillusionment with the war on poverty.

Jobs for poor persons were a serious problem throughout San Diego County. Prior to the war on poverty, traditional employment agencies attended this problem in the county. In the city of San Diego, the Mayor's Committee for Jobs was organized in an attempt to cope with it. One complaint was that the committee served the blacks better than the Mexican-Americans. It was hoped that war on poverty job training programs would distribute job opportunities more equitably. All the war on poverty manpower training programs immediately fell under control of the blacks. Mexican-Americans complained that when slots were opened in federal job training programs they were either systematically excluded or told to obtain a certain quota of slots from the blacks.[20]

In general, individuals and organizations in each of the several poverty habitats in San Diego County had to apply for programs to assist their area. The programs were many and the funds were limited. Hostility to the war on poverty increased. The community action program in Northern San Diego County wanted to sever relationships with the EOC because its members believed that they might succeed better alone. By and large, the north county community action program was composed of Anglos and Mexican-Americans. Rather than adding coherence to the program in San Diego County, their severence would tend to increase the fragmentation of the total program. Officials argued that if this was permitted it would drain already scarce resources from the urban area. It was a thorny and divisive problem that was not resolved during my research.

The Model Cities Program was scheduled to come into San Diego County in 1969. San Ysidro, originally excluded, was incorporated into the program at the height of conflict in the arena. Some EOC officials argued that the PFTA tactics had little to do with the Model Cities Program incorporating San Ysidro; others said it was a most significant factor. Regardless, even prior to the inclusion of San Ysidro in the Model Cities Program, several black CACs and the one Mexican-American CAC from Southeast San Diego (the original Model Cities Program area) were in conflict over how the resources and facilities of the program would be divided. The inclusion of San Ysidro suggested this problem because, even though special monies were allocated to San Ysidro, the blacks feared its inclusion would eventually drain funds from them.

The general strategy of the war on poverty was to initiate projects and policies which would eliminate poverty. Early in the war on poverty there was, as noted previously, the expectation of an increase in funds and resources to do the job. As resources were withdrawn, fear increased that the program would be abolished. Any confrontation between a war on poverty agency and another institution which might rock the boat, such as the local schools, was deplored. "Safe" programs became the watchword and the few CACs in the area which actually attempted to eliminate or reduce poverty by eliciting changes in traditional American institutions were considered "threats" to the future of the program. Information on such problems quickly fed upward in the war on poverty bureaucracy and incurred pressures from the regional and federal OEO lest the program develop a worse image than it already possessed. Divisiveness among the CACs developed as a result, the "safe" CACs deploring the actions of those which embarrassed the program.

What should have been a concentrated effort against poverty was fragmented even more. Few persons or areas were served well by this strategy. Those few CACs which did undertake programs disruptive to traditional American institutions feared that the EOC might close them down. The attempt by the EOC to sever relations with the CACs was regarded by them as a means by which the EOC could not only avoid responsibility for their activities but continue to exist at their expense. This fear is not without some substantiation. CACs spoke openly and frequently of succumbing to such a fate, especially as the November elections approached. Several believed that since they represented the "action component" of the community action program in San Diego County, they would either be sacrificed so that the EOC might survive, or they would be closed by federal action because of their activities and reputation. It is perhaps more a credit to the effective neutralization of the war on poverty as a potentially revolutionary force in American society than to any success it achieved in its attenuated battle against poverty that the Republican administration saw fit to maintain the bureaucracy and institutions—even the CACs—which comprised it.

3. Cooptation. As well as being aware that reductions in the resources available to the war on poverty was creating interethnic divisiveness and hostility, ethnic groups were also aware that indigenous leadership was being coopted in the service of the "mandates of administrators at higher levels of government" rather than serving the desires of their poor constituents. Blacks refer to such individuals as "Uncle Toms"; Mexican-Americans refer to them as "Tio Tacos" or "Tio Toms."

Although the war on poverty may be credited with stimulating Mexican-American leadership at the local level, it also did its share to absorb leadership in the service of the bureaucracy, and the drain of leaders into this or other bureaucracies has been obvious to concerned Mexican-Americans for some time.[21] During the conflict in San Ysidro, the director of Area Development, Delia Garcia, Mr. Flores, Yolanda Chaca, the local priest, Mr. De La Torre, Mr. De Leon, and others were considered "Tio Tacos" and identified by the poor Mexican-Americans as part of the establishment. Although much of such rhetoric was propaganda in the service of the PFTA, the drain of Mexican-American talent into the national culture was obvious and resented.

In San Diego County there is one Mexican-American organization known as IMPACT which is dedicated to the purpose of reclaiming such individuals for the Mexican-American community. It was organized and is led by the vice president of the EOC board of directors. Recently in San Diego County a large federation of all Mexican-American groups in the area has organized in order to coordinate Mexican-American political activities in the city and county of San Diego. Many of its founding members were participants in the war on poverty, and it has attempted to bring together politically radical, conservative, and middle-of-the-road Mexican-Americans in order to impede this talent drain and develop a firm basis for Mexican-American political activity.

AFTERMATH

In light of the various tactics and strategies employed by the contestants in the arena and the way they are conditioned by available resources, any integration of poverty habitats into the national culture will have to take place in terms of the values and ideologies of that culture. This will be terribly difficult to achieve without basic changes in the institutions of American society.

Tactics and strategies of the poverty habitats were always mediated by the fact that information and communication regarding their activities flowed upward through the bureaucracy much more easily than did information regarding the strategies and tactics at that level flow down to the poverty habitat. Contestants in poverty habitats had to make expedient adaptations to this condition. Demonstrations, letter campaigns, and exaggerations, were the means by which they attempted to influence the policies of the national culture of which they had little knowledge and less control. They gambled constantly that their activities would not elicit a forceful negative response from the establishment. Many poverty contestants probably overestimated their importance and underestimated the ability of the national culture to absorb their activism.

Truly serious agitations, as among the blacks in Watts, Detroit, and Newark (there was none comparable in San Diego County) elicited responses that were rather paternal from antipoverty agencies; a few concessions to the issue, such as one more project, but very little that ever got to the real cause of such agitation; that is, the very causes of poverty itself. Radical elements in the society and those disillusioned with the war on poverty often rightfully considered the program so much pap; at best a temporary palliative, but nothing which would result in the alleviation of poverty, or any meaningful integration of poverty habitats into the institutional structure of American national culture.

Bloomberg and Schmandt (1968) have argued that we are failing to reduce poverty to anywhere near the degree our resources would seem to permit because poverty, as well as the ideology which underwrites and gives meaning to the existence of the national culture, is part of the fabric of our social system, institutions, and political arrangements. In other words, the existence and perpetuation of poverty habitats may be considered as serving some purpose in American society. Some of these purposes may be indicated.

For example, in San Diego County, a welfare accountant informed me unofficially that it takes eight taxpayer's dollars to administer every one dollar paid out in welfare. Poverty seems to be important if for no other reason than to maintain and support the middle-class caretaker strata of American society. As well as providing a rationale for the perpetuation and existence of caretaker institutions, in a very subtle way, perpetuation of persons in a state of relative deprivation within the affluency of the United States supports the national ideology of the Protestant ethic. It provides meaning for the existence of the middle class by offering a counterpoint to their affluency and well being and by perpetuating the notion visibly demonstrated by their failure that through thrift and hard work anyone can "make it" in the society if they really want to. It effectively precludes any belief on their part that some drastic changes and alterations may in fact be in order for America's institutions.

Strategies and tactics of expediency by persons in poverty habitats, in response to calculated strategies of agents of the national culture, are going to have to change if the goals of the American national cultural ideology are to be achieved. This will come about with increased skill and knowledge among concerned and active participants in America's antipoverty organizations. One major problem is that by this time ethnic minorities may well be using such skills to propagate nationalistic separatist movements within the United States rather than effect any sociocultural integration. Such movements are already widespread among certain black populations and are emerging among the Mexican-Americans. The implications of this, as well as continued agitation by persons in poverty habitats, for the future culture of American society are vast. Despite conservative tendencies, it presages significant alteration in America's institutions.

Chapter Seven

Inequality Mañana: Conclusions

INTRODUCTION

In his work *The Political System,* David Easton (1953) delimits three levels of political theory by which generalizations that attempt to explain social phenomena may be distinguished. The first refers to singular generalizations. These are statements of observed uniformities between two isolated and easily identified variables. The second is synthetic or narrow gauge theory which consists of a set of interrelated propositions that are designed to synthesize the data contained in an unorganized body of singular singular generalizations. The third and highest level refers to broad gauge or systematic theory, the conceptual framework within which an entire discipline is cast.

This study, which is essentially a case study concerned with political activity, lends itself primarily to the development of singular generalizations. Many such generalizations regarding the nature and use of power, political activity among poor and ethnic categories of persons vis-à-vis other social categories, and other generalizations, have been suggested throughout this work. From my point of view much of the significance of this work has been its attempt to go beyond a mere case study of local level politics and indicate interaction between and influences upon political organizations from a variety of levels within American society, as well as contributing to an understanding of the war on poverty and the politics of persons in poverty as well as those in relative affluence. Because I believe that a social scientist should attempt to be bold and imaginative in the analysis of his data, I am going to carry my analysis beyond the data, to an extent which at times may strain its empirical credibility. I do this because I also believe a study should stimulate others to respond and undertake investigations which ultimately, through increasing refinement, will permit the development of Easton's third level of theoretical abstraction, that within which an entire discipline may be cast.

The central concern of this work was to understand some of the processes by which a complex society attempts to achieve and maintain socio-cultural integration. All societies, it was argued earlier, have to do this if they are to maintain their socioculture integrity; because of cultural heterogeneity, population size, different adaptations among populations within the nation, and other factors, this is a special concern of state systems. While I am aware of the limitations of my data, in order or generalize about the integrative process, I am going to attempt to generate hypotheses increasing in scale and scope from singular generalizations to those which may have systematic applications for the discipline of anthropology as a whole. If this sounds ambitious, it will be in keeping with the basic design of this study which has been to carry the analysis of empirical observations from the specifics of the poverty habitat to a level of cultural abstraction and adaptation represented by the national state system.

SINGULAR GENERALIZATIONS

At the least inclusive theoretical level Easton posits, I have attempted in this study to demonstrate, from the perspective of the political activity inherent in the United States' war on poverty, some of the forces at work which may influence the integration of a complex social system. I suggest that we have observed in this work not merely the functions of an institutional complex dedicated to a war on poverty, but political strategies of adaptation of the participants involved in this war.

I contend that the war on poverty itself represents an adaptation to the threat to the integrity of the United States manifest in the recent ghetto riots and agitations by the nation's ethnic minorities. I argue that the war on poverty was not dedicated to the elimination of poverty for any altruistic reasons. Rather, it was an attempt to achieve a more unified nation and a more cohesive national sociocultural integration.

I focused on the political field of activity as manifest in the institutional complex of the war on poverty because I believe that political institutions are one of the most significant in the integrative process. In order to stress the interrelatedness of the contestants, the issues over which they came into conflict, the population affected by this conflict, and the various tactics and strategies by which contestants who represent different levels of organization in the society sought to achieve thier goals, I set the study in the framework of "political ecology." Spokesmen for the "processual school" of political anthropology have argued the need for understanding political processes in terms of the interrelationships between the various sectors and compenents of the society which may be involved.[1] Yet very few political anthropologists have attempted to apply the notion with any regularity and it largely remains a suggestion without implementation. I attempted to demonstrate this suggestion by delimit-ing a tentative model of a poverty habitat within an environment circumscribed by the national boundaries of the United States. In this way I hoped to demonstrate the significance of the ecological framework by indicating the interrelatedness of activities within the poverty habitat and between the poverty habitat and the national culture generally.

The poverty habitat also serves as a political arena. This represents an environmental space within which a variety of contestants intrinsic to the sociopolitical field of activity in the arena vie for control of resources and over certain goals they pursue. The field is composed of those contestants who interacted with or were influenced by the war on poverty institutions in San Diego County. I described the statuses and roles of the personnel which make up the several concerned organizations in order to clarify the position of the groups they comprise within a larger social context. The values and ideologies represented by their collective statuses were discussed and were significant in understanding the goals they pursued and the means by which they attempted to achieve them. The interaction of these organizations with each other and the covert and overt influences they brought to bear in their political activity may be used as points of departure by which a variety of generalizations can be made regarding the political activity of persons in poverty habitats vis-à-vis organizations which exist apart from, but exert influence upon, poverty habitats.

For example, from my vantage point of the war on poverty in San Diego County, and following the theoretical lead of other social scientists, I suggest that relatively few persons in any community are actively involved in the decision-making process which affects their lives.[2] Democratic principles inherent in the ideology to which most persons in the society subscribe seem all too frequently surrendered by default to special interest groups. I argue that political power derives from the control of resources and suggest a variety of bases upon which political power is founded. A correlation also exists between the statuses of groups within the social system and the amount of power they control. The least power is controlled by the lowest status groups in the social hierarchy. Frequently, in the conflict in which the participate, they are forced to develop power and the means of implementing it through improvisations as the conflict evolves. Conversely, the most power is controlled by those with the higher statuses.

Persons involved in political activity at the local level also give primary allegiance to those contestants who represent the values and ideologies to which they are committed. However, it is also true that many Anglos in the Border Area CAC participate in organizations whose values and ideologies are antithetical to their own, but they do so for reasons of "civic duty." I suggest that organizations involved in political activity are ranked according to their statuses and power bases and that this structures the nature of the political activity in the arena. Many of those contestants with power manifest a disdain for the political activities of persons in poverty, viewing their tactics as "dirty" or unfair. The political activities of persons in poverty, I argue, really must be understood as the only viable adaptations to the reality of their social condition and the paucity of resources available to them.

It is within the arena that the strategies and tactics they utilize in pursuit of their goals are revealed as adaptations to the amount of resources each contestant controls. Political strategies and tactics will vary with respect to the amount of power contestants control. At each level above the poverty habitat contestants will control more resources and power than the one below. The political field itself extends far beyond the arena of San Ysidro and contestants and influences from other arenas flow in and out of it. The events within the arena generate a "cybernetic" condition in which political decisions and policies and the strategies and the tactics by which they are implemented by one contestant in the arena elicits a series of responses at all other levels. These responses feed back through the war on poverty bureaucracy and associated institutions and stimulate a variety of counterresponses, some of which serve the integrative process; most, however, serve only to neutralize the revolutionary potential of the war on poverty.

Organizations involved in the process within the arena, such as the Border Area CAC, will function efficiently to the extent that the arena accommodates them. Theoretically, the arena may expand indefinitely; processes within an arena may develop more smoothly if certain contestants can be accommodated by another arena. For example, the Border Area CAC was too large for the arena; too many contradictions were built into its composition: population size, ethnic diversity, social status differences, city-county distinctions. Forces such as those emanating from the planned development of San Ysidro exerted tremendous although covert pressures upon the arena and stimulated conflict along lines of the CAC's intrinsic contradictions. In retrospect, had the Border Area CAC at its inception served only San Ysidro, it is likely much of the conflict would have been avoided. The lesson to be drawn from the Border Area CAC and one which should be considered in planning any future programs of a similar type is that the war on poverty at large was too poorly thought out; it was too highly structured for many of the groups who actively sought change in the national culture, and not structured enough either in terms of the reality of the poverty habitat where positive guidance and leadership was a necessity, or for the conservative elements which desired to maintain control over the program and the political activities of the poor. This latter consideration provided another irreconcilable contradiction in the fabric of the war on poverty.

I also suggest that enthusiasm was the first, and perhaps only, resource available to contestants from the poverty habitats of America at the inception of the war on poverty. Although this enthusiasm has demonstrably declined, events that have developed in San Ysidro since my research suggest that enthusiasm among persons in this poverty habitat, now augmented by increased political expertise as a result of previous conflicts, may still be a viable com-

ponent of the political activity in that arena. Persons trained in the hard knocks
of the previous year's conflict now are attempting to thwart the building of a
major freeway through the community. Most of this activity seems to be organized by concerned citizen groups outside the war on poverty institutions in
the area.

There also seems to be a real as well as cognitive space between
persons in poverty habitats and those agents who represent the values and
ideologies of the national culture. For example, the San Ysidro Planning Group
generally disdained communication with the people of San Ysidro. The current
conflict over the San Ysidro development plan might have been avoided had the
San Ysidro Planning Group been willing to work with the community. The
statuses individuals in the group hold and the ideology to which they adhere not
only impeded this, but is characteristic of the gulf between the poor and more
affluent in the society. Also, in the conflict over the EMR program the school
personnel demonstrated a vast ignorance of the war on poverty institutions in
their area. Had they known more about them, either through participation or
interest, they probably would have recognized that they were being intimidated
by the proverbial paper tiger.

The war on poverty did not facilitate sociocultural integration by
reducing the real social space between contestants. Rather it seems to have forced
a closer identity of persons in poverty habitats with the federal government
and bureaucracy upon whom they are increasingly dependent for real change in
their sociocultural condition. Despite attempts by the current administration to
effect integration through the efforts of private industry and enterprise within
the United States, it is predictable that there will be an increasing articulation
between poverty habitats and the federal government at the expense of intermediate structures such as the city or many of the institutions so representative
of American national culture.

Finally, I attempt to point out the significance of ethnic symbols as
an element in the conflict in the arena. I suggest that this may serve as a significant power resource by giving specific identity to those of like ethnic background
involved in a fight with those of unlike ethnic background. Ethnic identity may
also be culturally defined; to Mexican-American contestants in San Ysidro symbols of Mexican-American identity—language, cultural, poverty—served as important means for obtaining support and maintaining boundaries by which the
contestants could be separated and by which a united front of poor persons could
maintain a viable identity against more powerful contestants. Through the
rhetoric and propaganda of the PFTA, ethnic identity also served as a significant
resource by which they were able to develop increased power in the arena.

Despite the contention in the final report of the war on poverty in
San Diego County that "inter-ethnic conflict is not viewed as a problem either
in the communities or in the Community Action Councils,"[3] ethnic hostility
was an important element of the conflict in San Ysidro. However, in San Ysidro

and elsewhere, the ethnic conflict also has overtones of a class conflict. Kramer (1969) suggests that one result of such ethnic-class conflict is the total lack of credibility between ethnic categories which represent different social classes in the war on poverty. I pointed out that some ethnic hostility was evident between poor blacks and Mexican-Americans in the war on poverty in San Diego County. In most cases they recognized it and viewed it as a means by which agents of the national culture attempted to put into effect the technique of divide and rule. To their credit, they also generally recognized the need to continue to work together in order to develop a more effective power base for the poor in America. As this develops, and it currently is, though by fits and starts, its implications for the traditional political process in American society and culture as well as the processes by which a complex system attempts to achieve socio-cultural integration will be vast.

At a somewhat further removed level of empirical analysis, I have, in this study, moved increasingly from the specifics of the war on poverty in the arena of San Ysidro to a consideration of cultural forces which result from the decisions and policies of the state government and institutions. Following Steward's (1955:65) argument that "The national institutions (of the United States) have functional and structural aspects which are distinguishable from the cultural behavior of the people connected with them . . . ," I have dichotomized these differences in terms of the political activity representative of the national culture of the United States and that representative of persons within poverty habitats in order to cope with this vast and complex problem. I argue that power, that is the availability, control, and manipulation of resources, and the tactics and strategies by which it is implemented, are part of the cultural content of the level of integration to which populations adapt. Persons who are members of that society utilize the power and means of implementing it as a consequence of the cultural adaptations they have made to their sociophysical environment and the opportunities and characteristics—material objects, values, symbols, organizations of human relationship—which that level of cultural adaptation affords them. In this context a variety of factors influence the integrative process.

The most important is the power which is controlled by agents of the dominant culture and the ideology, values, and symbols which provide a rationale and meaning for the utilization of this power. Because of this power concentration, I argue that integration will be in terms dictated by agents of the national culture. This means that all too frequently the ends or goals of those agents will be served rather than those of the contestants from the poverty habitats.

For example, the development of a community may destroy a particular poverty habitat, but without altering the condition and cause of poverty this simply forces it to re-emerge some place else. Although the war on poverty held promise to alter this condition, it did not provide the poor with

either the time or the resources necessary to do the job. Rather, in a variety of
subtle ways, it undermined their purpose.

Many poor became discouraged. Others were absorbed by the
establishment and were made "respectable." Others, now functioning primarily
outside the antipoverty program, still are attempting to work within the system
and effect change in American society so that poverty habitats may be better
articulated with the national social structure.

Many others, especially the youth, are becoming disillusioned. Some
are talking of revolution, and there is a growing tendency toward separatism
(cultural plurality is a more neutral term) within the nation among ethnic
minority youth. Although the result of this has been the emergence of ethnic
identity as an increasingly potent political force in the United States, much of its
potential is lost due to the cross purposes toward which many of the groups
work and the apparent increase in national sociocultural heterogenity.

All this points to a considerable degree of sociocultural heterogenity
in the United States currently. Apparently some degree of cultural heterogenity
is necessary in the integration of a state system because it provides elements
within the society which the state and elite power groups can play off one against
the other in the service of national sociocultural integration. The United States
seems to be no exception to this, and it will have implications for the future
sociocultural integration of the United States. I think it significant to mention
that, for better or worse and despite disclaimers, much of this received initial
impetus from the war on poverty.

Still, vast segments of our ethnic minority populations will remain in
a condition of poverty. The changes necessary in the nation's institutions in order
to get at the cause of poverty will take a massive confrontation between the
poor and their supporters and the agents of the national culture. So far, all the
odds in such a struggle seem to favor the establishment. In fact, there is a continuing dilution of agencies originally designed within the war on poverty to
serve the integration of ethnic minorities, and other viable organizations by which
such change might be promoted have not yet achieved a substantial degree of
either legitimacy or legality in the United States, and this certainly impedes their
effectiveness. This double pronged strategy of dilution and protraction is proceeding with the sanction of the national ideology—the Protestant ethic—so avidly
espoused by the current administration of the United States.

For example, the "War on Poverty" has been changed to the "Anti-
Poverty Program." The loss of the dynamic impact of a "war" of sorts not only
presaged, but was the result of, significant alterations in the program at large.
Some of the war on poverty programs have gone by the wayside. Funds for the
Job Corps were cut drastically and the program emasculated. Headstart was
"spun off" to the Department of Education; manpower training programs were
"spun off" to the Department of Labor. By incorporating such programs into
traditional federal bureaucracies their potential for stimulating significant

change in America's educational and economic institutions was certainly
mitigated. The establishment of the OEO and its community action programs as
an acceptable segment of American society is a tribute to their effective neutralization as a force for change in American society.

The new administration expressed a concern for enabling low-income
Americans to develop small business in the free enterprise tradition through
assistance from the National Association of Businessmen (NAB). As one person
in the war on poverty suggested, when one considers the vast subsidization of big
agriculture and big business by the federal government, this policy seems to foster
cut-throat capitalism for the poor (another principle of divide and rule) and
socialism for the rich. He and others did not regard this as a very satisfactory
strategy for eliminating poverty. The initial enthusiasm stimulated by the
notion of maximum feasible participation of the poor and the promise of the
war on poverty generally is dead. The unmistakable trend toward services rather
than toward community action undermined the maximum feasible participation
of the poor and has perpetuated their dependency upon caretaker institutions.

Although the actual quality of life of the poor has been little
affected by the war on poverty, there are still some positive aspects which
resulted from the war on poverty. The problems of poverty have been put before
the nation. The intricacies of the problem through its linkages with a variety of
institutions in American society are recognized by more people than before.
Ethnic minorities gained more expertise in how to confront the establishment
and realized that they no longer have to bow passively before its wishes. To what
extent the power structure of American society is willing to work with these
aspiring ethnic groups, or attempt to do something about the problems of poverty
is as yet an unanswerable question. The ideology of agents of American national
culture still seem to hark back to that sentiment expressed by Charles Wilson
when, as a member of President Eisenhower's cabinet, he remarked that "what is
good for General Motors, is good for the country." Is it really the case that
what is good for the San Ysidro Planning Group is good for San Ysidro? As a
result of skills learned and acquired through the hard knocks of the war on
poverty battlegrounds, such as San Ysidro, persons in poverty habitats may no
longer be quite so willing to concur with these sentiments.

NARROW GAUGE THEORY

From the generalizations derived from these data I now will attempt to elicit
theory relevant to Easton's second level, synthetic or narrow gauge theory.
Easton suggests:

> . . . synthetic or narrow-gauge theory . . . consists of a set of inter-
> related propositions that are designed to synthesize the data con-
> tained in an unorganized body of singular generalizations. But in

the process of synthesis, the theory that is developed goes beyond
the actual data included in the original cluster of generalizations.
It becomes possible to understand not only the phenomena to
which these generalizations originally related, but also other
phenomena which hitherto had been shrouded in doubt. (1953:56)

In the course of my research Mr. Flores, vice president of the EOC board of
directors, president of the National City CAC, and skilled in the tactics of union
organization as a result of over thirty years experience, outlined to me three
phases through which, according to him, the evolution of leadership in any organization passes.

In the first phase there is no real leadership. Persons capable of
becoming leaders have to be discovered. They have to be trained and their skills
developed. Because of the unfamiliar roles potential leaders are attempting to
fulfill, and the confrontations with shrewd and skillful establishment leaders
that they experience, their job mortality rate is high. Leadership remains
shallow for a long time. Mr. Flores referred to this as the "floundering stage" of
leadership evolution. Some organizations never achieve viable leadership and as
a result do not move to the second phase. For example, the intense conflict
in the Border Area CAC inhibited its shift to the second phase.

In the second phase persons who survive the first phase become
increasingly secure and knowledgeable in their role as leaders. They are challenged by events and work for their organizations. They are willing to take
risks in the service of their constituency. They move out into the community
and expand the base of their power by developing larger support networks. Skill
has developed and is important because it is necessary to manipulate a variety
of issues in order to maintain interest and support.

Slowly, however, problems begin to set in. The constituency becomes
stable; dissenting membership has shifted allegiance. Issues become less intense.
The leader in turn becomes less challenged by events. He is in increasing accord
with those with whom he was originally in conflict. His identity as a leader
becomes firm; his job more secure. He begins to serve others in upper echelon
positions with whom he increasingly identifies and, perhaps, depends upon for
his job.

In phase three, leadership becomes stable and the constituency
relatively dependable. Issues become stereotyped; higher wages, better fringe
benefits, and the like with reference to unions; and stop signs, school lunches,
service projects, and the like with reference to community action programs. The
leadership becomes a perpetual part of a self-perpetuating organization.

As an American of Mexican descent and very dedicated to the cause
of his people, Mr. Flores carried this analysis one step farther. He pointed out
that one problem which confronts Mexican-Americans is that they begin to serve
the upper echelons of the organization of which they are a part better than their

original constituency. This, he argued, is because Mexican-Americans are able to pass easier than blacks into white middle-class American society. The result has been a tremendous drain upon Mexican-American leadership at the barrio level. IMPACT, an organization he and others founded, and more recently the Chicano Federation of San Diego County, have dedicated themselves to retrieving this lost leadership for the Mexican-American community as well as maintaining the dynamic leadership which is developing.

However imperfect Mr. Flores insight may be, it is based on over thirty years of experience in a variety of arenas and is, I think, remarkably accurate. To what extent it was influenced by readings in sociology is difficult to say; Mr. Flores had a ninth grade education from a barrio school. Rather than criticize his analysis, I suggest his viewpoint is applicable by analogy to general principles inherent in other organizations, such as the Border Area CAC, the EOC, the war on poverty institutions of San Diego County and the nation at large, and that it bears upon the integrative process.

Models of the sort described are generally produced by sociologists. Scott Greer (1960) discusses the ascending order of the size of organizations from household to municipalities in which persons in suburban habitats become involved, and the accompanying shifts from face-to-face types of activities to participation in political activities through representation. Roland Warren (1963), in discussing organizations involved in community action and development, posits a five-stage model from inception to either (a) dissolution, or (b) transformation through which the various structures involved in these processes progress. As noted earlier, Turner (1957) suggests a phase development from breach to resolution of conflict through which political actions progress at the local level. Based upon data presented in their work, a similar phase development concerning the empirical regularities through which the war on poverty organizations in San Diego County progressed has relevance for understanding the integrative process within a complex social system such as the United States.

Phase one, similar to that concerned with leadership, may be considered a pioneering phase. In offering suggestions on techniques by which social action programs may be evaluated, Hyman and Wright discuss it this way:

> It is certainly reasonable to assume that the program is not yet functioning at maximum efficiency, but . . . enthusiasm fires the new enterprise. The staff has not yet become stale and tired. They are often bold and innovative and willing to risk their livelihood on something new, although there is also the possibility that they are castoffs who cannot find positions elsewhere. Where entry is voluntary, the first cohort of subjects may also be highly committed, since they are entering something new and unproved. (1967:751)

Each of these characteristics is indicative of the community action program in San Diego County. At its inception enthusiasm ran high. Many of the early staff of the EOC and its delegate agencies previously had been teachers, disgruntled welfare personnel, or professional people who quit their jobs to assume the challenge of the war on poverty. Many others were social castoffs, ex-prostitutes, ethnic minority persons, school dropouts, and so forth. CACs were almost exclusively staffed in their early phases by social castoffs who represented pariah groups within American culture. Commitment to the war on poverty was intense.

Phase two is characterized by increasing stability within the organization. In part this sets in because, as Bullock points out, "Poor people are not immune from the selfishness and careerism which pervades our society; indeed the daily struggle for survival leaves little room for any other concern" (1968: 67–68). Also, enthusiasm begins to wane among persons other than the poor as it becomes necessary to come to grips with the increasingly mundane problems that have been spawned by phase one. The goals of the organization have to be reanalyzed in the face of current reality and in terms of the internal and external demands placed upon the organization. Some of the initial, dynamic staff becomes molded to the program; for many others the excitement is tempered by the necessity of fulfilling perfunctory organizational obligations. This causes them to resign and seek new fields of excitement. The personnel generally begins to settle into their career positions and routine becomes the watchword.

Although several CACs, such as the Border Area CAC, never developed beyond the pioneering phase, several others in their dedication to administering services rather quickly achieved phase two. In the EOC the resignation of many staff members, the director, the head of the Area Development, and others, characterize the shift from phase one to phase two. As suggested by the protracted turmoil which has beset the EOC, this need not be an orderly transition. Also, as the current condition of the EOC suggests, it is entirely possible that an organization may not survive the transition from phase one to phase two.[4] However, if it does, phase three begins.

In phase three the organization stabilizes. It assumes its duties perfunctorily and at best becomes enmeshed in solutions to a multitude of petty but gnawing problems. Most of the dynamic personnel have left, been neutralized, or are thinking of leaving. Risks become an anathema to the structure, and threats to its orderly operation are viewed with fear. In a real sense the organization has become respectable. It now serves best those who will best facilitate its survival as an institution. Among war on poverty organizations it withdraws in cognitive and real space from its original constituents, the poor, in favor of identity with the more traditional agents and institutions of American society upon whom its existence increasingly depends.

Several of the CACs in the area had reached this phase of respectability and stability. The threat to local government by the war on poverty so feared by city halls across the nation is long past. As the Final Report of the War on Poverty in San Diego County suggests,[5] membership in most CACs has stabilized. Because the establishment views them as a kind of safety valve, a means by which the voices of the poor can be heard, they now represent organizations that are acceptable to the establishment.

Even if, as has been so often threatened, CACs are phased out of existence it is very probable that some other form of community action organization will replace them and that the funds necessary to sustain them will be made available, at least in part, by the federal government. Should this eventuate certain problems which are significant for the integrative process could well develop. For example, such local action organizations would probably be distributed unevenly among the nation's poverty habitats, since it is unlikely that each current community action agency would survive. Reduction of local action agencies might also promote development of more umbrella-type agencies which attempt to incorporate broader areas than are currently served; they would be further removed from the grass roots of the poverty habitat. In this case their role in promoting community action would have to be exceptionally efficient in order to reach all the needs of the area, and such efficiency is unlikely. It is also likely that action-oriented agencies that are dependent upon traditional sources of funding and which persist in attacking sacred national institutions would be abolished and probably replaced with service agencies.[6]

Phase four may be characterized as one of overadaptation. By this time the organization has fallen fully under the control of those who have vested interests in its survival. With reference to community action programs, Bullock points out the inevitable tendency for action programs with a radical bent at their inception to become "bastions of conformity" (1968:65). The goal of the organization is to persist at all costs. Its members adapt and conform to the ideology and value systems of the culture.

The essential difference between phases three and four is one of persistence. Although some war on poverty institutions will pass by the wayside, others will become part of the expanding bureaucracy of American society and pursue different goals than those to which they were originally committed. Local level politics may no longer reside exclusively at the level of city hall; but neither will it reside, as the war on poverty promised, at the grass roots level of the poverty habitat. Poverty habitats will remain. Organizations such as CACs or the EOC originally dedicated to changing them will simply become one more buffer zone between the poverty habitat and the dominant institutions of American society. Services along traditional lines from these institutions will prevail and their strategies will be dictated by the demands of institutions representative of the national culture.

Although this phase development suggests a unilineal progression, not all war on poverty organizations develop at equal rates. Some become arrested in one stage or other. Others progress through the phases more rapidly. As with other institutional complexes, some are more dynamic, others less so. A multitude of factors, many of which have been suggested in this work, such as internal and external political pressures, the nature of the personnel involved, the specifics of the habitats they represent, and so forth will affect their phase development. An analysis of these factors would demand a separate work, and a few attempts have been made to cope with some of them (viz., Warren 1963).

The data presented in this work suggest that the United States has come full circle in its battle against poverty under the current antipoverty programs. Persons living in poverty and/or concerned with its problems were propelled out of a state of inertia by the war on poverty to attack it and attempt to eliminate it. Still, the war on poverty was a failure. The program itself has been neutralized. A few persons who existed in poverty have been integrated, perhaps assimilated is a better term. The poverty habitats of the nation remain. Their populations seem at best only slightly depleted in number, and they are still not structurally integrated into the cultural patterns of the larger society.

From a body of singular generalizations I have attempted to build a model to reveal certain processes which, in Easton's terms, may have been shrouded in doubt. Implicit in the model is the theory that institutions will progress from a pioneering action phase to one of overadaptation. This will depend upon the degree to which personnel make adjustments to the institution's structure rather than to its functional intent. These adjustments are made in response to the survival imperative of the personnel in terms of the careers and identities the institutions afford them. Oscar Lewis's (1966) contention that the poor have no identity beyond themselves simply is not so. They know of the larger society and aspire to its desiderata. The war on poverty offered them organizations in which, for a few, these aspirations could be achieved.

Finally, it may be theorized that to the extent that issues relevant to the interests of the original dynamic staff can be maintained, the organization will more likely be responsive to its original constituency and founding purpose; conversely it will achieve overadaptation to the extent that potential issues lose their relevancy and dynamic personnel are assimilated or forced out in favor of increasing the institution's respectability and services to a broader constituency representing other levels of cultural adaptation and integration within the system. From this theoretical premise it is predictable that the integration of a poverty habitat into the social structure of the United States is not to be expected from any program designed by professional bureaucrats because it will be destined to attack the poverty habitat and not the causes of poverty. The dilemma is that the poor cannot be expected to do the job either, because under any such program they are essentially requested to attack and change the adaptations they have made as a result of their exclusion from the national culture and alternatives to their adaptation are not readily available within the system at large.

SYSTEMATIC THEORY

While this theory may help to explain factors inherent in the institutionalization process, it is only by extrapolating from the data at yet a higher level of theoretical abstraction that the integrative process within the nation at large may be understood. I suggest that there are forces within the social system, generally reminiscent of those inherent in institutions which are currently at work, that function to inhibit the integration of American society. The traditional articulation between its structural parts through redistributive, political, educational, service, and other programs will be precluded by these forces. Instead a realignment of the social system will develop and result in an increasing amount and complexity of the levels of sociocultural adaptation internal to it. In order to demonstrate this hypothesis, it is necessary to turn to the highest level of theory posited by Easton. This level is distinguished from the previous two primarily in terms of its scope. Easton suggests:

> At the highest level, there stands broad-gauge or systematic theory, the conceptual framework within which a whole discipline is cast. Since no social scientist can be interested in all the facts, the most general order of facts that enlists his interest will depend upon the conceptual framework used . . . a conceptual framework consists of those theories and assumptions which an investigator uses in understanding an analysis within a given field. It serves as a theoretical model to test the relevance of succeeding research. It is a system of working hypotheses, adopted and used only as long as it helps to orient empirical research in such a way that socially significant problems are better understood. There is nothing sacrosanct about a theoretical scheme such as this, and the same one need not be adopted to help understand different problems. The supreme test is its utility in understanding phenomena. (1953:57)

One body of anthropological theory which complements Easton's suggestion is that concerned with sociocultural evolution. One significant characteristic of evolutionary theory is the differentiation and specialization of roles and the larger institutions which they comprise. The primary causes of evolution are not my concern; I wish, rather, to suggest briefly first, the creative forces inherent in cultural evolution which sustain impetus in the differentiation and specialization of institutions once the initial process has been triggered, and, second, the forces which tend toward inertia and homeostasis in the process.

For example, Eisenstadt (1964a, 1964b) suggests the notion of the institutionalization of culture change; that is, the more institutionally complex a society is, the more potential it has to change as a result of interaction between its institutional components. Nadel suggests that models of physical equilibrium must be abandoned if the concept of integration as a "dynamic component in its own right . . . an impetus toward creative action" (1953:165, 347) is to be ascertained. Along similar lines, and with specific reference to the evolution of culture, Y. A. Cohen argues for an equally creative content to the process of cultural adaptation; that is, the "processes by which a population alters its relationship to its habitat" (1968a:34-4). I also suggest that in a complex state system the impetus for creative change of the sort the previous authors spoke of is stimulated primarily through the action of the society's political institutions. In other words, national culture change and the adaptations institutions make to it is stimulated by the political institutions of the nation.

A concomitant of this process is the necessity for the state to maintain the nation's sociocultural integrity by providing a workable articulation between its institutions and the variety of habitats which they serve within the nation: cities, suburbs, poverty habitats, industrial, or agricultural areas, etc. Integration in this context is stimulated by political decision concerned with the allocation of national values, symbols, ideologies, and resources throughout the nation. In this way, augmented by the material abundance of the nation, social distance between most sectors of the nation is at least cognitively reduced and allegiance to the nation and conformity to its values, symbols and ideology is ensured. MacIver (1947) has referred to this as the web of government; Cohen (1969) has spoken of it as the vertical entrenchment of a sociopolitical system. One functional attribute of this process is the reduction of sociocultural hetero-geneity in the service of national integration.

However, there is another quality inherent in this process which was evident in the models concerned with the phase development of leadership and war on poverty organizations. I refer to the quality of overadaptation, the state in which creative impetus is lost and stability and equilibrium within a system prevails.

The concept of overadaptation is couched in a variety of synonyms: stability, cohesion, equilibrium, and has been described in numerous ways. Some scholars have discussed it in terms of some kind of mutual adjustment between human needs and the institutions of the social system.[7] Others refer to a clustering of values into some "pattern" or "configuration" within that system.[8] Still others refer to the interrelationship of personalities, groups, and social systems which results in adjustments of members of the society to the values, attitudes, and procedures of that society.[9] Several authors also refer to the inherent conservatism of social institutions, that once they are formed they tend to persist.[10] Instead of getting to the heart of the specifics which cause overadaptation, most of these suggestions stress some kind of vague interaction between parts of a social system which eventually, somehow, tend to stabilize it.

Overadaptation from my point of view is based upon the extent to which the variety of statuses individuals hold in a society are functionally assimilated or incorporated into the institutions of that society. A high degree of assimilation will be at the expense of the pioneering activities which stimulate the creativity and change implicit in the concepts of adaptation and integration. Cohen describes this phenomenon quite well:

> Cultural adaptation refers to major alterations in the relationship of societies to their habitats that result in different levels of adaptation, from foraging to industrialism. Cultural adjustments refers to the "homeostatic" changes that occur within a society at a given level of

> adaptation; these changes result in a better "fit" or articulation
> between the group's technology and its institutions, ideologies, and
> customary behavior. Adjustments represent conservative forces,
> not forces for evolutionary change. (1968b:57)

In this context, overadaptation is caused from the adjustment that increasing
numbers of individuals make to the institutions in which they participate. At a
high level of theoretical abstraction the result of this process is explained by
Elman Service's "Law of Evolutionary Potential." He states:

> . . . the law of Evolutionary Potential is a simple one. The more
> specialized and adapted a form in a given evolutionary stage, the
> smaller is its potential for passing to the next stage. Another way of
> putting it which is more succinct . . . is: Specific evolutionary
> progress is inversely related to a general evolutionary potential.
> (1960:97)

Specific evolutionary progress is a matter of the degree to which a potential for
creative action is maintained within the social system. When, as Walinsky
suggests (1965:159), "four-fifths of a population is roughly satisfied with things
as they are," a condition I refer to as overadaptation may well be setting in.
Ideologies which support this phenomenon gain in popularity. "America: Love it
or leave it" prevails at the expense of a less popular counter ideology, such as
"America: Change it or lose it." What percentage of the population adheres to
these ideological principles is not of itself important. However, all societies have
to make adaptations to the size and density of the population within their
boundaries. The vast majority of America's citizens may be classified as, for lack
of a better term, middle class. As a result of the adjustments that increasing
numbers of America's population make to this middle-class way of life, its value
and belief system, overadaptation seems to be setting in.

The war on poverty institutions reflect this. Differentiation and
specialization within the context of adaptation refer to the development of "new"
institutions which are better suited to the demands of a changing society. The
war on poverty institutions, however, were simply a recapitulation of institutions,
a mere recasting of traditional structures under new nomenclature. Once a
recapitulation of structures becomes a regular part of the institutionalization
process, it reflects Leslie White's (1949) suggestion that a society's structure gets
in the way of sociocultural change, and the result is overadaptation.

As a result the differentiation of roles and institutions alters in
character. The institutionalization of change to which Eisenstadt (1964a) refers
becomes caught up in the recapitulation of organizations and structures which
serve best the vast majority of the population. Integration and adaptation, as
dynamic processes, manifest increasing homeostatic qualities as the adjustments
persons make to the institutions of the society reflect an increasing enslavement
to tradition and custom. Specialization becomes extreme. The quasi-networks of

social relationship out of which potentially new roles and new institutions may evolve are absorbed by the recapitulation of the nation's institutions. The recapitulation continues to serve the increasing number of persons adapting to the level of abstraction represented by those institutions and their role players. Populations representing other adaptations within the society find ingress into these institutions difficult, if not impossible. Economic expansion, educational innovation, political stimulus for change serve the majority; in the process of adaptation a few within the society are selected against. In the United States they represent those sequestered in poverty habitats. Integration gradually shifts to equilibrium; adaptation to overadaptation.

A theory may now be posited. I suggest that integration and adaptation function as creative processes in a national social system in inverse relationship to the degree and extent of the collective statuses held by social aggregates of persons within the nation's institutions; that is, the greater the adjustment of the nation's population to statuses within the nation's institutions, the more the institutions will respond to and serve that particular population at the expense of those who have not made like adjustments. When the majority of the population is so integrated into the nation's social structure, its institutions will cease to differentiate and through increased specialization merely recapitulate existing national institutional models. Those members of the society who for a variety of reasons—lack of skills, ethnic or racial background, low educational attainment and so forth—are not absorbed into the nation's dominant institutions will be forced to make adaptations outside this complex.

More drastic measures than those provided by the recapitulated bureaucracy of the war on poverty will have to be taken to alter this condition. More significantly, the real foe of the integrative process will have to be confronted and attacked; that is, the institutions of the dominant society. This is made difficult because the resources and ideologies of the nation serve the majority. The institutional representatives of the majority are the architects of planned change, the decisionmakers determining the kind of integration the society will reflect. It cannot be expected that they will seriously plan change at the expense of the adaptation they have made and the institutions which serve them so well.

Daniel Moynihan has been a significant policymaker in the present administration of the United States. He has argued that there are sociopsychological pathologies inherent in black culture—and by extension the culture of poor ethnic minorities throughout the United States generally—which can only be alleviated by some national action. The major problems of persons in poverty, however, are not due to something inherent in their culture. They are, rather, the result of pathologies inherent in the increasing overadaptation of the institutions representative of the dominant culture.

Although I argue that the integration process is dependent upon the political institutions of the nation and the national action which Moynihan suggests, in order to survive themselves these institutions have increasingly adapted to the demand—or inertia—of the majority of America's population, and, if general affluence is a gauge, their decisions and policies seem to be serving this majority rather well. They may give lip service to change regarding the institutions which represent the dominant national culture, but it is always in favor of the agents and participants of that culture. Individual persons in poverty may be absorbed into these institutions, but the population of persons in poverty as a whole will not be.

Still, the war on poverty did stimulate a kind of change that may represent a new process of integration with which American culture will have to contend. Although currently it seems subculturally specific to Mexican-Americans, blacks, and a few dissident white youths, we may be witnessing a differentiation and specialization of habitats as opposed to institutions.

Mexican-Americans, blacks and white youths are displaying nationalistic and separatist tendencies within the United States. As a result of their inability to gain ingress into the institutions representative of the national culture, they are developing new adaptive strategies. It may be predicted that as a result of exclusion from the nation's dominant institutions, and the impetus for change stimulated in large part by the nation's war on poverty, a variety of subculturally specific adaptations within the nation's environment will develop. These will, however, only be slightly similar to the more traditional subcultural habitat of the nation represented by curious customs and quaint folksy ways with complacent populations awaiting exploitation economically and politically by agents of the national culture as the situation demands. The current discussion of a volunteer army suggests one of the first responses by the nation's political institutions to this condition. A reasonable guaranteed annual wage may represent another. Regardless, these adaptations also will only be slightly similar to the prognostication of the Kerner Report (Report of the National Advisory Commission on Civil Disorders, 1968) of two separate and unequal nations existing within the national boundaries of the United States.

More likely new ethnic habitats will emerge in which ideologies, such as "Black is Beautiful" or "La Raza Unida," give meaning to the existence of their populations. They will maintain a loose articulation with the national culture but will resist any firm integration with the nation. They will attempt to gain local control of their institutions, educational, economic, political, and law enforcement apart from those of the national culture. The result will be a realignment of levels of cultural adaptation within the nation.

Relative economic deprivations will also certainly be a part of it; poverty, in the sense of apathy, disillusionment, and isolation from a larger cultural tradition may well not be. The degree to which this will be accomplished will, of course, depend upon the actions of the national political institutions. I think, however, if they wish to alter this process by any means other than direct suppression by force, they will have to recognize that the battlegrounds will have to be the institutions of the culture they represent and not the habitats of the ethnic minorities of the United States.

Chapter Eight

Epilogue: Who Won?

THE CAC

On January 16, 1969 the Economic Opportunity Commission of San Diego County split the Border Area Community Action Council into two separate agencies. The official reason given by the EOC for the split was that the incorporation of county and city communities into one CAC presented too many problems regarding the funding of projects for each area. Residents knew better. No one regretted the action.

The Border Area CAC was maintained but its jurisdiction was restricted to San Ysidro. Another CAC was established in Otay and Woodlawn Park. There was resistance, especially in Otay, to this new CAC because of past experiences. But due to the fact that San Ysidro would not be affiliated with it, considerable community support was acquired and it was generally agreed that the CAC organization and concept should be given one more chance.

Sally Horton became executive secretary of the Otay-Woodlawn Park CAC and she set about to establish a workable organization. She immediately ran into difficulties. Although community enthusiasm for the new CAC was generally high for the first few months, support from the EOC was lacking. The funds used for the previous Border Area CAC were divided between the two. This simply was not sufficient to hire a staff for either agency. Mrs. Horton did acquire an office for the new CAC. She never acquired a staff. Somehow funds were made available to the Border Area CAC for a staff. It was obvious that the EOC wished to placate and avoid any more trouble with this CAC. This discrimination irritated persons in Otay and Woodlawn Park and influenced adversely their commitment to the CAC.

After a short while factionalism began to emerge in Woodlawn Park. The people argued over who should represent the community on the CAC board and over the kind of programs the community needed. Arguments at meetings over who should get what piece of the war on poverty pie, when in fact the plate was empty, alienated responsible and influential persons in both communities. It was a replay of the conflict they had come to detest. Gradually they withdrew their support from the CAC. Nothing was being accomplished; nor did it appear likely anything would be. Just a little over a year after it opened the EOC closed down the Otay-Woodlawn Park CAC.

In San Ysidro for a short period of time things went well with the Border Area CAC. The PFTA and CAC were fused inasmuch as most of the new members of the CAC board of directors were also members of the PFTA. Ramon Cervantes was elected vice president, Mrs. Mercado was elected president, and Esmerelda Hurtado was hired as executive secretary. Conflict was reduced simply by the withdrawal of some contestants from the field, the Anglo board members, Sally Horton, Otay and Woodlawn Park representatives, John Diaz, and others. However, this proved to be a mere *caesura* in the conflict. Disturbances in the sociopolitical life of the arena reemerged with a new gusto in a very short time. Many of the primary contestants remained, the MAAC Center, the PFTA, the CAC, the San Ysidro Planning and Development Group, the EOC, and others. Within months new field contestants, such as the No-freeway committee, emerged and once again augmented the complexity of the arena.

Prior to the re-emergence of conflict, the Border Area CAC did make some positive gains for the community. Almost all were couched in the social service "caretaker" ethic which the PFTA and Mrs. Hurtado had stressed throughout their careers in the arena. The CAC organized its own service center and duplicated the functions and activities of the MAAC service center. They attempted to develop a food and clothing bank for needy persons, to organize a transportation service, and to establish a skill center in which the youth of San Ysidro could acquire training in woodworking, auto mechanics and small appliance repair. Their programs were unorganized, lacked community support, and were short lived. The community action program in the sense of organizing the community toward a set of positive goals ceased to exist. This CAC failed as had its predecessors to do anything about the housing problems, the dislocation of populations, unemployment, and the impending plan to develop San Ysidro.

Other problems also developed which served to undermine the CAC. Many of the new board members spoke no English. As a result, the Border Area CAC placed no representatives on the boards of the delegate agencies in its area, nor did anyone really know the intricacies of the war on poverty policies, guidelines, and procedures. Much had been said by the PFTA of the vast waste of funds by the CAC. Several members of the PFTA who became CAC board members thought these were salaried positions. They were much chagrined to find that they were not. Some were also under the illusion that EOC funds came directly to the CAC for its use. They were surprised to discover that this also was not the case. Divisiveness began to develop along several lines within the CAC.

Over the next nine months the board personnel and CAC membership underwent several changes. By November 1969 Mrs. Hurtado, Ramon Cervantes, and other PFTA members had been permanently excluded from the CAC board. The PFTA was also falling apart. This was due largely to the fact that PFTA support came from persons whose homes were being acquired by the state for the freeway route. As these people became resigned to their fate, apathy began to set in. Many families began to move out of San Ysidro. Support for the PFTA declined accordingly and new elements emerged.

By November a pro-freeway contingent had taken control of the CAC. However, the CAC staff had also been fired during the fights of the preceeding months and EOC refused to permit the hiring of another. It mattered little. This CAC board was favorably disposed to the route and construction of the freeway. They were committed to the development of the area because they wanted the old and unsightly housing removed and believed that jobs would be brought into the area. Most of these people represented a more "middle class" strata of San Ysidro citizenry. They were less cynical than the poor regarding the possibility of improved employment opportunities in the area. They were merely another set of caretakers of the poor.

During this period the CAC did complete the establishment of a food commodities program for San Ysidro. However, its stand on the freeway brought it into conflict with other groups. From November 1969 to July 1970 fights raged in private and in public between those opposed to the freeway and those in favor of it and the development of San Ysidro. The CAC and its supporters, notably now the San Ysidro Planning and Development Group, were reviled in the local Chicano press and by others who saw something immoral and unethical in the dislocation of poor persons and the break up of a community. They argued for other solutions. As a formal body the CAC was removed from these battles in July 1970 when it, along with all the other CACs in San Diego County, was closed by order of the regional OEO office in San Francisco. The community action program in San Diego County had been officially proclaimed a failure.

THE EOC

Throughout 1969 and beyond, the EOC experienced a series of structural and organizational problems of its own. In the spring and early summer of 1969, the regional OEO in San Francisco questioned some of the projects the EOC had approved for funding. They threatened to cut off war on poverty funds in San Diego County unless certain problems were resolved in these projects. Eventually they were, but only after much time and effort had been expended. This not only inhibited the EOC from better assisting the Border Area and Otay-Woodlawn Park CACs, it affected the war on poverty generally in San Diego County. Once again the EOC negotiated with an agency in San Francisco for the purpose of providing antipoverty agency staffs in San Diego with training in the hope of developing leadership and viable community programs. Neither was accomplished.

Another crisis developed around the EOC directorship. Shortly after the head of Area Development resigned, the director of the EOC also resigned. A new deputy director had been hired shortly before this. He hoped to become the new EOC director. The press discovered that he had an extensive criminal record and made an issue of this. They questioned the wisdom of his being placed in charge of a program that allocates some $4.5 million in federal funds. Governor Reagan threatened to cut off the state's contribution to the EOC if he was appointed. He held offfice for a while, but he was not appointed permanently.

An attempt was made during this period to impose a strong leadership on the EOC. It ended in failure. During the several months when the deputy director was more or less in charge, he attempted to tighten up the EOC structure and reorganize several of its departments into more efficient units. He attempted to develop better lines of communication between the EOC and its delegate agencies. He also took firm stands on issues, a quality previous directors had not demonstrated.

For example, one issue that emerged in San Ysidro after the CAC was split again involved Esmerelda Hurtado. Shortly after she became executive secretary the board of directors fired her because, as usual, she refused to follow directions. The board itself then went through a shake up and Ramon Cervantes and other PFTA members were impeached and removed from office. Another board was elected and it promptly rehired Mrs. Hurtado. The new EOC director claimed that she was rehired through illegal procedures and that she had been given more than ample opportunity to prove herself. He insisted that she be removed from office permanently. At the height of the turmoil over this issue he went to San Ysidro to confront the CAC board. So intense were the feelings against his position that he had to be escorted from the meeting by the police. He never returned to San Ysidro. But Esmerelda Hurtado was not rehired as executive secretary.

His actions became increasingly dictatorial and he offended a number of people. Many of the original EOC staff resigned. This could have provided a good chance for the organization to recruit a fresh, dynamic staff. Enthusiastic and dynamic replacements were not to be found. Apathy was now a general characteristic of the war on poverty in San Diego.

Throughout the late summer and fall of 1969, the local press made much of these matters and claimed that the EOC was guilty of mismanagement, unfair hiring practices, and gross misuse and application of funds. These accusations received support by the revelation that a shortage of some $15,000 existed in the MAAC project budget. Although no charges were brought, John Diaz resigned his directorship because of this. The comptroller of the EOC also resigned as a result of implications that he was involved in this fraud.

Shortly thereafter the executive director resigned. He was replaced by a more traditional sort who provided no leadership at all. Model Cities was gaining influence in community programs at the expense of the EOC. And the regional OEO in San Francisco gradually began to dictate policy to the EOC. These policies centered around the de-emphasis of the community action program and culminated in San Diego with the closing of the CACs.

The community action program generally had been judged a failure and it was the state OEO which ordered through a "special condition" in its policy that the CACs of San Diego County be replaced by four neighborhood corporations, each of which would be responsible for a large area and a vast population. It was an attempt to centralize control of the antipoverty program. The allocation of resources to local groups was ended, and this precluded any community action in poverty habitats through the structure of the war on poverty. The intention was now to provide services and to promote something only vaguely defined and understood as "affirmative action programs."

In the summer of 1972 support and leadership from the EOC was at an all time low. Resources for the programs which the neighborhood corporations tried to develop were almost nonexistent. As had been the case with the CACs, the neighborhood corporations were being threatened with disenfranchisement from the antipoverty program and constantly encouraged to seek funding on their own. Such support was hard to acquire. The local people were sick of the antipoverty program. They no longer believed in it. One neighborhood corporation worker in North county organized 150 persons into a child care cooperative on the understanding that the EOC would have funds for the project. At the last minute funds were not allocated. Understandably the people were angry and the worker was reluctant to confront them again. Sally Horton, who had become director of the South Bay Neighborhood Corporation, had all but given up. In the summer of 1972 the rumor was rampant that after August first the neighborhood corporations would receive no more federal support and that the EOC staff would be reduced by one-third. I found no one who really cared.

URBAN DEVELOPMENT

Although the citizens of San Ysidro had been aware for some time of the impending freeway, it was only during the winter of 1969–1970 that the Mexican-American community suddenly was made aware of the fact that a general plan for the development of San Ysidro had been drawn up by the San Ysidro Planning Group and the San Diego Planning Department. In February 1970 the *San Ysidro Plan* was presented to the people of the community at a public meeting. It was vigorously opposed by the three hundred persons who attended.

For the first time the full extent of the intentions of the San Ysidro

Planning Group for San Ysidro were public knowledge. Residents are quoted in the press as saying that prior to the public meeting they had never heard of the development plan. The Mexican-American community quickly sized up the effect it would have upon San Ysidro—higher taxes, high density population zoning, the establishment of localized welfare communities, the transformation of Mexican-American residential areas into industrial zones, the intrusion of land speculators into the area—and recognized the extent of the threat to the integrity of their community. The final fight had begun.

The Chicano press of San Diego County, *La Verdad*, published names and background information of several members of the San Ysidro Planning Group. It discussed the deleterious effect the freeway would have upon the community and compared the fate of San Ysidro to that which had previously befallen black and Mexican-American areas of Southeast San Diego as the result of a similar freeway system; the displacement of ethnic minority populations, community fragmentation, higher taxes, and relocation into poorer housing for higher rents. One of the new contestants in the arena was the No-Freeway Committee of San Ysidro. For a while Mrs. Hurtado was the head of the committee. This committee and other groups brought into San Ysidro influential Mexican-Americans, such as Dr. Ernesto Galarza, a professor at San Jose State College and author of *The Merchants of Labor*, to speak against the community development plan. The Chicano Federation of San Diego County came to the support of the No-Freeway Committee. They demanded that the freeway be routed around San Ysidro and that the housing project allocations in San Ysidro be investigated by federal officials.

One young Chicano who was employed by the San Diego Planning Department became involved in this issue. He supported the residents of San Ysidro and was instrumental in having the freeway plans modified so that the freeway would run at ground level rather than elevated over the community upon a huge heap of earth. He became an embarrassment to the planning department and lost his job. However, sufficient pressure was brought to bear so that the director of the San Diego Planning department proposed in August 1970 an alternate freeway route which would by-pass San Ysidro. It was a route that could have been taken much earlier. The mayor also ordered a temporary halt to freeway construction so that an alternate route might be studied. By that time plans were too far along, too much property had been acquired, and too much had been invested to so radically alter the route. Nothing was changed.

At the height of the conflict twenty-two organizations were protesting the freeway and development plan. Most of them came from outside San Ysidro. There was little coordination between them and many were involved merely for the purpose of making noise in order to promote their interpretation of Chicano nationalism. Almost no Anglos came out in support of the Mexican-Americans. Most Anglos were in favor of the community's development and the removal of the poor Mexican-American areas.

Advantages that were provided to the opponents of the freeway, such as the study of an alternate route proposed by the mayor, were not followed up. Arguments that the land which the state highway department had acquired for the route could be resold at a profit were never acted upon. Gradually the opposition faded away. Many persons tired of the fight. Most decided it was hopeless. There was no specific point at which the battle could be said to have ended. The forces with power simply waited out the turmoil.

Some of the poor did acquire 235 housing in the area. Ramon Cervantes and a few other PFTA members did. Many in San Ysidro accused them of selling out for a house. They have no following today, and they have been very quiet since moving into their new homes. The rent subsidy complex named Villa Nueva was completed in 1970. It apparently took quite a number of local residents, although exactly how many people left before the complex was completed is difficult to determine. And Villa Nueva has had a large turnover. By 1972 the vast majority of the nearly 2,000 people in Villa Nueva came from places other than San Ysidro, some from as far away as Los Angeles. The population in Villa Nueva is 82 percent Mexican-American and 17 percent Anglo. Eighty percent of this population is on welfare. Ninety percent of the welfare recipients are Mexican-American. The county welfare department expects Villa Nueva to become a 100 percent welfare community—a poverty habitat—in the very near future.

By the summer of 1972 the number of dwelling units in San Ysidro had increased from 1,664 total units in 1970 to 2,473; the population had increased from almost 6,000 to almost 8,500. Most of the homes are for middle-class persons who have flocked into the area; 235 units of housing for the poor are localized in a few areas. Services—health, education, police, sanitation, transportation—have not been able to keep up with the population growth. The residents are now reluctant to accept any more low-income housing in the area. Employment opportunities have not improved and unemployment among the Mexican-American population is at least as high as it was in 1968.

The war on poverty in San Diego County and in San Ysidro accomplished very little. The poor are still with us. In San Ysidro people sneer when the war on poverty is mentioned. They want nothing more to do with it.

There has been, however, some positive change in San Ysidro. Most poor persons do have better living units now. A well-equipped health center sponsored by the EOC and Model Cities and constructed with an OEO grant and county funds has opened. The poor also have a louder voice now than before the war on poverty was declared. They recognize that they have some potential as a political force in the society. They have acquired organizations and leadership which did not exist previously. This is true in San Ysidro and elsewhere. Perhaps the first real manifestation of their effect upon the sociopolitical institutions of the larger society will be when the persons in poverty habitats, such as San Ysidro, are able to thwart the private interest of agents of the national culture and force them into actions which will directly serve the needs of the poverty habitat.

San Ysidro Community Survey
San Diego, California

This survey and report was prepared during the summer of 1968 by the following college students employed and supervised by the San Diego City Planning Department, Community Planning Division A, Team B: Frank Cervantes, Daniel LaBotz, and Robert Carrillo.

INTRODUCTION

The San Ysidro Planning and Development Group has the responsibility of working with the city of San Diego in formulating a long-range community plan that will guide growth in San Ysidro. In preparing the community plan, it became apparent that San Ysidro had problems that were unique because of the ethnic composition of the residents, its isolation from San Diego urban centers, and its proximity to Tijuana, Baja California, Mexico.

Although the Planning Department had a general understanding of the particular problems that exist in San Ysidro, it was felt that there was a lack of knowledge about many of the more human facets of the community. In order to gain understanding of San Ysidro's problems and to better integrate the solutions into the community plan, a special approach to the problem was needed. It was, therefore, decided that a canvass of the area would provide a better understanding of the physical needs and the attitudes of residents. The findings of the survey would be taken into consideration in attempting to provide planning that would improve the living environment of the people of San Ysidro.

The team which conducted the survey was made up of three males, two Mexican-Americans and one Anglo-American,[1,2] all in their early twenties. The team was occasionally assisted by two Mexican-American adult females who were working with the San Ysidro Community Action Council.

In choosing the survey team, special care was taken to select people

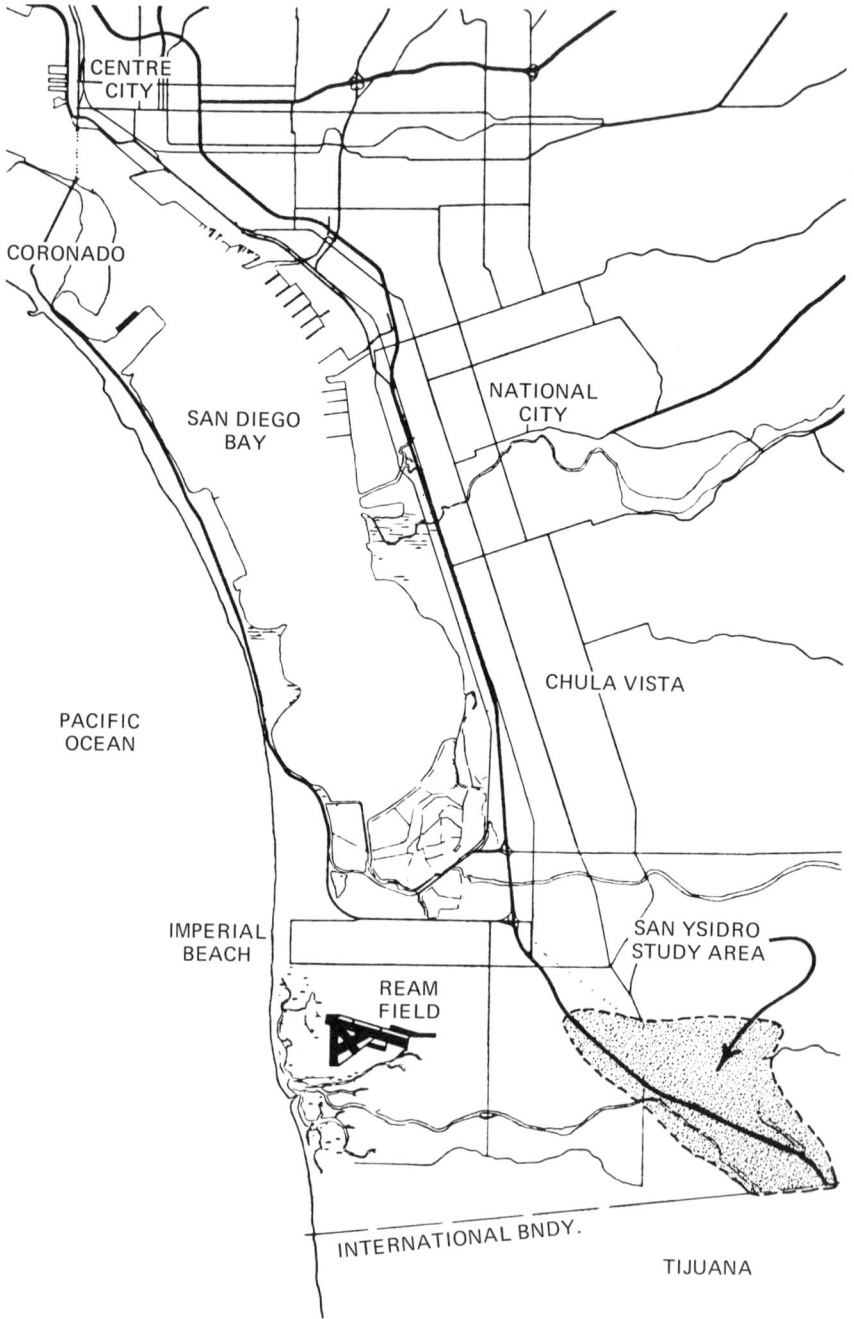

Figure A.1.   The South San Diego Bay Area.

who were bilingual, had some knowledge of Mexican-American customs and cultural patterns, and had experience in working with the public. The attempt was made to choose people who showed cognizance of and sensitivity toward the type of social conditions that appeared to exist in San Ysidro, but at the same time to find people who were as much as possible open-minded and unencumbered by biases that would impede their accurate perception of San Ysidro's problems.

SUMMARY

Population Characteristics
About two-thirds of all households contacted were Mexican-American.

Thirty-one percent of all respondents spoke only Spanish.

Almost half of the adults contacted in San Ysidro were not U.S. citizens.

Social
Many Mexican-Americans have strong attachments to Tijuana.

Housing
Twenty-six percent of the dwelling units in San Ysidro appeared to be substandard.

Seventy-three percent of the Mexican-American people presently renting housing would prefer to live in single-family dwelling units.

Sixty-four percent of all respondents renting housing would prefer to own their homes.

Seventy-one percent of the respondents pay rent of less than $100 per month. Generally, the residents felt they could not afford to pay more.

Churches
Most of the respondents felt that church facilities were adequate.

Employment
The unemployment rate for the Mexican-Americans living in San Ysidro is over three times the national average.

Fifty-five percent of the Anglo-Americans interviewed in San Ysidro are retired.

The most common job experience indicated by the Mexican-Americans contacted was agriculture.

Education
Respondents had virtually no complaints about the educational

system; however, their responses indicated they may not be knowledgeable of the system.

Twenty-six percent of all Mexican-American respondents expressed a desire to take citizenship classes.

Forty-two percent of all respondents indicated a desire to attend adult education classes.

Fifty-three percent of the respondents stated that the existing library is not adequate; many who said it is adequate thought it would not be in the near future.

Recreation

An overwhelming majority of the respondents states that there were inadequate recreational facilities in San Ysidro.

A majority of the respondents felt that San Ysidro's greatest recreational need was a swimming pool.

Transportation

A fourth of all responding households had no car.

One of the primary complaints of the respondents was the lack of adequate bus service.

Seventy-four percent of all respondents stated that they would ride public busses if more adequate service were provided.

Commercial

Respondents do much of their shopping outside of San Ysidro, with Chula Vista receiving a large part of their commerce.

Most of the people interviewed felt that the facilities now under construction will help alleviate some of San Ysidro's commercial problems.

Medical

Only fourteen percent of the respondents obtain medical services in San Ysidro.

Public Facilities and Services

Some respondents felt that San Ysidro had been better off under the administration of the County.

SURVEY METHODOLOGY

The survey was conducted during the months of July and August 1968 on weekdays between 8:30 in the morning and 9:00 in the evening. The surveyors attempted to contact all the permanent residents of San Ysidro, including those residing in houses, trailers, apartments, hotels, motels, and courts.[3]

The surveyors used a city of San Diego vehicle and wore printed badges identifying them as "Survey Enumerators" of the City of San Diego. Sometimes the residents who were contacted were first presented with a statement, in Spanish and English, explaining the nature and purpose of the survey (see Survey Questionnaire, p. 000); at other times the surveyors identified themselves orally and explained the survey.

If no one was home, or if on the first or second call the resident indicated that he or she could not reply at that time, the surveyors made arrangements to return at a more convenient time, calling back as many as three times to complete the interview. If the neighbors indicated that a person worked during certain hours, that was taken into consideration in an attempt to reach all the people possible.

For several reasons the surveyors, and not those being interviewed, filled out the questionnaire. The first reason for this was to save time. The second was because many of the questions would seem ambiguous without a knowledge of the question's intent. Third and most important was because the surveyors wanted an opportunity to get into an informal discussion with the respondents, feeling that in an informal situation people would more fully reveal the type of information being sought.

In attempting to become as knowledgeable about the community as possible, important individuals and organizations within the community were contacted. In particular, the San Ysidro Planning and Development Group was contacted in the initial formulation of the questionnaire and their help was sought in assessing the most effective way of carrying out the survey. The team worked in close association with the Community Action Council and with Assistant Professor Donald Kurtz of San Diego State College, an anthropologist conducting a study of the Mexican-American culture in San Ysidro. The surveyors received coopration and assistance from Fred Martinez of the United Farm Workers Organizing Committee (AFL–CIO) in San Ysidro, from persons in the Mexican-American Advisory Committee Neighborhood Service Center, as well as the San Ysidro Teen Post. The surveyors used the office of the Community Action Council as a local headquarters in San Ysidro during much of the study.

Additional Data

Several other surveys were being conducted in San Ysidro at about the same time that this survey was being undertaken. The Community Action Council was conducting a survey, also related to the living conditions, but primarily oriented towards the problems of particular families. That survey took the names and addresses of all the households contacted, as well as the names of the children, their ages and the schools they attended. The CAC survey was also directed towards determining the interest of the people in attending CAC meetings and in generally taking an active part in the political life of the city.

Assistant Professor of Anthropology Donald Kurtz of San Diego State College was conducting a survey to ascertain to what extent the Mexican-Americans living in San Ysidro are caught up in a life style which has been described as "culture poverty." This questionnaire attempted to determine to what extent the Mexican-Americans were involved in the community of San Ysidro and in the city of Tijuana, Baja California, Mexico. Questions included "How often do you go to Tijuana? Do you go there to shop? for food? for clothing? Do you go to the barber or beauty salon there? Do you have relatives living there that you visit? Comadres or compadres?"

Western Behavioral Sciences Institute also conducted two surveys in San Ysidro during the month of August.[4] They did a survey of thirty people who had attended two or more Community Action Council meetings to determine their attitude towards the poverty program. They also did a Poverty Area Community Survey to gather sociodemographic characteristics of the poverty area in order to evaluate the Office of Economic Opportunities' War on Poverty Program. The latter survey involved fifty randomly selected households. The results of these two surveys were not available at the date of publishing this report.

The Mexican-American Advisory Committee Neighborhood Service Center conducted a survey at approximately the same time of the people being displaced by Freeway 805, to find out their attitudes and problems.

In recognition of the numerous inquiries being conducted in San Ysidro during the summer of 1968, an attempt was made to avoid irritating people by conducting the City Planning Department's survey, the CAC survey and Professor Kurtz's survey simultaneously whenever it was feasible.

In spite of this, many people were understandably disturbed by the repeated calls of interviewers. Typical was the statement of the man who told the surveyors, "Get the hell out of here; I answered a bunch of questions like this just the other day."

VALIDITY OF THE SURVEY

There are several factors involved in the taking of the survey which may invalidate some of its results. To begin with the appurtenances which were to vouch for the legitimacy of the surveyors, the official car, white shirts and badges, may actually have intimidated many people. Several people said that because of the green car they thought the surveyors "were the border patrol." One small child ran ahead of the surveyors telling people that they had better come out because "the police are here." It has been frequently estimated that half of the Mexican-American adults in San Ysidro are not citizens, and many are recently immigrated. Consequently many of the people contacted were made afraid or anxious by the interview. For example, some attempted to show their immigration papers to prove that they were not illegally entered, others were too agreeable and attempted to tell the surveyors what they sensed the surveyors wanted to hear.

Conducting the survey in the summer also undoubtedly had an effect on its validity. There are some seasonal workers, field workers, packers and sorters, grooms and trainers, living in San Ysidro, and there may have been a greater or lesser number during the summer months. San Ysidro also has some summer dwellers who reside elsewhere in the winter. There was nothing on the survey to account for these types of residents. Probably the most important problem arising from conducting the survey in the summer relates to the school children. According to the San Ysidro School District Superintendent, Jack Sherman, every fall San Ysidro is inundated with school children from Mexico. Since this survey was conducted during July and August, the absence of these children may have affected the information that was gathered concerning the average number of children per family.

Another factor influencing the accuracy of the survey, was the fact that the surveyors were called upon to make certain estimations and approximations. For example the surveyors had to estimate the condition of the housing, and frequently the age of the respondent. Occasionally they had to judge whether or not it would be wise to omit a certain question, the answer to which seemed to be implied, rather than irritate an already exasperated respondent. To minimize these problems and increase the validity of the results, estimates of the housing conditions were based on a criteria used by all the surveyors while estimates of age only had to be within ten years.

The greatest problem in conducting the survey was that virtually all of the people being questioned had had no forewarning of the interview. They were not in many cases prepared to answer the questions. Perhaps they had never thought about the things being asked, at least in the way it was asked. This led to the almost inevitable problem of leading respondents in their answers. The surveyors would go to a home and ask, "What sort of recreational facilities are needed in San Ysidro?" Perhaps the person being questioned had just been called away from her housework, she'd respond, "I don't know, what do you mean?" The interviewer would respond, "Well, do you think a movie theater would go over in San Ysidro, or a new bowling alley?" the interviewee would answer, "Yes, we could use a movie theater or a bowling alley."

Once they became aware of these problems the surveyors were able to solve some of them. When they realized that Mexican-Americans sometimes neglected to mention that they shopped in Tijuana, they would specifically ask them if they ever shopped there, rather than simply asking them where they shopped. Once they realized that they had been inadvertently leading people, they tried to repeat or further explain the question, rather than give examples. Consequently they were able to counteract to some extent the problems encountered in the taking of the survey.

Despite the problems, the survey is felt to be successful in eliciting the opinions, attitudes, and problems of the people. Because of the loose structure of the survey and because the questions were open, rather than offering certain "choices" the people would often begin talking rather than simply answering, giving their feelings rather than mechanical responses.

Another of the benefits of this loose conversational approach was that the surveyors were often invited into the homes of the people of San Ysidro, giving them a greater insight into the actual living conditions of the people. Being in the homes also gave them an opportunity to find out the attitudes and opinions of several of the members of one family, including the children who may be more knowledgeable about some areas of the community than the adults.

GENERAL CONCLUSIONS

Population Characteristics

Part of the survey attempted to determine the ethnic composition of the San Ysidro area, information which is invaluable in understanding the community's problems. There were 778 households contacted (this figure does not include vacancies and people on vacation). Of these, 516 or 66.3 percent can be considered Mexican-Americans, and 262 or 33.7 percent of the people contacted can be considered Anglo-Americans or people belonging to some other ethnic group (only about five households would not fit into the Mexican-American and Anglo-American classifications). Forty percent of the Mexican-American families interviewed were, in their own opinion, bilingual, while 31 percent felt themselves to be competent in Spanish only. Of the Anglo-American households contacted, only 73.3 percent responded to the survey while 97.7 percent of all Mexican-Americans cooperated.

Among the English-speaking members of the community, half the residents contacted who responded to the survey were male and half were female. The Spanish-speaking and bilingual respondents, however, were predominantly female, about three-quarters were female and one-quarter were male. This difference in the sex of the respondents is believed to be due to the fact that the Anglo-American community in San Ysidro is made up largely of retirement age people, while the Mexican-American community is much younger. When the first calls were made during the day many more male Anglo-Americans were home, being retired, than were male Mexican-Americans. The ages of the respondents also reflects this difference in the make-up of the community; more than 70 percent of the Anglo-Americans contacted were over fifty, while around the same percentage of Mexican-Americans contacted were under fifty.

The San Ysidro School District's 1967 statistics on the ethnic composition of their students also help give a picture of the area: 86 percent of the students are Mexican-Americans (identified by Spanish surnames), while 13 percent are Anglo-Americans and 1 percent are of some other ethnic background.

San Ysidro School District Superintendent Jack Sherman indicates that the Mexican-American student population rises approximately 3 percent annually.

The Mexican-American families in San Ysidro are, according to the survey, considerably larger than Anglo-American families. The Anglo-American family surveyed in San Ysidro has an average of .36 children per household. The Mexican-American families average 2.30 children per household. Of those families having children, a larger percentage of Mexican-American families have women as the head of the household than do Anglo-American families. About 10 percent of the Anglo-American families with children have women as the head of the household, while about 15 percent of the Mexican-American families with children have women as heads of household. Of these women who were heads of households with children, it seemed to the surveyors, that a disproportionate number were widows.

Social

Many of the Mexican-Americans living in San Ysidro are recent arrivals from rural areas of Mexico. Thus, the Mexican-American community is not quite as stable as the Anglo-American community. However, a larger percentage of Mexican-Americans indicated an intent to stay in the area than did the Anglo-Americans.

Many, if not most, of the Mexican-Americans living in San Ysidro have relatives living in San Ysidro and Tijuana—consequently they have very strong attachments to the community. The San Ysidro Mexican-American community, in terms of its interests, activities, and sentiments, may be more strongly attached to Tijuana than to San Diego, according to the preliminary results of the survey of Donald Kurtz.

Although most Mexican-Americans surveyed live in poverty,[5] there is a growing segment of middle-class Mexican-Americans, most of whom live in new housing developments. These new developments, west of Otay Mesa Road and north of Vista Avenue, while they encompass a small area at the present time, will become more important as San Ysidro grows. Although most of the occupants of this new housing are Mexican-Americans, they have, on the whole, no ties with the "old" San Ysidro. Most of them never lived in San Ysidro before, and many are recently immigrated from Mexico. They are primarily from the middle or upper-middle class, while many of the people residing in "old" San Ysidro are of the lower-middle or lower class. The housing is better in terms of size and quality and much more expensive than the rest of the housing in San Ysidro. It is certainly financially out of the reach of most of the people living in "old" San Ysidro.

The people living in the older housing in San Ysidro do not consider the houses part of their town, nor do the people living in the new developments identify themselves with San Ysidro. The new developments are not commonly referred to as "San Ysidro," and people speak of going "back to San Ysidro."

The typical family living in the new housing may work in Tijuana, shop in Chula Vista, and send its children to parochial schools in San Diego proper. They are skilled or professional people; they own more than one automobile and live in above average quality housing. Though they are of Mexican descent, they tend to identify themselves with the Mexican upper class rather than with the Mexican-American community in San Ysidro.

Of the households contacted by the survey, about a third were Anglo-American. More than half of the Anglo-American respondents were retired, and many were single. Like many of the Mexican-Americans, many of the retired Anglo-Americans seem in a rather precarious financial position, social security or pensions comprising their sole means of support.

The retired Anglo-Americans appear to be less a part of the community of San Ysidro. Several factors would account for this. They are the minority and for the most part they do not speak Spanish. Unlike the Mexican-Americans, they do not generally have family ties in San Ysidro or in Tijuana. Some of them actually live in San Ysidro only a few months of the year, while many others live in trailer parks where circumstances often foster a feeling of isolation or separation from the community.

Despite their rather tenuous relation to the community, the Anglo-American community is very stable. Almost 24 percent of the Anglo-Americans surveyed have lived in San Ysidro between ten and nineteen years, and about 27 percent for more than twenty years. About 78 percent indicated they intended to stay in San Ysidro.

The military personnel and their dependents form the smallest group within the community. However, considering the proximity of naval facilities in the area, one of them being Ream Field, one of the largest helicopter facilities in the world, this population may grow considerably larger in the near future. Also included in this group, are the Border Patrol officers and their families.

These employees and families are, by and large, Anglo-Americans. They have not been in the area very long, and it is presumed they probably do not intend to stay, nor to return. They have located in San Ysidro, usually because they could not find housing in Imperial Beach or Chula Vista. They are not very active in civic affairs, since they appear to feel no real attachment to the community.

The Mexican-American population of San Ysidro is not rigidly isolated from the Anglo-American population. Mexican-Americans can be found living in houses, trailers, and apartments in almost every area of San Ysidro. Some Anglo-Americans, however, expressed a degree of animosity toward the Mexican-American, as exemplified by some of the following observations. One Anglo-American, living in a comfortable house said, "They should close down the border and not let any Mexicans come across to shop or to work. My wife's been looking for a job all over the South Bay area and she can't get one cause she don't speak Spanish." Another Anglo-American man said, "Every September all these Mexican kids come up here to get an education, and I don't think I should have to pay for it." An older Anglo-American man who has been coming to live in a San Ysidro hotel every summer for several years said, "I used to like it here, but now the Mexicans are trying to run the town; a white man doesn't stand a chance here. I don't think I'm coming back anymore." A young Anglo-American woman who was being interviewed by one of the Mexican-American surveyors told him that she "hated Mexicans," and that that was one reason her family was moving out of San Ysidro. The survey also indicated that in some cases, middle-class Mexican-Americans also expressed contempt for the poorer Mexican-Americans.

Housing

One of the outstanding problems in San Ysidro is the lack of adequate supply of sound housing. This fact has been established through previous census studies and is reinforced by this survey. Twenty-six percent of the total housing surveyed in San Ysidro appeared to be inadequate.[6] Because the people living in this poor housing are primarily the Mexican-Americans who have the larger families, it is estimated that about half the people in San Ysidro are living in housing judged to be less than standard. Due to the somewhat restricted scope of the survey it was not possible to examine in detail the condition of housing. However, it was possible to observe clues which might indicate that a house had a high potential of being a threat to the health, safety, and well-being of the occupants.

The Mexican-Americans in San Ysidro appeared to live in poorer housing than their Anglo-American neighbors. Using the criteria of the 1960 census, 31 percent of the Mexican-Americans live in housing that could be classed as substandard while only 13 percent of the Anglo-Americans live in housing that could be so classified.

Problems which the survey indicated to be typical of the San Ysidro area are overcrowding, outdated or substandard plumbing and electrical wiring, lack of screening, dilapidated porches, crumbling plaster, and general evidences of physical disrepair, such as lack of paint, broken walkways, driveways, and windows. While not documented by the survey, pests and vermin are also considered a serious problem in San Ysidro; as an employee of the State Employment Agency in San Ysidro said, "The strongest union in San Ysidro is the United Cockroaches."

The housing problems seem to be the result of many factors. First, the existence of many very old structures, which were built many years ago, when the area was still an unincorporated portion of San Diego County with very few building regulations. Second, there is an inadequate supply of new structures in San Ysidro in the lower price ranges available to persons with low incomes. Third, there is a desire expressed by many of the people interviewed to continue living in a Mexican neighborhood near the border. Fourth, there is a low vacancy rate in housing throughout San Diego which contributes to maintenance of high rent levels.

There were also many more subtle things helping to perpetuate poor housing conditions. According to the 1968 survey of the Community Action Council, half the adults in San Ysidro are not citizens and are not familiar with actions which they might take to improve their housing conditions. Because of their citizenship status many tend to feel intimidated by government officials and agencies and as a consequence avoid calling attention to themselves by complaining about problems.

Whether justified or not, some tenants actually fear deportation should they challenge their landlords by some sort of legal action. One man with no electricity in his home was, for six months, forced to run an extension wire from the next apartment to his. He told the surveyors that his landlord said he wouldn't repair the wiring and that if the tenant had it repaired and billed to the landlord, the tenant would be evicted. In the words of the tenant, "He (the landlord) said he'd have me evicted, but I think he might even try to have me deported." The survey revealed that the threat of deportation is very real to many of the Mexican-Americans in San Ysidro and makes it difficult for such organizations as the Community Action Council, the Renters and Poor People's Association, or others to organize and work effectively towards correcting housing deficiencies.

Inasmuch as inspection and enforcement of codes are largely made in response to complaints from citizens and since the above circumstances make such citizen complaints often unlikely, there results an ever-growing inventory of housing deficiencies. On the other hand rigid enforcement of all governmental codes and regulations would undoubtedly cause considerable local hardship in view of the shortage of alternative standard housing in the area.

Ninety-two percent of the Mexican-American respondents prefer to live in a single family dwelling, while less than 3 percent prefer apartments. As one Mexican-American lady put it, she didn't think apartments would be very popular because, "Mexican people want a little place to plant their 'cilantre e yerba buena' (herbs), and they won't have that in an apartment house."

Approximately one out of six dwelling units in San Ysidro will be eliminated to make way for the new Interstate 805 and for the widening of Interstate 5.[7] Consequently about one-fifth of San Ysidro's population will be forced to move. A 398-unit federal rent-subsidy housing development is proposed to begin construction in the near future. It is hoped that this program will provide housing for most of the people to be displaced by the freeways. Many people interviewed expressed a concern, however, that this housing development would not be completed before they were relocated by the freeway and that they would, therefore, be forced to leave San Ysidro, despite their expressed desire to stay.

Churches

Most of the respondents felt that church facilities were adequate. Those few who didn't indicated that they felt that it was the responsibility of the particular denomination in need of better church facilities to solve their own problem.

Employment

Another significant problem is unemployment, often causing or contributing to the housing problem. To understand the magnitude of the problem one must see it in comparison to the problem of the United States or San Diego County as a whole. The federal government announced that the national unemployment rate for the month of August 1968, the same month in which the San Ysidro survey was conducted, was 3.5. Based upon the survey respondents, the unemployment rate in San Ysidro was estimated as high as 8.2, or better than twice the national average and the overall unemployment rate for the Mexican-Americans interviewed was estimated at 10.6. The *San Diego Labor Market Bulletin* indicated that the county rate of unemployment for the month of June 1968 was 4.1 (seasonally adjusted).

The survey indicated that there are several factors contributing to the unemployment problem. Most obvious is the inability of the residents of the area to speak English. Another very important factor is the low educational attainment of many members of the Mexican-American community; many have only a sixth grade education in Mexican schools, that is, in a country with different customs and a different language.

Added to the low level of educational attainment is the fact that San Ysidro is far from most of the employment centers in the county, a real problem in an area with a lack of rapid, handy economical transportation. The survey indicated that many people in San Ysidro are seasonally employed: field workers, sorters, packers, cannery workers, track workers, and others. Many of these people indicated to the surveyors that they are being employed only part time, when actually they are in need of full-time work. Several people told the surveyors that they must accept unskilled or semi-skilled work simply because skilled employment for which they believe they are qualified has not been available to them.

The most common job experience among San Ysidro males is agriculture. Thirty-eight Mexican-American respondents are working or have worked as farm laborers. Other common job experiences were mechanic, gardener, construction worker, factory worker, custodian, sales clerk, and painter.

The most common female job experience was equally divided between seamstress and secretary. Twenty-nine respondents were employed or have experience in each category.

Many of the people interviewed felt that the employment problems would be alleviated by bringing industry to the area. There was also a lot of interest manifested in industrial employment for women.

The people interviewed also expressed an interest in trade schools and on-the-job training. "Electronics" and "mechanic" were the two most common skills preferred by men. Sixty women, mostly Mexican-American, would like to learn the skills of a seamstress. It is possible, however, that some women would use the skill in home occupations and would not intend to be employed as a seamstress. Secretary and nursing were also popular choices. A few of the people interviewed were already receiving some sort of training, through "Jobs Now" or other welfare program.

Education

The people surveyed in San Ysidro felt that there was very little problem in education. The Community Action Council survey of 1968, also reported that only 5 out of 504 households indicated that there was a problem in education at any level. However, indirect responses of those interviewed and observations of the surveyors may indicate otherwise. In many cases the respondents have been educated in the grammer schools of Mexico and are not familiar with the English language, American educational customs, or teaching methods. As a consequence they are not familiar with the opportunities or shortcomings of the educational system in the United States. They have little time to attend meetings concerning education, and they may not have transportation to take them to meetings. Some respondents indicated that they were self-conscious about their poor clothing and consequently too embarrassed to attend meetings.

Despite the evident satisfaction of the parents with the educational system, the surveyors encountered students who were less satisfied. Speaking with teenagers at the San Ysidro Teen Post, the surveyors found that many of them felt that they had been discriminated against by teachers and especially by counselors. Some felt that they had been suspended or expelled without sufficient reason. The majority of the students interviewed indicated that they had problems with the English language. A large number seemed to have no respect for the educational system and were not much interested in continuing their education.

In addition to the comments above, the surveyors learned of various activities and/or programs to deal with the problem of education in this Mexican-American community including Pre-school or "Headstart" programs, bilingual classes, and adult educational programs. It was beyond the scope of this survey to investigate and comment on these efforts.

The adults in San Ysidro indicated that they were very anxious about improving their education. Of the Mexican-Americans, 50 percent were interested in adult education and 26 percent in citizenship classes. Only 21 percent of Anglo-Americans were interested in some sort of adult education. Those who spoke only Spanish had the greatest need for higher education and expressed the greatest desire for it. It is reasonable to assume that many more might have been interested had they really thought it possible for themselves.

Fifty-three percent of the respondents felt that the library was inadequate. Many of those who considered that it was adequate felt that it would not remain so for long. Typical of the responses were the following: "the library is not open nearly long enough" (it is presently open only 15 hours a week); "it's much too small"; "the selection of books is poor, especially for adults"; "there are not enough books in Spanish."

Recreation

While they might not agree on the nature of the improvements needed, the need for better recreational facilities in San Ysidro was something that members of both the Mexican-American community and the Anglo-American community agreed upon. The Mexican-Americans interviewed expressed the desire to see better recreational facilities for their children. They were especially concerned about the need for better facilities for teenagers, though they by no means thought that there were adequate facilities for younger children. Most of the Anglo-Americans, on the other hand, felt that there was a real need for improvements in recreational facilities for the elderly members of the community, although many expressed a realization of the importance of facilities for teenagers. Even families without children, in both the Mexican and Anglo communities, were anxious to point out need for facilities for teenagers.

The renovation of San Ysidro's park will go a long way towards improving San Ysidro, but the survey indicates that the renovation will not completely solve recreation problems. Some of the renovations will be very valuable for younger children, and the landscaping of the park, the lawn and trees, will be very appealing to families and to the elderly members of the community. Some respondents did not approve of the proposed tennis courts and suggested that some other type of equipment, such as a pool table in the recreation hall, might be more used and more appreciated.

The existing hall in the park while it may be sound and large was not very attractive to the citizens. It was frequently viewed as functionally deficient because it could not, for example, be divided for meetings by the Senior Citizens' Club and young peoples' groups. Some people also felt that it was an eyesore.

The San Diego City Recreation Department employs a director in the San Ysidro Recreation Center located in the hall who supervises activities. The programs of the Recreation Department are aimed primarily at young people. There are not really many facilities to work with, however, and the people surveyed had very little to say one way or another about it.

Larson Athletic Field, located at Ensenada Street and Boston Avenue, is not only far from much of San Ysidro, it is in very poor repair and virtually useless for sports events. It is little more than a stone strewn vacant lot and many people were unaware of its existence. Lucky Waller Field, located approximately at the intersection of Palm Avenue and North Vista, while it has a small lawn, has no real facilities and is located much too far from the existing San Ysidro population to be of any value at the present time.[8]

The Mexican-American Advisory Committee is responsible for the existence of a San Ysidro Teen Post which serves as a gathering place and provides some entertainment for teenagers, such as a Ping-Pong table, a small dance hall, and trips to the swimming pool in Chula Vista. However, at the time of the report, the building in which they have been located is being razed and they have not yet made suitable arrangements for another location. Many people in San Ysidro expressed the feeling that this Teen Post was a step in the right direction, but that it was not adequate in size or variety of recreational opportunities.

There is virtually no commercial recreation such as theaters, bowling alleys, etc., in the area. Many people indicated that when they want entertainment they leave San Ysidro. Many of the Mexican-Americans said that they frequently went to the parks of Tijuana, Chula Vista, National City, and to Balboa Park. Many Mexican-Americans also said they go to Tijuana for commercial entertainment, and Anglo-Americans indicated that they often cross the border to attend the horse races.

The people surveyed repeatedly expressed the desire for a swimming pool. They felt that this would be good for both young children and teenagers. There is no swimming pool closer than Imperial Beach or Chula Vista and many people do not have the time, money, or transportation to take their children that far. They often pointed to the success of the temporary pool which was set up at Sunset School for a short period this summer, as evidence that the pool would be well used and appreciated.

Other recreational facilities which the people were anxious to see were an athletic field and a movie theater which would show Mexican movies. The athletic field they suggested would be for baseball, football, and soccer. They were also interested in a bowling alley, a roller rink, and in a dance hall for adults as well as teenagers.

Transportation

Nearly all the people interviewed felt that there is a severe transportation problem in San Ysidro. It is served approximately half-hourly round the clock by Western Greyhound Line, but the bus stops are limited on the northbound route, and the southbound Greyhound stops only at the border—or as much as two miles from some parts of San Ysidro. Services are also provided every two hours from seven in the morning until five in the afternoon by San Diego Economy Lines Incorporated, but like Greyhound the number of stops are few. In addition to the stops being poorly located, people surveyed said that the fares were too high for many of the people in San Ysidro, especially for the elderly, the retired, and the unemployed. Since San Ysidro does have a large percentage of retired people, many of whom are too old to drive, there is a great demand for adequate bus service. The surey indicated that about one-quarter of the families interviewed owned no private automobiles.

Commercial

It was the opinion of most of the people interviewed that any current shopping problems would soon be alleviated by the new commercial center going in on northern San Ysidro Boulevard. San Ysidro has for many years lacked any significant variety of businesses, being served mostly by numerous small, independent grocery stores. The grocery stores cater to shoppers from Tijuana; they have little variety and frequently carry poorer quality merchandise. Despite the economic drawbacks, many Mexican-Americans in San Ysidro indicated that they prefer to shop in San Ysidro because Spanish is spoken in the stores, there is personal service, and Mexican merchandise is featured. In addition, some of these grocery stores extend credit. Then again, many people indicated that they shop in San Ysidro, only because they have no transportation to travel to the shopping centers in Imperial Beach, Chula Vista, National City, and San Diego. Many Mexicans and some Anglo-Americans shop in Tijuana, especially for such items as beef and tortillas.

The people again and again indicated the need for a supermarket, and they also repeatedly expressed the desire for another drug store, a five-and-dime and a shoe store—all of which should be available in the new shopping center. Two other types of stores which were repeatedly mentioned as needed were clothing stores and hardware stores. Also many of the Mexican-Americans surveyed indicated that they prefer to shop in discount houses where they can shop for their groceries, clothing, hardware, and household items and make only one trip.

Medical

Many respondents expressed concern that their community did not have adequate medical care.

At the time of the survey there were two doctors in San Ysidro, one a general practitioner and one a specialist in chronic diseases. There was also a dentist and a pharmacist. The Mexican-American Advisory Committee Service Center provided emergency medical transportation, and city police and fire department emergency facilities were available. In addition the area was served by the Bay Ambulance Company. The San Diego County Department of Public Health provided its "Child Health Conferences" (commonly known as "well-baby clinics") at the MAAC Center.

While this may seem to be adequate medical care for the area, San Ysidro residents were of the opinion that it is not. The new pharmacy in the shopping center under construction on San Ysidro Boulevard should help meet local needs. Even though there was no question about needed medical facilities on the questionnaire, many people expressed the desire to have a medical clinic or perhaps a hospital in San Ysidro, as well as another pharmacy. Others thought that the presence of a nursery would help solve some health problems in San Ysidro, since nurseries usually provide medical care. Thirty-five percent of the Mexican-Americans interviewed felt that they would have personal use for the nursery. It was also mentioned that a year round Headstart program for children from three to five years old, since Headstart provides some medical care, would help to alleviate the problem.

At the present time, because of a lack of medical facilities in San Ysidro most people go to other cities for service. Only 17 percent of the Mexican-Americans and 8 percent of the Anglo-Americans obtain medical care in San Ysidro. The others stated they go to Tijuana, National City, Chula Vista, Imperial Beach, and other places out of necessity, not preference. Many people, both Anglo-Americans and Mexican-Americans, go to medical facilities in Tijuana, especially the dentist, because of the lower cost. Many others, because of a lack of money and transportation, may not be receiving proper health care when they need it.

Public Facilities and Services

The survey disclosed some dislike for the city of San Diego, even among those who were not losing their homes to the freeway. Many people felt that the town of San Ysidro had been better off under the administration of the county. Some people felt that the Mission Bay Park area had been improved at the expense of the taxpayers of San Ysidro who have seen, in their opinion, no significant improvement in their community in many years.

There were many complaints about the lack of proper traffic signals, signs, pedestrian crosswalks, and street lighting in San Ysidro.[9]

The surveyors several times heard the story of the stop sign at Sunset and Smythe Streets that was knocked down and never replaced. People told the surveyors of almost daily accidents, which may never have been reported, at the corners of Sunset and Smythe, and Alverson and Smythe. Sunset Elementary School is located between those two intersections. For reasons of safety, it was felt that signs should be in both languages.

Because it represents a problem for the proper dispatch of police and fire department officers, as well as for the dispatch of mail, many respondents felt that street names and numbers should be put in order. It is not uncommon in San Ysidro to find odd and even numbers on the same side of the street, houses with two numbers, no numbers, or numbers out of sequence.

Many people also expressed concern over the lack of lighting on some streets which creates a hazard to pedestrians and motorists. The poor condition of the streets in San Ysidro, the lack of curbs and sidewalks and the narrowness of many of the streets adds to local safety conditions. There is a need for pedestrian walkways and crosswalks on a few of the streets in San Ysidro which are traveled daily by school children, which was often cited by respondents. North Vista, for example, is a high speed street with only a rather narrow shoulder for a walkway and with virtually no crosswalks and those very poorly marked. Some of the people interviewed expressed a very urgent need for a pedestrian tunnel, overpass, or for street light at points where pedestrians must cross Interstate Highway 5.

Another possible danger about which some people expressed concern was the Willow Street pedestrian underpass of the freeway. They said that it was poorly lit, unpatrolled, and that the tunnel floor was covered with broken glass.

Others felt that while the railway crossings do not seem a significant problem at the present, they may become a problem in the future. Underpasses, overpasses or flashing lights may be necessary at some crossings.

The survey team noted many loose dogs in San Ysidro. Proximity to Tijuana makes the area especially susceptible to rabies.

There were complaints about the infrequency of garbage pickup.

While the great majority of the people felt that the police were doing a good job in San Ysidro, some people felt that San Ysidro Boulevard, Frontage Road, and a few other streets could be better patrolled in order to curtail speeding and racing.

TABLES

Table A-1. Language and Sex of Respondents

Sex	Spanish only	Spanish Spanish & English	Total Spanish		English		Total	
Male	45	91	136		96		232	
Female	170	182	352		100		452	
Total	215	31.4%	273	39.9%	488	71.3%	196	28.7%	684	100.0%

Table A-2. Age of Respondents

Age Group	Mexican-American		Anglo-American		Total	
10–14	14	3.1%	0	0.0%	14	2.2%
15–19	21	4.6	1	0.6	22	3.5
20–29	75	16.5	15	8.4	90	14.2
30–49	208	45.8	35	19.6	243	38.4
50–64	103	22.7	63	35.2	166	26.2
65 & over	33	7.3	65	36.2	98	15.5
Total	454	100.0%	179	100.0%	633	100.0%
Not noted	34		17		51	

Table A-3.   Years in Area

Years	Mexican-American		Anglo-American		Total	
Less than 1	53	11.0%	19	10.1%	72	10.8%
1–2	48	10.0	11	5.9	59	8.8
2–4	116	24.1	26	13.8	142	21.2
4–10	109	22.7	36	19.1	145	21.7
10–20	93	19.3	45	23.9	138	20.6
20 and over	62	12.9	51	27.2	113	16.9
Total	481	100.0%	188	100.0%	669	100.0%
No response	7		8		15	

Table A-4.   Intent to Stay in Area

Intent	Mexican-American		Anglo-American		Total	
Yes	392	89.5%	133	78.2%	525	86.3%
No	46	10.5	37	21.8	83	12.7
Total	438	100.0%	170	100.0%	608	100.0%
No response	50		26		76	

Table A-5.   Number of Children, and Average Number of Children Per Household

Number/Average Per Household	Mexican-American		Anglo-American		Total	
Number	1,122	94.0%	71	6.0%	1,193	100.0%
Average per household	2.30		0.36		1.74	

Table A-6.   Head of Household

Head	Mexican-American		Anglo-American		Total	
Male	377	81.1%	158	80.6%	535	80.9%
Female	88	18.9	38	19.4	126	19.1
Total	465	100.0%	196	100.0%	661	100.0%
No response	23		0		23	

Table A-7. Head of Household With Children

Head	Mexican-American		Anglo-American		Total	
Male	291	84.3%	35	89.7%	326	84.9%
Female	54	15.7	4	10.3	58	15.1
Total	345	100.0%	39	100.0%	384	100.0%

Table A-8. Observed Condition of Housing

Condition	Mexican-American		Anglo-American		Total	
Adequate	264	69.5%	119	86.9%	383	74.1%
Substandard	116	30.5	18	13.1	134	25.9
Total	380	100.0%	137	100.0%	517	100.0%
Not observed	108		59		167	

Table A-9. Ownership of Housing

Own/Rent	Mexican-American		Anglo-American		Total	
Own	148	32.8%	63	45.0%	211	35.7%
Rent	303	67.2	77	55.0	380	64.3
Total	451	100.0%	140	100.0%	591	100.0%
No response	37		56		93	

Table A-10. Ownership Preference of Renters

Preference	Mexican-American		Anglo-American		Total	
Own	185	73.4%	21	30.9%	206	64.4%
Rent	67	26.6	47	69.1	114	35.6
Total	252	100.0%	68	100.0%	320	100.0%
No response	51		9		60	

Table A-11.   Housing Preference

Preference	Mexican-American		Anglo-American		Total	
Single Family	290	92.1%	60	57.1%	350	83.3%
Duplex	7	2.2	1	1.0	8	1.9
Apartment	7	2.2	16	15.2	23	5.5
Trailer	11	3.5	28	26.7	39	9.3
Total	315	100.0%	105	100.0%	420	100.0%
No response	173		91		264	

Table A-12.   Monthly Rent

Amount	Mexican-American		Anglo-American		Total	
Less than $50	11	3.7%	9	13.4%	20	5.5%
50–59	18	6.1	7	10.4	25	6.9
60–69	32	10.8	9	13.4	41	11.3
70–79	45	15.2	12	17.9	57	15.7
80–89	56	19.0	5	7.5	61	16.8
90–99	48	16.2	6	9.0	54	14.9
100–109	38	12.8	5	7.5	43	11.8
110–119	22	7.4	4	6.0	26	7.2
120 and over	26	8.8	10	14.9	36	9.9
Total	296	100.0%	67	100.0%	363	100.0%
No response	7		10		17	

Table A-13.   Feasible Monthly Rent

Amount	Mexican-American		Anglo-American		Total	
Less than $50	5	1.9%	7	10.8%	12	3.6%
50–59	18	6.7	4	6.2	22	6.6
60–69	22	8.2	7	10.8	29	8.7
70–79	59	22.2	13	19.9	72	21.8
80–89	58	21.7	11	16.9	69	20.9
90–99	39	14.6	2	3.1	41	12.3
100–109	30	11.2	7	10.8	37	11.1
110–119	12	4.5	3	4.6	15	4.5
120 and over	24	9.0	11	16.9	35	10.5
Total	267	100.0%	65	100.0%	332	100.0%
No response	36		12		48	

Table A-14. Employment Status

Status	Mexican-American		Anglo-American		Total	
Employed	345	73.5%	70	37.2%	415	63.1%
Retired	58	12.3	104	55.4	162	24.6
Disabled	17	3.6	10	5.3	27	4.1
Unemployed	50	10.6	4	2.1	54	8.2
Total	470	100.0%	188	100.0%	658	100.0%
No response	18		8		26	

Table A-15. Predominant Job Experience—Male

Skill	Mexican-American	Anglo-American	Total
Farm Laborer	38	0	38
Mechanic	30	5	35
Gardener	28	2	30
Construction Worker	24	6	30
Factory Worker	17	2	19
Custodian	17	1	18
Sales Clerk	16	2	18
Painter	13	2	15

Table A-16. Predominant Job Experience—Female

Skill	Mexican-American	Anglo-American	Total
Seamstress	26	3	29
Secretary	16	13	29

Table A-17. Predominant Skills Desired—Male

Skill	Mexican-American	Anglo-American	Total
Electronics	14	1	15
Mechanic	12	1	13

Table A-18. Predominant Skills Desired—Female

Skill	Mexican-American	Anglo-American	Total
Seamstress	57	3	60
Secretary	19	2	21
Nursing	16	3	19

Table A-19. Education Desired

Education Desired	Mexican-American		Anglo-American		Total	
Adult	245	50.2%	41	20.9%	286	41.8%
Citizenship	129	26.4	2	1.0	131	66.1
Not Needed	174	35.7	129	65.8	303	44.3

Table A-20. Adequacy of Library

Adequate	Mexican-American		Anglo-American		Total	
Yes	157	45.2%	59	50.0%	216	46.5%
No	190	54.8	59	50.0%	249	53.5
Total	347	100.0%	118	100.0%	465	100.0%
No response	141		78		219	

Table A-21. Method of Transportation for Going Shopping (Sample of 200 Mexican-Americans and 100 Anglo-Americans)

Method	Mexican-American		Anglo-American		Total	
Car	133	66.5%	62	62.0%	195	65.0%
Bus	43	21.5	16	16.0	59	19.7
Walk	46	23.0	20	20.0	66	22.0
Other	15	7.5	10	10.0	25	8.3

Table A-22. Method of Transportation for Going to Work (Sample of 200 Mexican-Americans and 100 Anglo-Americans)

Method	Mexican-American		Anglo-American		Total	
Car	111	81.0%	30	90.9%	141	83.0%
Bus	9	6.6	0	0.0	9	5.3
Walk	5	3.6	1	3.0	6	3.5
Other	12	8.8	2	6.1	14	8.2
Total	137	100.0%	33	100.0%	170	100.0%
No response	63		67		130	

Table A–23. Car Ownership

Ownership	Mexican-American		Anglo-American		Total	
Yes	350	76.4%	127	70.2%	477	74.6%
No	108	23.6	54	29.8	162	25.4
Total	458	100.0%	181	100.0%	639	100.0%
No response	30		15		45	

Table A–24. Prefer More Bus Service

Prefer	Mexican-American		Anglo-American		Total	
Yes	336	79.2%	91	59.1%	427	73.9%
No	88	20.8	63	40.9	151	26.1
Total	424	100.0%	154	100.0%	578	100.0%
No response	64		42		106	

Table A–25. Area Where Clothing Purchased
(Sample of 200 Mexican-Americans and 100 Anglo-Americans)

Area	Mexican-American		Anglo-American		Total	
San Ysidro	41	20.5%	3	3.0%	44	14.7%
Tijuana	30	15.0	2	2.0	32	10.7
Imperial Beach, Otay, National City, Chula Vista	145	72.5	69	69.0	214	71.3
Other	52	26.0	24	24.0	76	25.3

Table A–26. Area Where Food Purchased
(Sample of 200 Mexican-Americans and 100 Anglo-Americans)

Area	Mexican-American		Anglo-American		Total	
San Ysidro	124	62.0%	42	42.0%	166	55.3%
Tijuana	31	15.5	3	3.0	34	11.3
Imperial Beach, Otay, National City, Chula Vista	103	51.5	76	76.0	179	59.7
Other	5	2.5	5	5.0	10	3.3

Table A-27. Need Nursery

Need	Mexican-American		Anglo-American		Total	
Yes	163	34.8%	13	7.2%	176	27.2%
No	305	65.2	167	92.8	472	72.8
Total	468	100.0%	180	100.0%	648	100.0%
No response	20		16		36	

Table A-28. Area Where Medical Services Obtained
(Sample of 200 Mexican-Americans and 100 Anglo-Americans)

Area	Mexican-American		Anglo-American		Total	
San Ysidro	34	17.0%	8	8.0%	42	14.0%
Tijuana	58	29.0	4	4.0	62	20.7
Imperial Beach, Otay, National City, Chula Vista	77	38.5	50	50.0	127	42.3
Other	28	14.0	31	31.0	59	19.7

SURVEY QUESTIONNAIRE

This is the first part of a two-part questionnaire being conducted by the San Ysidro Planning and Development Committee and the San Ysidro Community Action Council. The answer to these questions will help determine the housing, recreational, commercial, employment and educational needs of the people of San Ysidro.

We have attempted to keep the first part of this survey as impersonal as possible. Neither your name or your address will be required. The CAC will be contacting you later for the second part of the survey. All information you give us will be kept confidential. Your help will be greatly appreciated.

Esta es la primera parte de un cuestionario que consiste de dos partes y que se llevará a cabo por El Comité de Planificación Y Desarrollo de San Ysidro y El Comité Pro-Acción de la Comunidad de San Ysidro. Las respuestas a éstas preguntas nos darán a conocer las necesidas de viviendas, recreación, comercio, empleo y educación de los residentes de San Ysidro.

Hemos tratado de que la primera parte de este cuestionario sea lo mas impersonal que sea posible. Su nombre y dirección no serán requeridos. El Comité Pro-Acción de la Comunidad se pondrá en contacto con usted en fecha próxima, para realizar la segunda parte de este cuestionario. Toda información que nos proporcione será estrictamente confidencial. Su ayuda será de mucho valor y muy apreciada.

Date_____

Interviewer_____

Area_____

San Ysidro Community Survey
City Planning Department

General
1.   Respondent—Sex: M_____ F_____; Age_____
     Language: Eng. _____ Sp._____ Other_____
2.   Sex of head of household: M_____ F_____
3.   Persons residing in household including relatives: Adults_____ Children_____

Residential
1.   Do you like living in this area: Yes_____ No_____
     Why?_____
     _____

2.   How long have you lived in this area? Yrs._____ Months_____
3.   Do you plan to remain in this area? Yes_____ No_____
4.   What type of housing would you prefer to live in and what would be your
     order of preference?
     a) Single family_____ b) duplex_____ c) 1 or 2 story apt. house_____
     d) trailer_____ e) high rise apt._____
5.   Your family needs_____bedrooms and_____baths.
6.   Do you own_____or rent_____your home? Which do you prefer?_____
7.   What do you presently pay a month for your home (including utilities)?
     $_____
8.   What do you think you could afford to pay a month for better housing if
     it were available? $_____
9.   Observed condition of home:_____
10. Do you make your own repairs? Yes_____ No_____
     If not, would you if given assistance? Yes_____ No_____

Commercial
1.   Where do you prefer to shop for food and groceries?
     S. Y._____Tj_____ N. C., I. B. or C. V._____ Other_____
2.   Does the ability to charge purchases help determine where you shop?
     Yes_____ No_____
3.   Where do you shop for clothing? S. Y._____ Tj_____N. C., I. B. or
     C. V._____ Other_____
4.   What stores do you feel are needed in San Ysidro that do not currently
     exist? _____
     _____

5.   Do you prefer large stores with a wide range of goods or smaller specialty
     shops? Large_____ Small_____ Why?_____
     _____

Recreational

1. What do you do in your leisure time for entertainment?_____
   _____

2. What type of entertainment facilities do you feel are needed in San Ysidro?
   _____

3. What types of games or activities are your children most interested in?
   _____

4. What types of facilities do you feel should be provided in public parks?
   _____

5. If more organized activities such as Boy and Girl Scouts, Little League, and
   cooking classes, etc. were provided, would your children participate?
   Yes_____ No_____ They already do_____

6. Would they still participate if this involved a slight cost per child?
   Yes_____ No_____

Schools

1. What problems do your children encounter concerning the education they
   are receiving? _____
   _____

2. In which of the following classes would you participate in, if any?
   Adult education_____ Citizenship_____

Transportation

1. How do you travel to work? Walk_____ Car_____ Bus_____ Other_____
2. How do your children travel to school? Walk_____ Car_____ Bus_____
   Other_____
3. How do you travel to your shopping? Walk_____ Car_____ Bus_____
   Other_____
4. Would you ride the public bus if adequate service was provided? Yes_____
   No_____

Employment

1. How are you currently employed?_____
   Your spouse? _____
2. What type of job skills do you have? _____
   Your spouse?_____
3. Are any of the children now living in this household working? Yes_____
   No_____
4. What type of skills would you like to learn? _____
   _____

Public Facilities and Service

1. Where do you get your medical and dental care?
   S. Y._____ Tj_____ N. C., C. V. or I. B._____ Other_____
2. Do you think that San Ysidro is a safe area to live in? Yes_____ No_____
   If not, why? _____
3. Are you involved in any way in civic affairs? Yes_____No_____

4. Would you use nursery facilities if they were provided? Yes_____ No_____
5. Are there adequate church facilities in San Ysidro? Yes_____ No_____
6. Are library facilities adequate? Yes_____ No_____
   If not, what could be done to improve them? _____
   _____
   _____

Notes

NOTES TO INTRODUCTION

1. See, for example, Liebow (1967), Hannerz (1969), Oscar Lewis (1959, 1961, 1966), Gans (1962), Valentine (1968).

2. Nathan Glazer (1971) points out that in New York City it is possible to find a culture of poverty among populations who are not poor as well as impossible to find a culture of poverty among some who are poor.

3. For the sense of this debate the interested reader should see, from among others, Gladwin (1961), Schorr (1964), Roach and Gursslin (1967), *Current Anthropology* (1967, 8:5; 1969, 10:2-3), Valentine (1968), Hannerz (1969), Ryan (1971), Winter (1971), Leacock (1971).

4. Hannerz (1969), Eames and Goode (1970), Liebow (1967), Valentine (1968).

5. Eames and Goode (1970).

6 See Rainwater and Yancey (1967), *The Moynihan Report and The Politics of Controversy.*

7. The problem is more far ranging and vicious than this simple causal statement suggests. In San Diego County, at the time a female whose husband had departed applies for welfare she is required to file a charge of non-support with the district attorney's office. The district attorney then issues a warrent for the husband's arrest. This warrant is rarely acted on unless the husband gets in some kind of trouble or is found in the household. However, should the husband acquire a job that will permit him to support his family and desire to return home he is unable to because at that time the district attorney will enforce the original writ. In this way the male is driven even further from the family. Thus the cultural pressures which create the matrifocal household in the first place conspire to perpetuate it. Also, should the female, who is a biological creature, satisfy her sexual desires in an illicit relationship, her activity serves to reinforce mainstream attitudes regarding the debased morality of the poor.

8. This is reported in a document (n.d.) prepared by the Very Reverend John H. Blethen of the Augustinian Order, which runs the low-cost housing project in San Ysidro.

9. I suggest that the reason the matrifocal household has not been discovered among urban poor whites is due to the fact that this category of people has not yet been well studied.

10. This proposition has been explored by a variety of authors. See, for example, Young, F. and R. (n.d.), Bendix (1964), Geertz (1963), Almond and Coleman (1960), Boissevain (1965), Adams (1966).

NOTES TO CHAPTER 1

1. Charles Valentine (1968) has suggested perhaps most strongly the unfortunate tendency for social scientists such as Oscar Lewis (1966) and Daniel Moynihan (1965) to perpetuate the notion of subcultural isolation in urban state societies.

2. The lack of interplay between poor people and the dominant society of which they are a part has been pointed out by Lewis (1966), Gladwin (1967), Valentine (1968), Hannerz (1969), and others.

3. This theory derives basically from Robert Mc. Adams work, *The Evolution of Urban Society*; it is supplemented by consideration drawn from Carneiro's (1968, 1970) and Fried's (1967) theory regarding the evolution of the state.

4. The history of San Ysidro has been pieced together from a variety of sources available in the California Room of the San Diego Public Library. Richard F. Pourade provides in his history of San Diego the best information available on San Ysidro (See Pourade 1964:224–25; 1965:111, 117; 1967:83).

5. Posters circulated by the Little Landers advertising their venture are available for investigation in the California Room of the San Diego Public Library.

6. This is a word of mouth estimate from "old timers" in San Ysidro. Census tracts for the area incorporate parts of San Ysidro into other communities and do not break down the population of the area into ethnic groups.

7. The San Ysidro Community Survey is an unpublished and controversial document which will be discussed in detail later in the proper context. While the content of the survey is considered by some, though not the author, to be grossly inaccurate, the tables are considered by most of the same dissenters to be generally correct. Since the survey and its accompanying tables represent the most comprehensive and current survey available for San Ysidro it will be utilized in this work. It is also reproduced as an Appendix in this volume.

8. The future development of San Ysidro and the San Diego Border Area generally is detailed in two documents available from the San Diego Department of City Planning. They are the San Diego Border Area Plan (1966) and the San Ysidro Community Plan (1970).

9. The rationale for the proposed route of the freeway through San Ysidro is discussed in the *San Diego Union*, June 23, 1963. Silver (1969) has argued before the Federal Highway Administration that freeways do not benefit the poor in obtaining jobs, for they do nothing to alleviate the critical job problems poor people face; lack of skills, underemployment, substandard wages, and the like. Freeways are more likely to be detrimental to poor people by displacing great numbers of them as they dissect their neighborhoods.

10. These schedules and prices are discussed in the San Diego Border Area Plan (1966:22) and the San Ysidro Community Survey (1968:33). Officials of the Comprehensive Health Survey Association of San Diego and Imperial Counties also pointed out that a one-way taxi fare from San Ysidro to San Diego costs $7.00 and a round-trip to the nearest health facility costs $2.00 by bus, as well as much time. The association was investigating San Ysidro as part of the Model Cities Program in which San Ysidro is scheduled to participate.

11. There are no good income figures for the people of San Ysidro, for people are unwilling to respond to this question on interview schedules administered by the author and the Community Action Council. Census tracts for San Ysidro are unreliable because they cover a large area which includes several communities. The 1960 census tract, Z-100, indicates, however, that San Ysidro is one of the two poorest areas in San Diego. See Steward and Austin, *Pockets of Poverty: A Study of Deprivation in Two Areas of the City of San Diego, California* (Community Welfare Council of San Diego County, August 1964).

12. The residential stability of poor peoples is discussed with specific reference to San Diego by Gillette (1967) and Johnson, Gillette, and Feldman (1966).

13. Despite the sentimental and economic bonds of the Mexican-American people of San Ysidro to Tijuana, there is also a high degree of hostility between peoples of the two areas. Many of the Mexican-Americans of San Ysidro are hostile to the green-card holders in Tijuana because they depress the job market along the border and contribute to the unemployment on the American side. Mexicans in Tijuana frequently display a cynical humor regarding the "better life" people lead on the American side of the border.

14. This is not to imply that all the social and economic relationships along the border are one-way, from the United States and San Ysidro into Mexico and Tijuana. Actually, an intense symbiosis more nearly describes the relationships which exist along the border. See John A. Price, (1968a) "Tijuana: A Study of Symbiosis", in "The Postindustrial City", *New Mexico Quarterly* 38, 3, pp. 8–18.

15. Even vital services in certain circumstances are dispersed variably in the community. In 1969 San Diego was the victim of a garbage collector's strike and emergency measures were instituted. Two trips which I made to San Ysidro during the strike indicated that garbage was being collected in the Anglo and more middle-class areas of San Ysidro, but with far less regularity and efficiency in the poorer Mexican areas.

16. This information is from the report of the Select Commission on Western Hemisphere Immigration (Washington, D.C.: United States Government Printing Office, January 1968).

17. There is vast literature regarding the education of Mexican-Americans in the United States. See, for example, Sanchez (1966), Glick (1966), Pickney (1963), Fogel (1965), Gebler (1967), Samora and Lamanna (1967), Forbes (n.d.), Manuel (1965), *The Mexican-American: A New Focus on Opportunity* (1967), and Swadesh (1968).

18. It is difficult to assess precisely the dropout rate in this particular district. Students who stop attending regular sessions are, by the district, automatically enrolled in their night school, one office of which is in San Ysidro, and thus not counted as official dropouts. The night school does not adjust its records accordingly and it is certain that most regular session dropouts never attend the night school.

19. As with most other census figures, San Ysidro is included in a much larger area. The figure estimated by the county welfare officials does, however, correspond generally to those arrived at by officials of the San Diego Model Cities Program who are concerned with the San Ysidro area.

20. Galbraith (1958) discusses this point generally and Johnson, Gillette, and Feldman (1966) verify his contention for the San Diego area.

NOTES TO CHAPTER 2

1. Several authors have contributed to understanding this process. See, for example, Geertz (1963), Bendix (1964), Easton (1959), Eisenstadt (1964a), Levy (1952), and Fallers (1965).

2. There is no real consensus among authorities regarding the particulars which underlie this statement, though there is general agreement among many regarding the sense of it. Many of the issues upon which this statement is based are clouded by imprecise semantics, confused definitions, and rhetoric. Moynihan, for example, states unemphatically and imprecisely that, "It *might be estimated* (emphasis added) that as much as half the Negro community falls into the middle class" (1967:75). President Johnson's Council of Economic Advisors argue that "One-fifth of our families and nearly one-fifth of our total population are poor. Of the poor, 22 percent are nonwhite; and *nearly one-half of all nonwhites* (emphasis added) live in poverty" (Weisbrod 1965:66). Moynihan seems to assume that all nonwhites are black; the statement of the President's Council implies that Indians and, perhaps, Mexican-Americans may also be included in their figures. Others argue, using gross figures, that between 20 and 50 million persons in the United States are poor (Weisbrod 1965:7). In light of these inconsistencies my statement seems at least as reasonable as others.

3. Antipoverty programs of one kind or other pre-date the war on poverty by a considerable period of time (Weisbrod 1965; Bremner 1967). The war on poverty, however, was the first American antipoverty program which attempted to involve as a general policy the poor in the decision-making processes to eliminate poverty. For a discussion of the reconsideration of the factors involved in economic distress in America see Cater (1964); the current history of the war on poverty is dealt with by Weisbrod (1965), Cater (1964), and James (1970).

4. Problems and processes similar to those in San Ysidro have been reported and analyzed by Kramer (1969) and Hayes (1972) in the San Francisco Bay Area.

5. Kramer (1969) makes this distinction with reference to other battles in the war on poverty program which he studied in the San Francisco Bay Area.

6. Bailey (1969) offers a most detailed and cogent analysis of the significance of resources for emerging leadership roles and political activity generally. Much of this discussion has to be attributed to influence derived from his work.

7. This statement has to be attributed to Ralph Nicholaus (1966) and is significant because it provides an alternative to more traditional consideration of political power. For example, political power is conceived generally by political scientists and philosophers as the ability of a person or group to determine through some form of coercion or force, or the threat of it if necessary, the decisions and actions of others in the direction of the former's own ends. However, the ability to coerce and the means of coercion are not intangible considerations; they are derived from real and explicit criteria that are frequently overlooked in the discussion of power. Following a tradition in the science of politics which dates back at least to Aristole and which has been carried on by such thinkers as James Harrington, (1924:1955), Karl Marx (1906) and other more contemporary social scientists, Ralph Nicholas (1966:53) suggests that, " 'Power' is control over resources, whether human or material . . . participants in political activity attempt to expand their control over resources; (for) control over material resources and men may be used to attain a greater variety of personal objectives." This seminal statement concretizes some of the explicit criteria, that is resources and their control by which a group or individual may be considered to have power.

8. While there is no universally acceptable way of classifying resources or other bases of power, Lasswell and Kaplan (1950:74–102) suggest eight basic values out of which power may emanate. These include power, the possession of which may lead to increased power, respect, rectitude or moral standing, affection, well-being, wealth, skill, and enlightenment. Dahl (1961: 229ff.) augments this list with complementary criteria which include the distribution of cash, credit, and wealth among people who are potentially and actually influential, access to legality, popularity, and the control by certain individuals of jobs and sources of information.

9. Harsanyi (1962a, and 1962b) discusses principles concerned with deferred allocation of resources; Bailey (1969) also deals with this and in greater detail.

10. In order to understand this concept, see the alternative views of Max Weber (1930) and R. H. Tawney (1926). Also, in recent cross-cultural analyses concerned with sexual activity and state controls, Y. A. Cohen (1969b) has suggested another dimension within which the Protestant ethic might be viewed. Peacock and Kirsch (1970) also presents a very good and succinct discussion of the Protestant ethic. In this work the concept is used in its simplest sense and refers to the situation in which an individual may extricate himself

from poverty and achieve a higher status in the American class structure through hard work, thrift, and perseverance.

11. The distinction between "deserving" and "undeserving" poor is made by James (1970) in a comparison of European American policy regarding the poor and needy in industrial societies.

12. Gans (1962) uses this concept to explain some aspects of the relationship between working class Italians and welfare institutions in Boston.

13. This is a difficult point to document, although in San Diego in the early days of the war on poverty the establishment did experience a real fear of the power of the poor. This is discussed in a variety of contexts in a series of reports on the war on poverty in San Diego County entitled, *The Action As Viewed From the Scene.* These reports were compiled by investigators from the Western Behavioral Science Institute in La Jolla, California. This phenomenon has been reported for other areas of the United States in *The Poverty War Report* (1965), and by Kramer (1969), Friendly (1966), and Moynihan (1970).

14. Several authors imply such a policy in America's relations with Mexican-Americans: McWilliams (1968), Steiner (1969), Galarza (1970), Swadesh (1968), Samora (1966). With the suggestive perspicacity for which nonintellectuals are often noted, a Mexican-American farmer of New Mexico quoted by Stan Steiner in his book, *La Raza: The Mexican Americans,* affirms his concern over the diminishment of his pasturage as a result of its incorporation into national forests in this way: "I think it is the unwritten policy of the Forest Service to get rid of the poor farmers" (1969:9). Analogous sentiments are expressed by many persons involved in the antipoverty programs of San Diego.

NOTES TO CHAPTER 3

1. About a year later, the sudden and full realization of what was going to happen to San Ysidro as a result of the freeway and the massive development planned for the community set off another wave of conflict from which many wounded sensibilities of individuals and groups in and outside of San Ysidro will be a long time recovering.

2. Of the fourteen original Community Action Councils, the ethnic preponderance of each is as follows (Crow and Johannsen 1969:B-3):

Council	*Ethnic Preponderance*
1	Negro
2	Mexican-American
3	Negro
4	Negro
5	Negro
6	White/mixed
7	Mexican-American
8	White/mixed
9	Mexican-American
10	Mexican-American

11	Mexican-American
12	White/mixed
13	White/mixed
14	Mexican-American/Negro (now closed down)

The physical boundary of the Border Area Community Action Council, as well as others in San Diego County, was based upon data and information available in federal census tracts and presented in a report of the San Diego Community Welfare Council, Pockets of Poverty (Stewart and Austin, 1964). Community Action Councils were established in areas of the county in which 20 percent or more of the families had incomes of less than $3,000 per annum.

3. The several explicit purposes of CACs in San Diego County were spelled out in detail in a paper issued by the EOC of San Diego County, March 9, 1966. They are as follows:

1. To involve residents and agencies serving the area into joint effort to identify the causes of poverty affecting individuals, families, and groups
2. To determine how to test effectively existing agencies and services are meeting the needs of the poor in the area
3. To prevent duplication of efforts in the area
4. To influence the redirection, extension, expansion or improvement in the use of existing agency services
5. To review and approve community action programs directly affecting the area served by the Community Action Council
6. To recommend projects to fill gaps in services which are not being met by existing services
7. To work for improved economic, educational, cultural, and social opportunities in the area
8. To select the community representative and alternates to sit on the Economic Opportunity Commission Board of Directors.

4. The Office of Economic Opportunity sponsored a variety of training and informational programs in order to inform the working staff of community action programs about the theory and practice of community organization and action. Most of those conducted during the period of this research were well attended in the San Diego area. With reference to the Border Area CAC, however, most of them were a waste of time. Most of the participants from this CAC either did not comprehend the complexity of community organization practices, were not interested, or were committed to the administering of services which did not demand this knowledge.

5. This figure is reported in *A Comprehensive Evaluation of the Community Action Program in San Diego County, California* (1967), which was conducted by The Western Behavioral Science Institute of La Jolla, California.

6. The figures in table 3.1 should be accepted critically. The people of San Ysidro were quite hostile to surveys and suspicious of the motives of the surveyors. During the course of my research the people of San Ysidro had

been or were being interviewed by a variety of agencies concerned with the development of San Ysidro, e.g., the California State Highway Department and the Planning Department of San Diego; the community action programs, e.g., the Community Action Council and service center; the Model Cities Program, and others. With some justification the people complained that despite all the interviews nothing positive was being done to improve their living conditions. Because of the wording of one questionnaire I circulated in San Ysidro my research assistant was evicted from eight of the first ten houses which agreed to respond because they regarded the questions as being too personal. Refining the instrument to a point where it was acceptable rendered it quite pointless.

However, the percentages in table 3.1 do not seem too far from reality. For example, no more than 200 people ever attended a CAC meeting. This number was present at the initial meeting concerned with the freeway and redevelopment of San Ysidro and included persons from Otay and Woodlawn Park, representing a total population I would estimate at about 8,000. This attendance represents about 2½ percent of the total population. The CAC meetings in San Ysidro were comparatively well attended, but rarely more than fifty persons appeared. This represents the average number of involved persons in each of the fourteen CACs in San Diego County (Crow, Erickson and Grissom, n.d.:70). In San Ysidro this attendance represents approximately 1 percent of the community, although Saul Alinsky has argued that a participation of 5 percent in any community "is a tremendous democratic phenomenon" (1945: 201). Also, the United Farmworkers representative in San Ysidro, in explaining political and union tactics in which he had participated over the previous thirty years, argued that without 50 percent of a community behind a program there was little chance of its succeeding. The events in San Ysidro would seem to bear out his argument.

7. See: Keith-Lucas, 1957; May 1964.

8. Each of the four agencies provides essentially the same services. Three of these agencies have more than one center in San Diego County. They are: The Neighborhood House Association, which has five centers in Southeast San Diego; the Mexican-American Advisory Committee of San Diego County (MAAC), which has four centers in the county; and the Catholic Family Service, which has four centers in San Diego County under the project name ACCESS (Areawide Community Centers, Employment Services, Self-Improvement). The Imperial Beach Community Economic Opportunity Center, Inc. (IBCEOC) served the communities of Nestor, Palm City, Coronado, and Imperial Beach.

9. The Community Action function of service agencies has been discussed by Perlman and Jones (1967), and in *Community Action: The Neighborhood Center* (1966).

10. While it might seem strange that a study concerned with Mexican-Americans to the extent this one is has nothing to say about the role of the priest and religion in the community, it is simply because the priest was totally uninvolved and uninterested in the activities with which this research was concerned. The local priest was not well liked by many of the poorer Mexican-Americans in the community. He was referred to cynically as "Father Plata" because of his constant pleas for money in order to build a new church in San

Ysidro. This church was under construction during the time I was conducting research. It was being built very near to the new housing development on the hill overlooking San Ysidro. This also antagonized many of the poor Mexican-Americans, because they did not consider this development a part of San Ysidro; it symbolized the "rich" elements of the community. The local priest seemed to affiliate more with the "influentials" of the community than with the poor. Prior to my research he had his assistant priest dismissed because he had become involved in organizing the poor Mexican-Americans for community action, and his philosophy is summed up by a statement posted outside his church:

> I am a Catholic Priest
> ... Never wrote for Saturday Evening Post
> ... Never organized a union for discontented priests
> ... Never had an identity crisis
> Just a happy priest thankful for the privilege
> of working full time for God.
> My life has meaning.

11. Political scientists such as Dahl (1961) have dealt most with this phenomenon; D'Antonio and Form (1965) and Klapp and Padgett (1960) have investigated it in Mexican–United States Border Cities.

12. As with the PFTA, the precise membership of the San Ysidro Planning and Development Group is hard to verify. However, only a few of this presumed number were active and for all practical purposes they alone comprised the development group.

13. In the more affluent beach area of San Diego where I lived after my study in San Ysidro ended, a member of its local planning agency told me that he could obtain the service of an inspector to investigate a complaint within 48 hours.

14. A sardonic joke circulating among the poor in San Ysidro was that the only active organization in San Ysidro was the United Cockroaches. A health study of Southeast San Diego, the poorest area of the city which included San Ysidro, pointed out severe health problems in San Ysidro. This study, *The Southeast San Diego Health Study* (1969), was done as a Model Cities project by the Comprehensive Health Planning Association of San Diego and Imperial Counties. Since then a health clinic has opened in San Ysidro under OEO funding.

15. Several highway constructions are affecting the area in and around San Ysidro. State highway 75 will merge with interstate highway 5 a few miles above San Ysidro. Interstate 5 will be widened from four to eight lanes as it approaches the Border. Interstate highway 805 will slice through San Ysidro, cross interstate 5 via an overpass and merge with it so to create sixteen lanes of traffic into the Border. This is to be completed by 1974, at which time the City Planning Department of San Diego estimates it will be obsolete given projections of increased border traffic.

16. Tex Stillman lost about one-third of his property to the freeway. In 1972 when I spoke with him he had dropped out of the Development Associa-

tion as well as all other civic and social groups in the area. All of them, he argued, were composed of individuals who merely sought to serve their own special interests.

17. Since this research terminated the category of consultant has been abolished by the EOC.

18. MAAC's personnel has changed considerably since this research terminated; the project director, assistant director, and others, have been replaced. However, I don't know what affect this has had on MAAC-CAC relations.

19. The Community Action Councils in San Diego County were abolished in July 1970; Regional OEO directives (along with a considerable amount of rumor) suggest that all delegate agencies in San Diego City will be phased out of existence by August 31, 1972 and that about one-third of the EOC staff will be let go. If this eventuates, those delegate agencies which are unable to acquire some other source of funding will simply become defunct.

NOTES TO CHAPTER 4

1. In 1968 there was talk among CAC, service center, and EOC personnel to seek an injunction on further highway construction until adequate housing for the displaced families was assured. Nothing came of this, largely because of the emerging conflict in the community which created inertia at all levels on other issues. By 1970, however, the Mexican-Americans of San Ysidro had savored the alternative housing projects erected for their poor people and were more cognizant of the total impact the highway was going to have upon the community: higher taxes, land speculation, increased population density. The year 1970 was a stormy one for the developers and planners. As a result of community clamor more low-income housing did come into the area, largely through Model Cities' efforts; the highway was changed from an elevated roadbed which would have separated sections of San Ysidro by a mountain of earth to a grade level roadbed; and at the height of the conflict the director of the city planning office proposed an alternative route for the freeway, but to no avail because of the heavy investment of time and money in the existing route. By 1971 the developers and planners had weathered the storm of community dissent and the freeway was well on its way.

2. For an assessment of the war on poverty in these terms see Hallman (1968), Shostak (1968), Keyserling (1967), and Kravitz (1968).

3. Bloomberg and Schmandt (1968) discuss such forces and some of the following discussion derives from suggestions in their work.

4. The notion of social distance is difficult to conceptualize as well as document. A variety of social scientists have dealt with the implications of social distance between communities, statuses, ethnic groups, and as an aspect of language (Bogardus 1929, 1959; Hall 1959; Loomis and Powell 1949; Festinger, Schacter, and Back 1950; Pickney 1963; Simienko 1964). In anthropology and sociology, scholars concerned with problems of cultural evolution especially have been significant in suggesting this phenomenon, although much is

left to intuit from their efforts. (See especially Cohen 1968a; Fried 1967; Sahlins and Service 1960; Adams 1966; Lenski 1966).

5. This is spelled out in detail in the Economic Opportunity Act of 1964, as amended (1967:30).

6. In 1972 the EOC in San Diego was still operating this way. There seemed to be less fear of amputation of the total program; the EOC expected to survive. However, local agencies under its auspices were increasingly fearful that they would be cut adrift because of the EOC was heavily in debt as a result of borrowing to keep the program operating and one way of making up this deficit would be eliminate cost at subordinate levels.

7. For general insight into these factors see Jacobs (1967), Bloomberg and Schmandt (1968), Kramer (1969), and Shostak (1968).

8. Antipoverty programs are generated from suggestions by persons and organizations active in the poverty habitat. Under current federal guidelines a funding period for such programs takes place once a year. In San Diego anti-poverty programs were first reviewed by the Community Action Council, its board and staff. If they accepted the program it was then transmitted to the EOC for review of feasibility and budgetary considerations. After passing the scrutiny of the EOC staff one copy of the program was transmitted to the regional OEO office in San Francisco and another to the state OEO office in Sacramento. However, not until November 1966 was it *required* that all applications for grants be sent to the governor's office (CAP Memo 51, 1966).

9. See Josten (1966) and Kramer (1969) for rather rare discussions of this phenomenon. While such concern in San Diego may not have been as overt as I suggest here, the local government did initially have similar concern regarding the influence of the poor upon city government policy.

10. This now rather famous observation of the status of the poor in affluent American society is attributed to Michael Harrington (1962).

11. Kramer (1969) suggests this in his analysis of the war on poverty in the San Francisco Bay area.

12. This is my observation from the level of the Community Action Council and poverty habitat. The relationship between these structures certainly became closer over time, although EOC personnel often complained of the lack of city support or interest. *The Final Report of the War on Poverty in San Diego County, 1967-69.* (Crow, Erickson and Grissom, n.d.) presents a somewhat more positive assessment of this relationship.

13. This quote and much of the preceding discussion of San Diego and the initiation of the war on poverty in that community comes from *The War on Poverty in San Diego County: Final Report,* by Crow, Erickson and Grissom (n.d.) of the Western Behavioral Science Institute, La Jolla, California.

14. In July 1970 funding for CACs was stopped by the EOC. This meant that to maintain their paid staff, offices, and equipment they would have to seek outside funding or cease to exist. Only one CAC, National City, survived and was still functioning in 1972, but without an office or staff. It served more as a community forum.

15. The training of the consultants is explained in detail by one of

them in an extended interview conducted for an evaluation of the war on poverty in San Diego County. It is summed up by the following excerpt: "What they (the EOC) did was dump us in a branch office and tell us to organize councils" (Crow and Gorman, 1967:4).

16. This point has been suggested in other Mexican-American inter-ethnic situations by Samora and Lamanna (1967:119) who state that while "the various ethnic groups seem to get along remarkably well from day to day, there are strong underlying feelings of hostility and mistrust that could surface at any time under certain circumstances." This describes rather exactly the situation in San Ysidro.

17. As Moore, Mittlebach, and McDaniel (1966) point out this is common in Southwestern communities.

18. See, for example, Hunter (1953), Lynd (1937), Mills (1964), Useem (1942), Warner (1949), and West (1945).

NOTES TO CHAPTER 5

1. This is a very similar situation to one encountered by Gans (1962) in his study of working class Italians in Boston. He points out that urban development is suddenly there, a cruel reality, before anyone knows it, and personal and group adjustments to it can be traumatic.

2. The housing development is to consist of four hundred units. This development was to be under construction by October 1968 and be completed in twelve to fifteen months. Construction, however, was just beginning in the early summer of 1969, approximately eight months behind schedule.

Low rent subsidy housing is regulated by the FHA according to standards determined by the Congress of the United States and there are several regulations which govern who may rent subsidized housing.

3. Where my family and I lived in Mission Beach, a relatively fashionable and rapidly developing tourist area, a member of the Mission Beach Planning Group remarked that he could get a member of the sanitation department to investigate any complaint on housing in this area within forty-eight hours

4. According to FHA regulations, nor more than two persons can share a bedroom, nor can siblings of different sex share a bedroom after a certain age. These restrictions excluded several larger families being displaced in San Ysidro from participating in the low rent subsidy housing.

5. The full blame for this action fell on the service center director because very few people knew as a fact that it was the superintendent of schools who had called the mayor. I found out only through a casual conversation with him. It matters little, because the service center director did essentially instigate his action. It seems significant only that despite all her self-proclaimed sophistication on the one hand and identity with the people of San Ysidro on the other, she contacted one of the community's Anglo influentials for advice as she began to doubt the wisdom of the demonstration.

6. The rent subsidy apartment complex was eventually named

Villa Nueva (New Town) and was purchased by the California Province of Augustinians who run the project as a nonprofit corporation. Villa Nueva consists of 90 two-bedroom units, 264 three-bedroom units, and 36 four-bedroom units.

7. There are a few errors in this report, to be sure, but my feeling is that it is generally sound. Most of the errors to which the San Ysidro Planning Group member alluded were matter of judgment and interpretation. I accompanied the enumerators on many of their rounds. In this way I obtained a view of a cross-section of the homes in San Ysidro and spoke with the people and listened to them express their views. I was in approximately 10 percent of the houses in San Ysidro, from the poorest to the more middle-class dwellings. In general, the Anglos were ruder than the Mexican-Americans. They also were considerably more blatant in their prejudice toward Mexican-Americans than Mexican-Americans were to them. Of the seventy-one persons who refused to respond, almost all were Anglo. The accusation of being radical that was leveled against the enumerators was, to some extent, true. They became angry at the conditions they saw in San Ysidro and at the plans and motivations of the San Ysidro Planning Group. I felt the report was remarkably free of the anger they frequently expressed to me.

8. Since this research terminated community pressure has in fact forced some reconsideration of the proposed development of San Ysidro. *The San Ysidro Community Plan* (1970) which was prepared by the City of San Diego Planning Department and the San Ysidro Planning and Development Group and in which the changes proposed for San Ysidro are presented was rejected by the people of the community on two different occasions. It is currently (June 1972) undergoing its third revision. Among other changes, as a result of community pressure more low-income housing has come into the area, the interstate highway was changed from an elevated route to one which proceeds now at ground level, and reconsideration is being given to the amount of park land proposed for the area and to altering the high density zoning which was prescribed for much of San Ysidro.

9. These public meetings were formally known as San Ysidro Informational Meetings; to the community they were known as the Mayor's Meetings because he was the principal speaker at the first meeting and did attend one or two others. A total of six meetings were held at two week intervals; the first one took place on September 11, 1968. They were concerned with the following topic:

1. First meeting: The principal speaker was the Mayor of San Diego. He presented the general program of the meetings, discussed the history of San Ysidro's relationship to San Diego since annexation, and responded to a list of questions which had been submitted to him previously and made up by the service center director, the Border Area CAC executive secretary, the head of the PFTA, the superintendent of the San Ysidro Elementary School District, and members of the San Diego Planning Department.
2. Second meeting: A summary of the city, state and federal governments as well as their responsibilities to the people was presented. Several departments of the city government of San Diego were presented with explanations of their responsibilities to the people

3. Third meeting: The problems of housing in the area were discussed as well as present approaches to solutions to these problems.
4. Fourth meeting: Representatives from the elementary, junior and senior high schools, which the children of San Ysidro attended, presented explanations of their programs and future plans for the area in general.
5. Fifth meeting: This meeting discussed existing employment opportunities and problems in the area and possible solutions to these problems.
6. Sixth meeting: The recreational facilities in the area generally were discussed as well as present facilities in San Ysidro and plans for future recreational programs and developments in the area.

10. It was argued by the city during the San Ysidro Informational Meetings that San Ysidro did not qualify for a swimming pool and that none was going to be built. I found out in July 1970 that a swimming pool is now scheduled to be built in San Ysidro through a joint local and federally funded effort. The pool that was finally constructed is, however, near the Villa Nueva rent subsidy apartment project and is quite distant from the old section of San Ysidro. It also has a recommended capacity of only 85 persons; Villa Nueva alone, however, has a total population of approximately 2,000 persons of which 1,200 or so are children, from infants to 19 years of age.

Bus service is still inadequate for the area and people complain that it is also still too expensive. Of great success has been a free shuttle bus service which was developed through Model Cities and which takes people to welfare and employment offices and to various medical and dental clinics in San Diego. The intense use of this service by the people of San Ysidro belies the city's argument that the people in San Ysidro do not use bus service and gives some credence to the people's argument that the price charged for existing service is too high for a good many of them.

11. Needless to say, Mrs. Horton was shaken by this since the first word she heard of the letter was in a long distance telephone call from her husband in Japan. He was enough aware of what was transpiring in San Ysidro through letters from his wife so that he was reasonably convinced of the falsity of the letter.

12. See the *Chula Vista Star News,* November 14, 1968.

13. See the *Chula Vista Star News,* October 20, 1968.

14. The conflict, however, did not terminate. The impending highway and relocation of population kept this issue alive and generated conflict within the CAC until July 1970, at which time all CACs in the county were severed from EOC affiliation. As noted, almost all CACs in the county had already ceased to exist at this point. Even without the CAC conflict between various factions in San Ysidro continued for about another year over these issues as well as others which arose over various Model Cities' Programs planned for San Ysidro.

15. Among other works, consult Manuel (1965), Sanchez (1966), Forbes (n.d.), *The Mexican-Americans: A New Focus on Opportunity* (1967), Swadesh (1968), Gebler (1967), Samora and Lamanna (1967), Burma (1970), and Moore (1970).

16. These figures were given to me by the superintendent of the San Ysidro Elementary School District and reaffirmed by one of the school principals.

17. The San Ysidro School District has recently hired a bilingual school psychologist. The 47 Mexican-American children in the EMR classes during the 1969–70 term had been tested only in English. In June 1970, when tests were conducted in both English and Spanish, the psychologist found only 23 children in the district to be educationally mentally retarded (*Chula Vista Star News,* August 6, 1970).

NOTES TO CHAPTER 6

1. For details on these models see, for example, Swartz, Turner, and Tuden (1966), Turner (1957), and Kramer (1969).

2. Among others who argue that very little planning or strategy went into consideration of the war on poverty are Moynihan (1966) and Madden and Miles (1965).

3. See, for example, a document published by the Western Center for Community Education and Development, *Community Organization: A Dialogue* (n.d.). This was the first in a planned series concerned with working with disadvantaged communities.

4. For another analysis of the quick dissolution of community organizations among the poor once an immediate problem is resolved, see Safa (1968).

5. This phenomenon has been investigated and suggested by a number of scholars in a variety of sociocultural contexts. Among others see Hymes (1968), Burling (1970), Sapir (1921), and Tyler (1969).

6. Hunter (1965) advanced this argument and Kramer's (1969) analysis of community action programs in the San Francisco Bay area tends to corroborate it.

7. The best examination of the complex nature of political support from an anthropological point of view is presented in the introductions to *Political Anthropology* (Swartz, Turner, and Tuden 1966) and *Local Level Politics* (Swartz, 1968) and other articles contained in these works, and in F. G. Bailey's profound little study, *Strategems and Spoils* (1969).

8. This point is made by Wolfe (1966) with reference to peasants and by Johnson, Gillette and Feldman (1966) with reference to poor in San Diego.

9. This point is made by Rubel (1966), Sheldon (1970), Lewis (1965), and Barbosa-Dasilva (1968).

10. This appears to be a myth which has been dispelled to a great extent by Haber (1967), Kramer (1969), Myrdal (1965), and Thaab (1966), among others.

11. This point has unfortunately been stressed out of proportion by a great number of writers. See, for example, Burma (1954), Rubel (1966), Glalarza (1970), Villarreal (1966), Rowan (1970), and Strauss (1968). Among those who take issue with both its historical and contemporary realty are

McWilliams (1968), Romano (1968), Martinez (1966), Sheldon, (1966), Swadesh (1968), Steiner (1969), Moore and Guzman (1966), and almost all the 1969–70 issues of *La Verdad*.

In fact, a resurgence of Mexican-American political activity has developed throughout the nation. Chicano student activists are organizing and coordinating activities throughout the Southwest and elsewhere (Kurtz 1969; *La Verdad*, April, June, September, November 1969). In San Diego County and elsewhere, Chicano political federations are bringing together previously disparate Chicano political groups for more concerted action. The Brown Berets, a paramilitary organization modeled after the Black Panthers, is active in Chicano barrios throughout the Southwest and elsewhere. Caesar Chavez, leader of the Delano Grape strike, serves as a symbol for much of this renewed activity. Reis Tijerina is another Mexican-American who also has provided a symbolic focus for Mexican-American political activity, and has developed a strong sense of Chicano nationalism in the Southwest (Steiner, 1969; Swadesh, 1968). Rudolfo "Corky" Gonzalez, and articulate and charismatic Chicano from Denver, has founded another nationalistic movement, The Crusade for Justice, which stresses Chicano beauty and pride and autonomy from the dominant Anglo culture through control at the barrio level of schools, economic institutions and the like (Kurtz 1969; Steiner 1969; *La Verdad*, April, June 1969). On Mother's Day, May 10, 1969, several hundred Chicanos marched through San Diego. It was an expression of Chicano unity and political determination (*La Verdad*, May 1969). It is worth noting that this march received no mention in the San Diego press or public media of communication. In the spring of 1969 there were massive Chicano walkouts and demonstrations in many of the city schools of San Diego in protest of the education of Chicano youth. Though this walkout of hundreds of minority students received press coverage, in the South San Diego Bay Area, where I did much of my research, incidents presaging these actions began in December 1968; Anglo-Chicano student rumbles; knifings, expulsions of Chicanos from school, and bombings. None of this was reported in the press either. In March 1970 a Chicano protest march against United States' involvement in Vietnam took place in Los Angeles; over 800 marched in San Diego (*La Verdad*, May and June 1970; also recorded on film available through Chicano activist organizations). Again, little notoriety was given these events in the press. Chicano political activism is emerging, though it is not receiving the notoriety it deserves. In a real sense, American society is sitting on a Chicano volcano that is beginning to seethe and belch smoke.

12. It is curious that the Anglo and black board members did not consider their tactic of holding the impeachment proceedings in Woodlawn Park "dirty" or unfair, even though it was the only meeting held in Woodlawn Park during my research, and it was certain that the house vote would be stacked against the PFTA members. Although the next scheduled CAC meeting should have been in San Ysidro, they explained that the move to Woodlawn Park was merely a means of avoiding trouble with the Mexican-Americans of San Ysidro.

13. At a meeting in the South Bay area held for the purpose of establishing funding priorities for the area for the next fiscal year, the Chicanos

suggested that if the schools did not alter their attitudes toward Mexican-American youth then the funds for war on poverty programs, such as Headstart and Preschool which the schools conducted, should be cut off and junior high and high school Chicano students should be encouraged to walk out in a protest strike. Several Anglos became furious and threatened to leave the meeting. After discussing the matter, a strong statement suggesting that the schools reconsider the education of the Chicano youth was inserted in the refunding proposal. This statement was later deleted by the EOC in the final funding procedures.

14. These quotes can be found in *Business Week,* March 22, 1969, and in Crow, Erickson, and Grissom (n.d.).

15. Detailed case studies of poverty habitats in the United States are relatively rare. Some are: *La Vida* (Lewis, 1966); *Spanish Harlem* (Sexton, 1965); *Tally's Corner* (Liebow, 1967); *The Social Order of the Slum* (Suttles, 1968); *Faces of Poverty* (Simon, 1966); *Soulside* (Hannerz, 1969). An excellent study of the evaluation of a poverty area has been done by Harry Caudhill (1962), *Night Comes to the Cumberlands.*

16. This development is spelled out in detail up to the year 2000 in a study, *The San Diego Border Area Plan* (1966), available from the Planning Department of the City of San Diego.

17. In 1972, 80 percent of the population in Villa Nueva, the Rent Subsidy Apartment Complex which was built in 1970 to accommodate those who were to be displaced by the freeway, was on welfare and the Welfare Department expected that to become 100 percent in the very near future. Unemployment, a sensitive indicator of poverty, in the San Ysidro area was as severe in 1972 as in 1968, and Human Resource Development personnel lament the fact that they have no good answers to the problem.

18. This tendency has been reported by Frank and Ruth Young (n.d.:27), who point out on the basis of research in Mexico that "the direction of community growth is always toward greater participation in the national social structure." This process is examined in detail by Rhienhard Bendix in his book, *Nation Building and Citizenship* (1964). With specific reference to the war on poverty Kravitz (1968:300) suggests that "The direction of community action programs seems to be clearly toward increasing bureaucratization and rapid absorption in the general system."

19. In their work *A Social Profile of a Poverty Area, A Study of Southeast San Diego,* Johnson, Gillette, and Feldman (1966) point out that one-third of the 391 respondents in their study had not heard of the war on poverty. This suggests that the war on poverty is not only not touching them, but that the hard core poor may be living in a greater state of isolation than imagined.

20. An on-the-job training (OJT) program designed especially for Mexican-Americans and known as Project SER was established in 1966 in various areas of the five southwest states (*Manpower Report to the President,* 1968). Project SER was funded in the San Diego area in late 1968 and shortly thereafter was training some sixty Mexican-Americans in auto body painting, uphol-stering, and mechanics. The other three job training programs in San Diego,

all black controlled and oriented, were funded for two hundred job slots for the next year. All these slots together would not absorb the unskilled unemployed in the San Ysidro area alone.

21. See for example Sheldon (1966), Martinez (1966), Galarza (1970), and Rubel (1966).

NOTES TO CHAPTER 7

1. The point of view of the processual school is presented best by Swartz, Turner, and Tuden (1966), Swartz (1968), and Bailey (1969).

2. For a discussion of this point of view see Presthus (1964), Dahl (1961), and D'Antonio and Form (1965).

3. See Crow, Erickson, and Grissom (n.d.:p. x) for this quote.

4. The EOC probably will survive and become a permanent institutional fixture in American bureaucracy. It will probably serve as a local experimental unit for programs devised by the nation OEO which has been delegated to a research and program development function. In order to ensure its stability the EOC severed any relationship with the CACs and is currently (June 1972) threatening to do the same with almost all other delegate agencies. In short, the EOC will not have to bear the onus of any boat-rocking these agencies engage in.

5. See Crow, Erickson, and Grissom (n.d.).

6. This analysis should not be attributed to any great perspicacity on the author's part. The events suggested here have been in the offing for some time. By June 1972 CACs had been severed from the EOC and all but one had become extinct. "Umbrella" neighborhood organizations which the state of California OEO and the EOC of San Diego County developed as CAC replacements are currently being threatened by a withdrawal of funding by the EOC and the expectation is that if they are to survive they will have to acquire funding for staff, office space, supplies, and so forth on their own. Community action programs also are now less acceptable and affirmative action programs are in vogue. These programs seem especially caretaker oriented and stress the delivery of services in which the poor participate but have a minimal voice in developing.

7. See Malinowski (1926:132–39), Kroeber (1948:288), and Murdock (1949:198).

8. See Benedict (1934:41–51) and Linton (1936:347–48).

9. See Firth (1951:56) and Parsons and Shils (1951:198–229).

10. See Kroeber (1948), Schumpeter (1947), and Mair (1965).

NOTES TO APPENDIX

1. "Mexican-American" refers to people of Mexican descent living in the United States who may or may not be citizens of the United States.

2. "Anglo-American" refers to Caucasians not of Mexican descent.

3. Hereafter, those living in hotels, motel or courts are included with those living in apartments; and those preferring to live in motels, hotels, or courts are included with those preferring to live in apartments.

4. 1121 Torrey Pines Rd., San Diego, Calif.

5. Conclusion based on earlier study *Pockets of Poverty*, by Community Welfare Council, 1964.

6. The definition of "inadequate" is based on the surveyor's observations and judgment as influenced by the 1960 census criteria that defined deteriorating and dilapidated.

7. San Diego City Planning Dept. Staff Study.

8. Since completion of the field survey, the city of San Diego has purchased a 10-acre park site in the area.

9. Since completion of the field survey the city engineer had indicated that new street lighting will be installed.

References Cited

Adams, Robert McC. *The Evolution of Urban Society: Early Mesopotamia and Prehispanic Mexico.* Chicago: Aldine Publishing Company, 1966.

Alinsky, Saul. *Reveille for Radicals.* Chicago: University of Chicago Press, 1945.

Almond, Gabriel, and James Coleman, eds. *The Politics of Developing Areas.* Princeton, New Jersey: Princeton University Press, 1960.

Bailey, F.G. *Stratagems and Spoils.* New York: Schocken Books, 1969.

Barbosa-Dasilva, J.F. "Participation of Mexican-Americans in Voluntary Associations." *Research reports in the social sciences* 11, 1 (1968):33–44.

Barth, Fredrik, ed. *Ethnic Groups and Boundaries: The Social Organization of Cultural Difference.* Boston: Little, Brown and Company, 1969.

Bendix, Rheinhard. *Nation Building and Citizenship: Studies of Our Changing Social Order.* New York: John Wiley and Sons, Inc., 1964.

Benedict, Ruth. *Patterns of Culture.* Boston and New York: Houghton-Mifflin Company, 1934.

Blethen, The Very Reverend John F. *Villa Nueva: A Case Study of One Religious Community Involved in the Field of Housing for Low-income Families.* Los Angeles, California: Province of St. Augustine, n.d.

Bloomberg, Warner, and Henry Schmandt, eds. *Urban Poverty: Its Social and Political Dimensions.* Beverly Hills, California: Sage Publications, Inc., 1968.

Blouner, Robert. "Black Culture: Myth or Reality?" In *Afro-American Anthropology: Contemporary Perspectives,* edited by Norman Whitten and John Szwed. New York: The Free Press, 1970.

Bodine, John J. "A Tri-ethnic Trap: The Spanish Speakers in Taos." In *Spanish Speaking People of the United States,* edited by June Helm. Proceedings of the 1968 annual spring meeting, American Ethnological Society. Seattle: University of Washington Press, 1968.

Bogardus, Emory B. "Second Generation Mexicans." *Sociology and Social Research* 13 (1929):276–82.

——"Racial Reactions by Regions." *Sociology and Social Research* 43, 4 (1959): 286–90.

Boissevain, Jeremy F. "Saints and Fireworks: Religion and Politics in Rural Malta." *London School of Economics monographs on social anthropology,* no. 30. London: Athlone Press, 1965.

Bremner, Robert H. *From the Depths: The Discovery of Poverty in the United States.* New York: New York University Press, 1967.

Bullock, Paul. "On Organizing the Poor: Problems of Morality and Tactics." *Dissent* 15 (1968):65–70.

Burling, Robbins. *Man's Many Voices: Language in its Cultural Context.* New York: Holt, Rinehart and Winston, Inc., 1970.

Burma, John H. *Spanish Speaking Groups in the United States.* Durham, North Carolina: Duke University Press, 1954.

Burma, John H., ed. *Mexican-Americans in the United States: A Reader.* Cambridge, Massachusetts: Schenkman Publishing Co., 1970.

Businessweek. "New Plants Dot the Black Slums," March 20, 1969.

Cahn, Edgar S., and Jean C. Cahn. "The War on Poverty: A Civilian Perspective." *Yale Law Journal* 78, 3 (1964):1317–52.

Carneiro, Robert. "Slash-and-Burn Cultivation Among the Kuikuru and its Implications for Cultural Development in the Amazon Basin." *In Man in Adaptation: The Cultural Present,* edited by Y. A. Cohen. Chicago: Aldine Publishing Company, 1968.

——"A Theory of the Origin of the State." *Science* 169, 3947 (1970):733–38.

Cater, Douglas. "The Politics of Poverty." *The Reporter* 30, 4 (1964):16–20.

Caudhill, Harry M. *Night Comes to the Cumberlands: A Biography of a Depressed Area.* Boston: Little, Brown and Company, 1962.

Chula Vista Star News October 20, 1968 issue. Chula Vista, California. November 14, 1968 issue. Chula Vista, California. August 6, 1970 issue. Chula Vista, California.

Cohen, Yehudi A., ed. *Man in Adaptation: The Cultural Present.* Chicago: Aldine Publishing Company, 1968a.

Cohen, Yehudi A. "Culture as Adaptation." In *Man in Adaptation: The Cultural Present.* edited by Y. A. Cohen. Chicago: Aldine Publishing Company, 1968b.

——"Ends and Means in Political Control: State Organization and the Punishment of Adultery, Incest, and Violation of Celibacy." *American Anthropologist* 71, 4 (1969):658–87.

Coleman, James S. *Community Conflict.* New York: The Free Press, 1957.

Community Action Program Memo 51. Office of Economic Opportunity, Washington D.C., 1966.

Community Action: The Neighborhood Center. Community Action Program. Offices of Economic Opportunity, Washington D.C., July 1966.

Community Organization: A Dialogue. First in a series on working with disadvantaged communities. The Western Center for Community Education and Development. (Booklet distributed through community action program offices in San Diego County, n.d.).

A Comprehensive Evaluation of the Community Action Program in San Diego County, California. Quarterly Progress Report No. 3 (July 15, 1967). La Jolla, California.

Crow, Wayman J. and Anthony Gorman. "The Action as Viewed from the Scene: Personal Profiles, Executive Secretaries and Consultants of the Community Action Councils." *Technical Report* No. 3 (July 15, 1967). Western Behavioral Sciences Institute, La Jolla, California.

Crow, Wayman J., and J. R. Johannsen. "Organizing the Poor in Their Neighborhoods." *Technical Report* No. 21 (October 15, 1969). Western Behavioral Sciences Institute, La Jolla, California.

Crow, Wayman J.; R. J. Erickson; and L. A. Grissom. "The War on Poverty in San Diego County: Final Report." Western Behavioral Sciences Institute, La Jolla, California, n.d.

Current Anthropology. "Book Review of the *The Children of Sanchez, Pedro Martinez,* and *La Vida,* by Oscar Lewis." *Current Anthropology* 8, 5 (1967):480–500.

——"Book review of *Culture and Poverty: Critique and Counter Proposals,* by Charles A. Valentine." *Current Anthropology* 10, 2–3 (1969):181–201.

D'Antonio, William, and William H. Form. *Influentials in Two Border Cities: A Study in Community Decision Making.* Notre Dame: University of Notre Dame Press, 1965.

Dahl, Robert A. *Who Governs? Democracy and Power in an American City.* New Haven and London: Yale University Press, 1961.

Eames, Edwin, and Judith Goode. On Lewis' Culture of Poverty Concept. *Current Anthropology* 11, 4–5 (1970):479–82.

Easton, David. *The Political System: An Inquiry into the State of Political Science.* New York: Alfred A. Knopf, 1953.

——"Political Anthropology." In *Biennial Review of Anthropology,* edited by B. Siegel. Stanford, California: Stanford University Press, 1959.

Economic Opportunity Act of 1964, As Amended. Office of Economic Opportunity, executive office of the President, Washington D.C., 1967.

Eisenstadt, S. N. "Institutionalization and Change." *American Sociological Review* 29 (1964a):235–47.

——"Social Change, Differentiation and Evolution." *American Sociological Review* 29 (1964b):375–86.

Fallers, Lloyd. *Bantu Bureaucracy: A Century of Political Evolution Among the Basoga of Uganda.* Chicago: University of Chicago Press, 1965.

Festinger, Leon; Stanley Schacter; and Kurt Back. *Social Pressure in Informal Groups: A Study of Human Factors in Housing.* Stanford, California: Stanford University Press, 1950.

Firth, Raymond. *Elements of Social Organization.* Boston: Beacon Press, 1951.

Fogel, Walter. *Education and Income of Mexican-Americans in the Southwest.* Mexican-American Study Project. Division of Research, Graduate School of Business Administration, University of California, Los Angeles. Advance Report 1, 1965.

Forbes, Jack. *Mexican-Americans: A Handbook for Educators.* Published by Far West Laboratory for Educational Research and Development. 1 Garden Circle, Hotel Claremont, Berkeley, California, n.d.

Fried, Morton H. *The Evolution of Political Society: An Essay in Political Anthropology.* New York: Random House, 1967.

Friendly, Alfred, et al. *Washington Post.* Series on the War on Poverty (January 30 through February 13, 1966). Washington, D.C.

Galarza, Ernesto. "La mula no nacio arisca." In *Mexican-Americans in the United States: A Reader,* edited by John H. Burma. Cambridge, Mass.: Schenkman Publishing Company, Inc., 1970.

Galbraith, John K. *The Affluent Society.* Boston: Houghton-Mifflin, 1958.

Gans, Herbert J. *The Urban Villagers: Group and Class in the Life of Italian-Americans.* New York: The Free Press, 1962.

——We Won't End the Urban Crisis Until We End 'Majority Rule'. *New York Times Magazine* (August 3, 1969).

Gebler, Leo. *The Schooling Gap: Signs of Progress.* Mexican-American Study Project. Division of Research, Graduate School of Business Administration, University of California, Los Angeles. Advance Report 7, 1967.

Geertz, Clifford, ed. *Old Societies and New States: The Quest for Modernity in Asia and Africa.* New York: The Free Press, 1963.

Gillette, Tom. *Re-analysis of a Social Profile of a Poverty Area.* Technical Report No. 2 (July 15, 1967). Western Behavioral Science Institute, La Jolla, California.

Gladwin, Thomas. *The Anthropologists' View of Poverty.* The Social Welfare Forum 1961. New York: Columbia University Press, 1961.

——*Poverty U.S.A.* Boston: Little, Brown and Company, 1967.

Glazer, Nathan. "The War on Poverty: The View from New York." In *The Poor: A Culture of Poverty or a Poverty of Culture,* edited by J. A. Winter. Grand Rapids, Michigan: William B. Eerdmans, 1971.

Glick, L. B. "The Right to Equal Opportunity." In *La Raza: Forgotten Americans,* edited by Julian Samora. Notre Dame: University of Notre Dame Press, 1966.

Gluckman, Max. *Politics, Law and Ritual in Tribal Society.* Chicago: Aldine Publishing Company, 1965.

Greer, Scott. "The Social Structure and Political Process of Suburbia." *American Sociological Review* 25, 4 (1960): 514–22.

Haber, Allen. "The American Underclass." *Poverty and Human Resources Abstract* 2, 3 (1967):5–19.

Hall, Edward T. *The Silent Language.* New York: Doubleday, 1959.

Hallman, Howard W. "The Community Action Program." In *Urban Poverty: Its Social and Political Dimensions,* edited by Warner Bloomberg and Henry Schmandt. Beverly Hills, California: Sage Publications, Inc., 1968.

Hannerz, Ulf. *Soulside: Inquiries into Ghetto Culture and Community.* New York: Columbia University Press, 1969.

Harrington, James. *Oceana.* Edited with notes by S. B. Liljegren. Heidelberg, 1924.

——*Political Writings: Representative Selections.* Edited with an introduction by Charles Blitzer. New York, 1955.

Harsanyi, John C. "Measurement of Social Power, Opportunity Costs and the Theory of Two Person Bargaining Games." *Behavioral Science* 7 (1962a):67–80.

——"Measurements of Social Power in In-person Reciprocal Power Situations."
    Behavioral Science 7 (1962b):81–91.

Hayes, Edward C. *Power Structure and Urban Policy: Who Rules in Oakland?*
    New York: McGraw-Hill Book Company, 1972.

Hughes, Charles Campbell. "From Contest to Council: Social Control Among
    the St. Lawrence Eskimos. In *Political Anthropology*, edited by
    M. J. Swartz, V. W. Turner, and A. Tuden. Chicago: Aldine Publish-
    ing Company, 1966.

Hunter, David R. *The Slums: Challenge and Response.* The Free Press of Glencoe,
    1965.

Hunter, Floyd. *Community Power Structure: A Study of Decision Makers.*
    Chapel Hill: University of North Carolina Press, 1953.

Hyman, Herbert H., and Charles R. Wright. "Evaluating Social Action Programs."
    In *The Uses of Sociology*, edited by P. H. Lazarfeld, William H.
    Sewell, and H. L. Wilensky. New York: Basic Books, Inc., 1967.

Hymes, Dell H. "Functions of Speech: An Evolutionary Approach." In *Man in
    Adaptation: The Biosocial Background*, edited by Y. A. Cohen.
    Chicago: Aldine Publishing Company, 1968.

Jacobs, Paul. "Poverty Today." In *Dialogue on Poverty*. The Campus Dialogue
    Series, general editor Robert Theobald. Indianapolis and New York:
    The Bobbs-Merrill Company, Inc., 1967.

James, Edward. *America Against Poverty*. London: Routledge and Kegan Paul,
    1970.

Johnson, Dale; T. Gillete; and D. Feldman. *A Social Profile of a Poverty Area.*
    Sociological Research Associates, San Diego, California, January
    1966.

Josten, Margaret. *Cincinnati Enquirer* (January 9, 1966), Cincinnati, Ohio

Keith-Lucas, Alan. *Decisions About People in Need: A Study of Administrative
    Responsiveness in Public Assistance.* Chapel Hill: The University of
    North Carolina Press, 1957.

Keyserling, Leon H. "Programs: Present and Future." In *Dialogue on Poverty*.
    The Campus Dialogue Series, general editor Robert Theobald.
    Indianapolis and New York: The Bobbs-Merrill Company, Inc., 1967.

Klapp, Orrin E., and L. Vincent Padgett. "Power Structure and Decision-making
    in a Mexican Border City." *American Journal of Sociology* 65, 4
    (1960): 400–06.

Kramer, Ralph M. *Participation of the Poor: Comparative Community Case
    Studies in the War on Poverty.* Englewood Cliffs, New Jersey:
    Prentice-Hall, Inc., 1969.

Kravitz, Sanford. "Community Action Programs in Perspective." In *Urban
    Poverty: Its Political and Social Dimensions,* edited by Warner
    Bloomberg and Henry Schmandt. Beverly Hills, California: Sage
    Publications, Inc., 1968.

Kroeber, Alfred. *Anthropology.* New York: Harcourt, Brace and Company,
    1948.

Kurtz, Donald V. "Chicano Student Activists: One Segment of Emerging Brown
    Power." Paper presented at the 68th annual meeting of the American
    Anthropological Association, New Orleans, 1969.

Lasswell, Harold, and Abraham Kaplan. *Power and Society: A Framework for Political Inquiry*. New Haven: Yale University Press, 1950.

La Verdad. All issues, San Diego, California, 1969.

——January through May 1970 issues. San Diego, California

Leacock, Eleanor B., ed. *The Culture of Poverty: A Critique*. New York: Simon and Schuster, 1971.

Lenski, Gerhard E. *Power and Privilege: A Theory of Social Stratification*. New York: McGraw-Hill Book Company, 1966.

Lewis, Oscar. *Five Families: Mexican Case Studies in the Culture of Poverty*. New York: Basic Books, 1959.

——*The Children of Sanchez*. New York: Random House, 1961.

——*La Vida: A Puerto Rican Family in the Culture of Poverty—San Juan and New York*. New York: Vintage Books, A Division of Random House, 1966.

Lewis, Oscar, with the assistance of Victor Barnouw. *Village Life in Northern India: Studies in a Delhi Village*. New York: Vintage Books, A Division of Random House, 1965.

Levy, M. J. *The Structure of Society*. Princeton, New Jersey: Princeton University Press, 1952.

Liebow, Elliot. *Tally's Corner: A Study of Negro Street Corner Men*. Boston and Toronto: Little, Brown and Company, 1967.

Linton, Ralph. *The Study of Man*. New York: Appleton-Century-Crofts, Inc., 1936.

Lipset, S. M. *The First New Nation*. London: Heinemann, 1963.

Loomis, Charles P., and Reed M. Powell. "Sociometric Analysis of Class Status in Rural Costa Rica—A Peasant Community Concerned with an Hacienda Community." *Sociometry* 12 (1949):144–57.

Lynd, Helen, and Robert Lynd. *Middletown in Transition*. New York: The Free Press, 1937.

MacIver, R. M. *The Web of Government*. New York: The Free Press, 1947.

Madden, Carl H., and John R. Miles. "Right of Center: A Battle Plan of Questionable Value." In *Poverty in Affluence: The Social, Political, and Economic Dimensions of Poverty in the United States*, edited by Robert E. Will and Harold G. Vatter. New York: Harcourt, Brace and World, Inc., 1965.

Mair, Lucy. *Introduction to Social Anthropology*. Oxford: Clarendon Press, 1965.

Malinowski, Bronislaw. *Crime and Custom in a Savage Society*. New York: Harcourt, Brace and Company, Inc., 1926.

Manpower Report to the President. Including a report on manpower requirements, resources, utilization and training: by the United States Department of Labor. Transmitted to Congress, April, 1968.

Manuel, Herschel. *Spanish-speaking Children of the Southwest: Their Education and the Public Welfare*. Austin: University of Texas Press, 1965.

Marris, Peter. "A Report on Urban Renewal in the United States." In *The Urban Condition: People and Policy in the Metropolis*. edited by Leonard J. Duhl. New York: Basic Books, Inc., 1963.

Martinez, John R. "Leadership and Politics." In *La Raza: Forgotten Americans*, edited by Julian Samora. Notre Dame: University of Notre Dame Press, 1966.

Marx, Karl. *Capital: A Critique of Political Economy.* Chicago: C. H. Kerr and Company, 1906.

May, Edgar. *The Wasted Americans: Cost of Our Welfare Dilemna.* New York, Evanston, and London: Harper and Row, Publishers, 1964.

McWilliams, Carey. *North from Mexico: The Spanish-speaking People of the United States.* New York: Greenwood Press Publishers, 1968.

The Mexican-American: A New Focus on Opportunity. Testimony presented at the cabinet committee hearings on Mexican-American affairs. El Paso, Texas, (October 26–28). Inter-agency committee on Mexican-American affairs, 1800 G. Street, N.W., Washington D.C., 1967.

Mills, C. Wright. "The Middle Class in Middle Sized Cities." *American Sociological Review* 11 (1946):520–29.

Moore, Joan W. with Alfredo Cuellar. *Mexican Americans.* Englewood Cliffs, New Jersey: Prentice Hall, 1970.

Moore, Joan W. and Ralph Guzman. "New Wind from the Southwest." *The Nation* 202, 22 (1966):645–47.

Moore, Joan W. and F. G. Mittleback, with the assistance of Ronald McDaniel. *Residential Segregation in the Urban Southwest.* Mexican-American Study Project. Division of Research, Graduate School of Business Administration, University of California, Los Angeles. Advance Report 4, 1966.

Moynihan, Daniel. *The Negro Family: The Case for National Action.* Washington: U.S. Department of Labor, 1965.

——"What Is Community Action?" *Public Interest* No. 5 (1966):3–9.

——"The Negro Family: The Case for National Action." In *The Moynihan Report and the Politics of Controversy.* Lee Rainwater and William Yancey. A trans-action social science and public policy report. Massachusetts Institute of Technology, Cambridge, Mass.: The M.I.T. Press, 1967.

——*Maximum Feasible Misunderstanding, Community Action in the War on Poverty.* New York: Basic Books, 1970.

Murdock, George P. *Social Structure.* New York: The Free Press, 1949.

Myrdal, Gunnar. "The War on Poverty." In *New Perspectives on Poverty,* edited by Arthur B. Shostak and William Gomberg. Englewood Cliffs, New Jersey: Prentice-Hall, Inc., 1965.

Nadel, S. F. *The Foundations of Social Anthropology.* Glencoe, Illinois: The Free Press, 1953.

Nicholas, Ralph W. "Segmentary Factional Political Systems." In *Political Anthropology,* edited by M. J. Swartz, V. W. Turner, and A. Tuden. Chicago: Aldine Publishing Company, 1966.

Parson, Talcott, and Edward A. Shils, eds. *Toward a General Theory of Action.* New York: Harper and Row, 1951.

Peacock, James L., and A. T. Kirsch. *The Human Direction: An Evolutionary Approach to Social and Cultural Anthropology.* New York: Appleton-Century-Crofts, 1970.

Perlman, Robert, and David Jones. *Neighborhood Service Centers.* United States

Department of Health, Education and Welfare, Welfare Administration Office of Juvenile Delinquency, Washington D.C., 1967.

Pickney, Alphonse. "Prejudice Toward Mexican and Negro Americans: A Comparison." *Phylon* 24 (1963):353–59.

Pourade, Richard F. *The Glory Years.* Commissioned by James S. Copley, Chairman of the corporation, the Copley Press, Inc. Published by the Union-Tribune Publishing Company, San Diego, California. Vol. II, 1964.

——*Gold in the Sun.* Commissioned by James S. Copley, Chairman of the corporation, the Copley Press, Inc. Published by Union-Tribune Publishing Company, San Diego, California. Vol. V, 1965.

——*The Rising Tide.* Commissioned by James S. Copley, Chairman of the corporation, the Copley Press, Inc. Published by the Union-Tribune Publishing Company, San Diego, California. Vol. VI, 1967.

Poverty War Report. In *The Economics of Poverty: An American Paradox,* edited by Burton A. Weisbrod. Reprinted by permission of the *Wall Street Journal* (January 18, 1965). Englewood Cliffs, New Jersey: Prentice-Hall, Inc., 1965.

Presthus, Robert. *Men at the Top.* New York: Oxford University Press, 1964.

Price, John. "Tijuana: A Study of Symbiosis." In *The Post Industrial City. New Mexico Quarterly* 38, 3 (1968):8–18.

Rainwater, Lee, and Wm. L. Yancey. *The Moynihan Report and the Politics of Controversy.* A transaction social science and public policy report. Massachusetts Institute of Technology, Cambridge, Mass: The M.I.T. Press, 1967.

Report of the National Advisory Commission on Civil Disorders. Special introduction by Tom Wicker of the *New York Times.* New York: Bantam Books, a subsidiary of Grosset and Dunlap, Inc., 1968.

Roach, J., and O. Gursslin. "On the Evolution of the Concept of the Culture of Poverty." *Social Forces* 45: (1967): 383–91.

Romano, Octavio I. "Minorities, History and the Cultural Mystique." *El Grito* 1, 1 (1967):5–11.

——"The Anthropology and Sociology of the Mexican-Americans." *El Grito* 2, 1 (1968):13–26.

Rowan, Helen. "A Minority Nobody Knows." In *Mexican-Americans in the United States,* edited by John H. Burma. Cambridge, Massachusetts: Schenkman Publishing Company, Inc., 1970.

Rubel, A. J. *Across the Tracks.* Austin: The University of Texas Press, 1966.

Ryan, William. *Blaming the Victim.* New York: Random House, 1971.

Safa, Helen I. "The Social Isolation of the Urban Poor: Life in a Puerto Rican Shanty Town." In *Among the Poor,* edited by Irwin Deutscher and Elizabeth Thompson. New York: Basic Books, 1968.

Sahlins, Marshall D., and Elman R. Service, eds. *Evolution and Culture.* Ann Arbor: The University of Michigan Press, 1960.

Samora, Julian, ed. *La Raza: Forgotten Americans.* Notre Dame: University of Notre Dame Press, 1966.

Samora, Julian, and R. A. Lamanna. *Mexican-Americans in a Midwest Metrop-*

olis: A Study of East Chicago. Mexican-American Study Project. Division of Research, Graduate School of Business Administration, University of California, Los Angeles. Advance Report 8, 1967.

Sanchez, George I. "History, Culture and Education." In *La Raza: Forgotten Americans,* edited by Julian Samora. Notre Dame: University of Notre Dame Press, 1966.

San Diego Border Area Plan. Prepared by the City Planning Department, City of San Diego, California. Available from the City Planning Department, San Diego, California, 1966.

San Diego Union. June 23 and 25, 1963 issues. San Diego, California.

San Ysidro Community Plan. Prepared by the San Ysidro Planning and Development Group and the city of San Diego, California. Available from the City Planning Department, San Diego, California, 1970.

San Ysidro Community Survey. An unpublished document commissioned by the Planning Department of the City of San Diego at the suggestion of the San Ysidro Planning and Development Group, 1968.

Sapir, E. *Language.* New York: Harcourt, Brace, 1921.

Schatzman, L., and A. Strauss. "Social Class and Modes of Communication." In *Communication and Culture,* edited by A. G. Smith. New York: Holt, Rinehart and Winston, Inc., 1966.

Schorr, Alvin. *Slums and Social Insecurity.* London: Thomas Nelson and Sons, 1964.

Schumpeter, Joseph. *Capitalism, Socialism and Democracy.* New York: Harper, 1947.

Scoble, Harry M. "The Political Scientist's Perspective on Poverty." In *Poverty: New Interdisciplinary Perspectives,* edited by Thomas Weaver and Alvin Magid. San Francisco, California: Chandler Publishing Company, 1969.

Service, Elman. "The Law of Evolutionary Potential." In *Evolution and Culture,* edited by Marshall D. Sahlins and Elman R. Service. Ann Arbor: University of Michigan Press, 1960.

Sexton, Patricia Cayo. *Spanish Harlem: An Anatomy of Poverty.* New York: Harper Colophon Books, Harper and Row, Publishers, 1965.

Sheldon, Paul. "Community Participation in the Emerging Middle Class." In *La Raza: Forgotten Americans,* edited by Julian Samora. Notre Dame: University of Notre Dame Press, 1966.

——"Mexican-American Formal Organizations." In *Mexican-Americans in the United States: A Reader,* edited by John H. Burma. Cambridge, Massachusetts: Schenkman Publishing Company, 1970.

Shostak. Arthur B. "Old Problems and New Agencies: How Much Change?" In *Urban Poverty: Its Social and Political Dimensions,* edited by Warner Bloomberg and Henry Schmandt. Beverly Hills, California: Sage Publications, Inc., 1968.

Silver, Laurens. "The Poor vs. Highway Construction." *Law in Action: A Monthly Account of the Legal Services Program* 3, 9 (1969):10–11.

Simienko, Alex. *Pilgrims, Colonists and Frontiersman.* New York: The Free Press, 1964.

Simon, Arthur. *Faces of Poverty.* New York: The Macmillan Company, 1966.

Southeast San Diego Health Study. A Model Cities Project Conducted by: Comprehensive Health Planning Association of San Diego and Imperial Counties, 3211 Jefferson St., San Diego, California 92110, 1969.

Steiner, Stan. *La Raza: The Mexican Americans.* New York: Harper and Row Publishers, 1969.

Steward, Julian H. *Theory of Culture Change.* Urbana: University of Illinois Press, 1955.

Stewart, Donald D., and Marge Austin. *Pockets of Poverty: A Study of Deprivation in Two Areas of the City of San Diego, California.* Community Welfare Council of San Diego County, 1964.

Strauss, Melvin P. "The Mexican-American in El Paso Politics." In *Urbanization in the Southwest,* edited by Clyde J. Wingfield. Public Affairs Series, No. 1. University of Texas at El Paso, 1968.

Study of Management, Organization and Administrative Practices of the Economic Opportunity Commission of San Diego County. Conducted under direction of: Records Management Division, National Archives and Record Service, General Services Administration, Region 9, San Francisco, California, 1968.

Suttles, Gerald D. *The Social Order of the Slum.* Chicago: The University of Chicago Press, 1968.

Swadesh, Frances L. "The Alianza Movement: Catalyst for Social Change in New Mexico." In *Spanish-speaking People of the United States,* edited by June Helm. Proceeding of the 1968 Annual Spring Meeting of the American Ethnological Society. Seattle and London: University of Washington Press, 1968.

Swartz, Marc J., ed. *Local-level Politics.* Chicago: Aldine Publishing Company, 1968.

Swartz, Marc J.; Victor W. Turner; and Arthur Tuden, eds. *Political Anthropology.* Chicago: Aldine Publishing Company, 1966.

Tawney, R. H. *Religion and the Rise of Capitalism: A Historical Study.* Gloucester, Massachusetts: Smith, 1926.

Thaab, Earl. "What War on Which Poverty?" *The Public Interest* 3 (1966):54.

Turner, Victor W. *Schism and Continuity in an African Society.* Manchester: Manchester University Press, 1957.

Tylor, Stephen A., ed. *Cognitive Anthropology.* New York: Holt, Rinehart and Winston, Inc., 1969.

Useem, John, and Ruth H. Useem. "Stratification in a Prairie Town." *American Sociological Review* 7 (1942):331–42.

Valentine, Charles. *Culture and Poverty: Critique and Counter Proposals.* Chicago and London: University of Chicago Press, 1968.

Villarreal, Jose Antonio. "Mexican-Americans and the Leadership Crisis." *Los Angeles Times West Magazine* (September 15, 1966).

Walinsky, Adam. "Keeping the Poor in Their Place: Notes on the Importance on Being One-up." In *New Perspectives on Poverty,* edited by Arthur B. Shostak and William Gomberg. Englewood Cliffs, New Jersey: Prentice Hall, Inc., 1965.

Warner, William Lloyd. *Democracy in Jonesville*. New York: Harper, 1949.

Warren, Roland L. "Toward a Typology of Extra-community Controls Limiting Local Community Autonomy." *Social Forces* 34, 4 (1956):338–41.

——*The Community in America*. Chicago: Rand McNally and Company, 1963.

Weber, Max. *The Protestant Ethic and the Spirit of Capitalism*. Translated by Talcott Parsons, with a forward by R. H. Tawney. London, 1930.

Weisbrod, Burton A., ed. *The Economics of Poverty: An American Paradox*. Englewood Cliffs, New Jersey: Prentice Hall, 1965.

West, James. *Plainville, U.S.A.* New York: Columbia University Press, 1945.

White, Leslie. *The Science of Culture: A Study of Man and Civilization*. New York: Grove Press, Inc., 1949.

Wilson, James Q. "Planning and Politics: Citizen Participation in Urban Renewal." *Journal of the American Institute of Planners* 29, 4 (1963): 242–49.

Winter, J. Alan, ed. *The Poor: A Culture of Poverty or a Poverty of Culture*. Grand Rapids, Michigan: Wm. B. Eerdmans, 1971.

Wolf, Eric R. *Peasants*. Englewood Cliffs, New Jersey: Prentice Hall, Inc., 1966.

Young, Frank, and Ruth Young. "A Theory of Community Development." *Science, Technology, and Development*, Vol. 7, n.d.

Index

About the Author

Donald V. Kurtz received his Ph.D. in anthropology from the University of California, Davis. He is presently Assistant Professor of Anthropology at the University of Wisconsin–Milwaukee. While conducting the research upon which this work is based he was a member of the Border Area Community Action Council and served on the San Diego County Geographic Review Committee to develop war on poverty priorities and program plans for 1969–1970. Professor Kurtz has presented papers and published articles on other aspects of poverty and politics.